THE ILLUSTRATED
ORIGINS
ANSWER BOOK

Concise, Easy-to-Understand Facts About
the Origin of Life, Man, and the Cosmos

by Paul S. Taylor

NOTE

The endnote numbers in the main text have been made bold and easy-to-find for your convenience in cross-referencing between the text and the Reference Section. References for boxed quotations can be found by using the index to look up the name of the person quoted and and then finding the full quotation.

Published by
Eden Productions
P.O. Box 41644
Mesa, Arizona 85274-1644

Revised Edition, First printing: Spring 1990.

Library of Congress Cataloging in Publication Data

I. ORIGINS Answer Book, The Illustrated – Revised Edition / Taylor

   Concise, Easy-to-Understand Facts About the Origin of Life, Man, and the Cosmos.
   Includes index and references.
   1. Creation-Evolution. 2. Evolution. 3. Life, Origin of. 4. Science - origin of the cosmos.

II. Taylor, Paul S., 1953-

Library of Congress Catalog Card Number: 90-081210

ISBN 1-877775-01-0 (paperback)

Printed and bound in the United States of America

The Origin of the Universe

Did Evolution on a massive scale produce the cosmos — everything from planets to animals to man?

In this century, many scientists have accepted Evolution, in part or in whole. However, there are significant numbers who have not. Many intelligent and experienced scientists either openly or secretly dismiss Evolution as highly unlikely or impossible. (See endnote *1*.) As *Science Digest* reported:

> "Scientists who utterly reject Evolution may be one of our fastest-growing controversial minorities... Many of the scientists supporting this position hold impressive credentials in science."*[2]*

One example is Dr. Arthur E. Wilder-Smith, an honored scientist with three earned doctorates.*[3]* He is exceptionally well-informed in the Creation/Evolution controversy, particularly in the biochemistry and physics involved. A former Evolutionist, Dr. Wilder-Smith has debated various leading scientists on the subject. In his opinion, the Evolution model does not fit as well with the established facts of science as does the Creation model.

> "The Evolutionary model says that it is not necessary to assume the existence of anything, besides matter and energy, to produce life. That proposition is unscientific. We know perfectly well that if you leave matter to itself, it does not organize itself — in spite of all the efforts in recent years to prove that it does.
>
> The common objection to the Creation model is that it's supposedly 'not scientific.' Some say, 'If you propose a god to explain the origin of energy, matter, and life, you are proposing something which you cannot examine in the laboratory.' That's quite true. But the Creation *model* can be examined in the laboratory and has proved itself... What we *do* need every time in order to get life is an injection of matter [with information code] from an intelligent being, be it god or man."*[4]*

model: a scientific framework of ideas used to help organize and understand facts in a meaningful way. A "scientific model" must be defended on the basis of evidence and experiments. A "model" is not equivalent to a "theory", as scientifically defined. Two main models are used to explain the origin of the cosmos — Evolutionism and Creationism.*[5]* It should be scientifically possible to examine these two models and decide which best fits the evidence; however, it is not possible to *totally* prove or disprove either view *scientifically.[6]*

cosmos: the universe and everything in it.

In Dr. Wilder-Smith's opinion, the Evolutionary model does not fit as well with the established facts of science as does the Creationist model.

evolution, evolve: a series of related changes in a certain direction; to develop gradually.

Evolution, Evolve: macroevolution; megaevolution; a theoretical naturally occurring process of change which produces increasing complexity from lower, simpler states to higher, more complex states — as in the supposed Evolution of single-celled creatures into multicellular creatures and ultimately to fishes, amphibians, reptiles, and mammals.

Evolutionist: One who believes in macroevolution in part or in whole. There are 2 basic types of Evolutionists: those who believe in a god (theists), and those who do not (agnostics or atheists).[7]

Theistic Evolutionists believe that a god created the natural laws, created the first life and set up the process of Evolution in some form. Some assume god stepped into the process at times to create radically new types of creatures or to redirect the process of Evolution.

In contrast, both atheistic and agnostic Evolutionists (also called naturalistic Evolutionists) rule out all supernatural causes.[8] They explain the origin, development, and meaning of *all* things in terms of natural laws and processes in operation today. Atheistic Evolutionists believe it is not necessary to suppose any reality outside matter and energy to produce life. They generally assume the universe began in a state of total randomness and has gradually become more ordered and complex over great ages of time.[9] Many Evolutionists suppose that wherever energy and matter exist life will eventually form, if the conditions are right. Further, they assume that life will always evolve upward to the highest forms suitable for the environment.

Evolutionism: sometimes called Total Evolutionism or transformism; belief in agnostic or atheistic Evolution; Evolutionism generally teaches that the creatures of today gradually developed into existence through billions of years of natural processes, and that all present life has descended from one (or a few) original form(s).

Creationism: the point of view of origins which says the elements and all living things were made by a creator for some purpose.

Creationist: In the context of this book, the term "Creationist" will be restricted to meaning one who rejects belief in macroevolution, and who believes that scientific evidence points to the existence of a powerful being who created a complete, fully-working cosmos. Creationists believe all major kinds of living things were created individually. They predict it should be possible to discover a basic fixity of kinds of animals, rather than a myriad of transitional forms between basic kinds. Many Creationists accept the book of Genesis as accurate history (including Genesis 1-2 and the worldwide flood catastrophe). Many Creationists allow for the possibility that Earth could be far younger than Evolutionists claim.

There are 3 common misconceptions about scientists: (a) Scientists are objective, (b) Scientists are unbiased, and (c) Science is infallible. That is, the attitude: "If a scientist says it, it must be true."

The Nature of Science and Scientists

How is it possible for reasonable, intelligent, well-educated people to hold such diametrically opposite views as Evolutionism and Creationism? Can both Evolutionists and Creationists be classified as true scientists? As shall be shown, the answer is undoubtedly "yes."

There is no different human species called *Homo scientificus*. Scientists are not separate from the rest of humanity. They are *not* some unique class of super-human; they are just people. None are all-knowing.

Being people, scientists do not always objectively seek truth, wherever it might lead. *All* people hold biases toward particular viewpoints.[10] Because scientists are human (subject to self-deception, pride, self-interest, etc.), there are those in both camps (Evolutionist and Creationist) who do not always practice *good* science. No person or institution is infallible or above all question.

*S*cientists... are emotional human beings who carry with them a generous dose of subjectivity into the supposedly objective search for The Truth.

Roger Lewin

Each person's particular set of biases is a result of personal life experiences, relationships, parents, schools, peers, teachers, personal practices, and the pressures of life. It is difficult for any person to deal objectively with evidence potentially destructive to one's own cherished beliefs or pride[11] — or detrimental to perceived personal security, in whatever form. (For further information on the fallibility of scientists, see endnote 12.)

In one way or another, bias and presuppositions[13] affect every scientist's theories, priorities, research, methods, decisions and interpretations. Whether it be molecules, test results or rocks, evidence cannot evaluate, prioritize, or interpret *itself*. It takes humans to create a meaning for evidence — interpreting it and building theories upon it.

The fossil of any ancient extinct animal can be used as an example. A fossil is a material fact having dimensions, texture, weight and shape. However, that is *all* it is, just a particular hard object with shape. It comes with no label detailing its *true* significance and meaning.[14] There are no attached photographs of the living animal showing its actual appearance, color, habits, environment or ancestors.

Detailed illustrations and colorful descriptions of long-extinct animals and their origins which are based merely on fossils are not ultimate truth. They are only the fallible, biased interpretations of human beings working with limited knowledge and no direct experience with the living animal.

The rocks and the fossils are facts. But labels such as "Cambrian," "Cretaceous," and the like are *interpretations*. There are no "time machines" to transport scientists into the past. Thus, in many ways, science is *very* limited in what it can know with certainty about the ancient past.[15] In all descriptions of origins, one must be very careful to discern between fact and fiction.

The Focus of this Book

Hundreds and thousands of volumes are already available to present a one-sided promotion of Evolutionary theories and ideology. Yet, there are other scientific viewpoints. The focus of this book is primarily on revealing fascinating new evidences and interesting alternate ways to interpret the data.

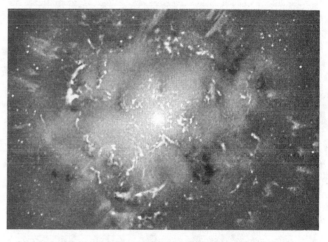

Many evolutionists support the theory that the cosmos was created by a gigantic explosion — the so-called "Big Bang".

THE BIG QUESTION: How Did It All Begin?

The Big Bang Theory

Many Evolutionists believe the stars and Earth owe their existence to a gigantic explosion. This is commonly called the "Big Bang Theory." The proposal is that all of the matter and energy in the universe were once concentrated in a single spot. The size of this site has sometimes been described as being no bigger than the head of a pin. "Big bang" promoters say this theorized object (source unknown) sat in the void of space for a time (length unknown) and then suddenly exploded. It is said that the stars, galaxies and planets eventually developed out of this explosion.

cosmogonies: theories about the origin of the cosmos (Note: Cosmogonies cannot qualify as *scientific* theories since they involve events in the distant past which could never be tested and duplicated in the here and now using scientific methods.)[16]

Fossils are not found with labels explaining their meaning. Meaning is assigned by people.

Light from objects moving away at very fast speed appears more red. Most galaxies are reddish. Is this convincing proof for the "Big Bang Theory"? Many scientists say no.

The main evidence used in support of the "big bang" is the so-called "redshift" of light coming from stars as viewed from the perspective of Earth.[17] Astronomical measurements of the spectrums of many (but not all) galaxies show their light appears to be shifted to the red side of the spectrum.

> **Doppler effect on light:** Light waves from a very fast-moving object can become slightly stretched or compressed depending on the perspective from which they are viewed. If the object is moving *away* from the viewer, the light is stretched out and therefore appears to be slightly more red. Conversely, an object moving *toward* the viewer is compressed and appears slightly more blue.

Some scientists believe the color shift observed in most galaxies is due to the Doppler effect and, therefore, evidence that galaxies are rushing outward from some center point (the source of the "big bang," they say). Of course, even if the universe is expanding, this is not definite evidence for Evolution or a "big bang."

Do uncontrolled explosions produce complex organization? No, they produce disorder.

Expansion of the universe can be accounted for by Creationist theories, also.[18]

Difficulties With the Redshift Evidence

- Some of the "more distant" stars have tremendously large redshifts. Are these stars, therefore, moving away at incredibly high speeds?[19] It seems quite doubtful.

  If these redshifts are not due to the stars' speed and direction, is there another cause for redshifts?

- Various galaxies have been discovered which are in pairs and separated by relatively little distance.[20] Some are even connected by a "bridge" of luminous matter. In some cases, one of the two galaxies in the pair has a radically different "red shift" from the other.[21] Does this mean there is an extreme speed difference between the two galaxies (for example, an impossible difference of 5 thousand miles per *second*)? This seems absurd, since these galaxies are either touching or extremely close together.[22] Could it be that the observed color difference has nothing to do with the Doppler effect?

- Another problem is the discovery of several *different* redshifts in the *same* object! Is the object moving at several different speeds at once?! Or, is the Doppler effect the wrong explanation?[23]

- Not all galaxies have redshifts; some have blueshifts.[24] This does not fit well with the "big bang" theory.

- The observed redshift may be the result of something other than receding motion: (a) Some think it could be evidence that the universe is rotating in a circular motion, instead of expanding. (b) Rather than moving away from us at high speed, some suggest the "red" galaxies might be relatively stationary.

- Other forces can cause light waves to be stretched out and reddened. Gravity, the attractive force between all matter, can cause light to redden. This was predicted by Einstein. Some say the tremendous gravitational forces inherent in immense objects throughout the universe could be the cause for much of the observed redshifting.[25] Another theory suggested by some astronomers is that "reddening" might be due to "photon decay" or "tired light."[26]

What Do Explosions Really Make?

Many scientists are quite unconvinced that any undirected series of events, including the "big bang," could ever form the cosmos.[27] Nowhere in the uni-

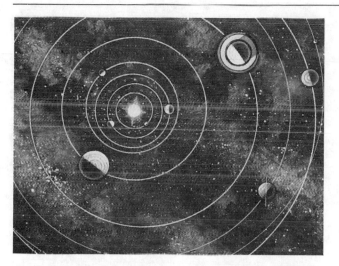

The ordered movements of the Solar System allow scientists to accurately predict positions of planets and comets years into the future, so probes can be sent to meet them.

Evolution and the "Big Bang" Versus a Basic Law of Nature

Scores of distinguished scientists have carefully examined the most basic laws of nature to see if Evolution is physically possible — given enough time and opportunity. The conclusion of many is that Evolution is simply *not* feasible. One major problem is the 2nd Law of Thermodynamics.

> **law of science:** basic, unchanging principle of nature; a scientifically observed phenomenon which has been subjected to very extensive measurements and experimentation and has repeatedly proved to be invariable throughout the known universe (e.g., the law of gravity, the laws of motion).

> **thermodynamics:** the study of heat power;[30] a branch of physics which studies the efficiency of energy transfer and exchange.

The 2nd Law of Thermodynamics describes basic principles familiar in everyday life. It is partially a universal law of decay; the ultimate cause of why everything ultimately falls apart and disintegrates over time. Material things are not eternal. Everything appears to change eventually, and chaos increases. Nothing stays as fresh as the day one buys it; clothing becomes faded, threadbare, and ultimately returns to dust.[31]

verse has science observed explosions producing complex, ordered arrangements. Explosions *destroy* complexity and produce disorder.

Imagine being witness to the massive volcanic explosion of a great mountain. As tons of flying rock and dust settled, what are the odds that the settling debris would land to produce an entire city of well-formed buildings? It is safe to say it would never happen.

Many feel it is even more far-fetched to believe that an explosion (the "big bang") could ultimately produce every wondrous galaxy, planet, and physical law, and ultimately lead to the existence of every creature and plant. The cosmos around us is far more marvelous and intricate than a city. Even some Evolutionists have begun to abandon the "big bang," labeling it a hopeless theory.[28]

Although there are random accidents and evidences of deterioration throughout the cosmos (stars burning out or exploding, mutations, etc.), many scientists and philosophers note an underlying sense of purpose in the brilliant design and interrelationship of all things.

The more scientists explore the cosmos, the more they discover evidence of great order, complexity and appearance of design.[29]

*R*ather than being totally random and chaotic in construction, the cosmos is abundant with order.

Everything ages and wears out. Even death is a manifestation of this law. The effects of the 2nd Law are all around, touching everything in the universe.

Each year, vast sums are spent to counteract the relentless effects of this law (maintenance, painting,

EVOLUTION: Upward trend — *Increasing* order and complexity.
2ND LAW OF THERMODYNAMICS:
Downward trend — *decreasing* order and complexity.

Massive buildings may appear to be capable of lasting almost forever, but they will not. The need for ongoing repairs stems, in part, from the 2nd Law of Thermodynamics.

The useable energy of the universe is decreasing. The most probable state for any natural system is one of disorder.

medical bills, etc.). Ultimately, everything in nature is obedient to its unchanging laws.

2nd law of thermodynamics: Physicist Lord Kelvin stated it technically as follows: "There is no natural process the only result of which is to cool a heat reservoir and do external work." In more understandable terms, this law observes the fact that the useable energy in the universe is becoming less and less. Ultimately there would be no available energy left. Stemming from this fact we find that the most probable state for any natural system is one of disorder. All natural systems degenerate when left to themselves.[32]

It is well known that, left to themselves, chemical compounds *ultimately* break apart into simpler materials; they do not ultimately become more complex. Outside forces can increase order for a time (through the expenditure of relatively large amounts of energy, and through the input of design). However, such reversal cannot last forever. Once the force is released, processes return to their natural direction — greater disorder. Their energy is transformed into lower levels of availability for further work. The natural tendency of complex, ordered arrangements and systems is to become simpler and more disorderly with time.[33]

Thus, in the long term, there is an overall downward trend throughout the universe. Ultimately, when all the energy of the cosmos has been degraded, all molecules will move randomly, and the entire universe will be cold and without order.

To create LIFE would require much more than raw energy and materials; it would require a huge amount of complex, organized INFORMATION.

To be true, the Evolutionary theory would require a universal law of *increasing* complexity and order. However, no such force has been discovered. To put it simply: In the real world, the long-term overall flow appears to be downhill, not uphill. Thus, the 2nd Law seems to have dramatic implications for the theory of Evolution, despite claims to the contrary.[34] All experimental and physical observation appears to confirm that the Law is indeed universal, affecting *all* natural processes.[35]

entropy: a term related to the 2nd Law of Thermodynamics; entropy is a measure of the level of disorder in the universe;[36] the greater the disorder, the greater the entropy. Eventually, the increasing entropy of the universe would reach a maximum point, leaving everything completely disorderly and random. There would be no life and no heat; the downward slide would be complete. No further change would take place after that point.

Naturalistic Evolutionism requires that physical laws and atoms organize themselves into increasingly complex and beneficial, ordered arrangements. Thus, over eons of time, billions of things are supposed to have developed *upward*, becoming *more* orderly and complex.[37] However, this basic law of science (2nd Law of Thermodynamics) says the exact opposite.[38] Complex, ordered arrangements actually tend to become *simpler* and more *disorderly* with time. There is an irreversible downward trend ultimately at work throughout the universe. Evolution, with its ever increasing order and complexity, appears impossible in the natural world.

If Evolution is true, there must be an extremely powerful force or mechanism at work in the cosmos that can steadily defeat the powerful, ultimate tendency toward "disarrangedness" brought by the 2nd Law. If such a massive force or mechanism is in existence, it would seem it should be quite obvious to all scientists. Yet, the fact is, no such force of nature has been found.

A number of scientists believe the 2nd Law, when truly understood, is enough to refute the theory of Evolution. In fact, it is one of the most important reasons why various Evolutionists have dropped their theory in favor of Creationism.

Is Energy the Key?

> **open systems/closed systems:** open thermodynamic systems exchange heat, light, or matter with their surroundings, closed systems do not. No outside energy flows into a closed system. Earth is an open system; it receives outside energy from the Sun.

To create any kind of upward, complex organization in a closed system requires outside energy and outside information. Evolutionists maintain that the 2nd Law of Thermodynamics does not prevent Evolution on Earth, since this planet receives outside energy from the Sun. Thus, they suggest that the Sun's energy helped create the life of our beautiful planet. However, is the simple addition of energy all that is needed to accomplish this great feat?[39]

Compare a living plant with a dead one. Can the simple addition of energy make a completely dead plant live?

A dead plant contains the same basic structures as a living plant. It once used the Sun's energy to temporarily increase its order and grow and produce stems, leaves, roots, and flowers — all beginning from a single seed.

If there is actually a powerful Evolutionary force at work in the universe, and if the open system of Earth makes all the difference, why does the Sun's energy

not make a truly dead plant become alive again (assuming a sufficient supply of water, light, and the like)?

What actually happens when a dead plant receives energy from the Sun? The internal organization in the plant *decreases*; it tends to decay and break apart into its simplest components. The heat of the Sun only speeds the disorganization process.

THE ULTIMATE INGREDIENT: Designed and Coded Information

The distinguished scientist and origins expert, Dr. A.E. Wilder-Smith, puts it this way:

> "What is the difference then between a stick, which is dead, and an orchid which is alive? The difference is that the orchid has teleonomy in it. It is a machine which is capturing energy to increase order. Where you have life, you have teleonomy, and then the Sun's energy can be taken and make the thing grow — increasing its order" [temporarily].[40]

Distinguished scientist Dr. Arthur E. Wilder-Smith.

teleonomy: Information stored within a living thing. Teleonomy involves the concept of something having a design and purpose.[41] Non-teleonomy is "directionlessness," having no project. The teleonomy of a living thing is somehow stored within its genes. Teleonomy can use energy and matter to produce order and complexity.[42]

Where did the teleonomy of living things originate? It is important to note that the teleonomy (the ordering principle, the know-how) does not reside in matter itself. Matter, itself, is not creative. Dr. Wilder-Smith:

> "The pure chemistry of a cell is not enough to explain the working of a cell, although the workings are chemical. The chemical workings of a cell are controlled by information which does *not* reside in the atoms and molecules."[43]

Creationists believe cells build themselves from carefully designed and coded information which has been passed from one life to the next since their original inception.

Creation: When Creationists refer to the term "Creation," they are speaking of the original creation of the cosmos in a fully-working form. Many Creationists accept the historical account in the book of Genesis which describes a unique, one-time creation event which it says resulted in a complete environment including sea and land, fully-formed trees, stars, Moon, birds, fish, land animals and man in one week (and in that order).[44] It should be noted that this order is in marked contrast to the order of first existence described by Evolutionism. For example, Genesis implies that Earth and its vegetation were fully formed *before* the existence of stars or the Sun and Moon.

---

*H*as the 2nd Law of Thermodynamics been circumvented? NOT YET
Frank Greco

THE BOTTOM LINE
on the origin of the universe

- The two most common ideas used to try to explain the origin of the cosmos are Evolutionism and Creationism.

- Neither concept can be totally proved or disproved using *pure* science, since both deal to a significant extent with remote past events which cannot be experienced or examined.

- There is no scientific proof that the universe began or evolved as "big bang" theorists propose. Quite to the contrary, there are serious scientific problems with the theory.

- There are experienced and intelligent scientists who find all forms of evolutionism exceedingly unsatisfactory in providing a credible explanation for the origin of the cosmos – based on the known facts and physical laws.

- The powerful 2nd Law of Thermodynamics appears to render naturalistic Evolutionism scientifically untenable.

The Earth, A Young Planet?

Earth, as seen from the Moon.
Not all scientists agree that the Earth and Moon are billions of years old.

How old is planet Earth? On this point there are enormous differences of opinion between Evolutionists and Creationists. Many Creationists believe the Earth may be only 6 to 7 thousand years old. Evolutionists give it an age of approximately 5 billion years. Evolutionism, of course, *requires* billions of years to support the plausibility of life's emergence and of subsequent Evolution from "amoeba" to man.

Scientists have proposed numerous age estimating methods. Surprising to some, many of these systems appear to give indications of a young age.

Most age estimating systems promoted by Evolutionists involve radioactivity.[45] Various radioactive elements are involved, including Carbon-14, Uranium-238, Thorium-232, and Potassium-40. It is important to understand that most rock strata "dates" were actually assigned long before the first use of radioactive age estimating methods in 1911.[46]

radioactive element: an atom with an unstable nucleus which gives off energy in the form of particles (or rays) when it decays; The rate of decay can be measured.

Estimating Age by Carbon-14 Content

The Carbon-14 age estimating method[47] can only be used to "date" *organic* materials[48]; things which were once alive.[49] The inventor of the Carbon-14 dating method was the Nobel Prize winner Willard Libby,[50] a committed Evolutionist.

In simplified terms, here is how the system works: Carbon-12 is carbon in its common, natural, stable form. It is not radioactive. All living things depend on it for survival. Plants get it from carbon dioxide in the

Carbon-14 dating laboratory in the Netherlands.
This method measures the amount of radioactive carbon left in dead plants and animals.

The Carbon-14 system is only useful for estimating the age of organic remains, not rocks or "petrified" fossils.

air. This carbon is passed on to animals through the carbohydrates which plants produce and animals eat.

Carbon-14 is a radioactive form of carbon and is much rarer. It is produced when cosmic rays strike Earth's atmosphere.[51] Carbon-14 is naturally absorbed by living plants and animals in the same way as Carbon-12. The normal ratio between Carbon-12 and Carbon-14 in living things has been calculated.[52]

When an animal or plant dies, no further Carbon-14 is absorbed — and then the ratio between Carbon-12 and Carbon-14 in the remains begins to change. The Carbon-14 decays gradually and disappears — decomposing back into nitrogen. Dr. Libby developed a method to compare the amount of Carbon-14 in a specimen with the presumed original level, in an attempt to calculate the elapsed time since death.

Carbon-14 dating is useful for much archaeological work,[53] when used with great care. As with all age estimating systems, many variables and assumptions are involved. (See endnotes 54 and 55.)

Creationist dating experts believe Earth was devastated by a worldwide flood cataclysm thousands of years ago. They stress that such an event would have to be taken into account to properly calibrate the Carbon-14 method. [See endnotes 56, 57 (tree ring and bristlecone pine evidence) 58 (C-14 errors.)]

Both Creationists and Evolutionists agree Carbon-14 would be useless for estimating the age of anything that is supposed to be millions of years old. Carbon-14 has a relatively short life, and there would be no useful measurable amount left in 30 to 100 thousand years.

Conventional Carbon-14 techniques appear to produce fairly accurate age estimates from about 1,000 B.C. to the present. However, when it comes to "dates" older than this, there appear to be some problems. Most Creationists seriously question the accuracy of radiocarbon "dates" older than 3 thousand years, and certainly any radiocarbon estimates greater than about 4 or 5 thousand years.[59]

Other Radioactive Age Estimations

The Carbon-14 age estimating method does not work on rocks or thoroughly mineralized fossils; it is only useful for relatively well-preserved organic materials such as cloth, wood, and other non-fossilized materials. Other methods must be used to estimate the age of rocks and minerals. Two of the most widely-known systems are the potassium-argon method and the uranium-lead method.

A radioactive form of potassium is found in minute quantities in some rocks. It disintegrates at a measured rate into calcium and argon. Similarly, the radioactive element uranium decomposes into lead and some other elements.

Generally, Creationists consider Carbon-14 age estimates to be legitimate and useful — a system in good agreement with Creationism WHEN PROPERLY UNDERSTOOD AND CALIBRATED.

How are these processes used to estimate the age of rocks? The principle is similar to that used with Carbon-14. The speed of the disintegration process is measured. A portion of the material is ground up and a measurement is made of the ratio of radioactive "parent" atoms to the decomposition products.

Age estimates which are obviously wrong or contradictory are sometimes produced.[60] For example, new rock in the form of hardened lava flows produced estimated ages as great as 3 billion to 10.5 billion years, when they were actually less than 200 years old.[61]

Assumptions and More Assumptions

Arriving at a "date" depends upon a chain of assumptions,[62] each link in the chain being an assumption. The validity of the calculated date can be no stronger than the weakest link (weakest assumption) used in the calculation. What are some of the assump-

An age estimating method is much like a chain. Each assumption represents a link. The validity of the estimate can only be as strong as the weakest of the links.

tions made by most Evolutionists in using these systems?

- **ASSUMPTION:** Evolutionists generally assume the material being measured had no original "daughter" element(s) in it, or they assume the amount can be accurately estimated. For example, they may assume that all of the lead in a rock was produced by the decay of its uranium.

  PROBLEM: One can almost never know with absolute certainty how much radioactive or daughter substance was present at the start.

- **ASSUMPTION:** Evolutionists have also tended to assume that the material being measured has been in a closed system. It has often been wrongly assumed that no outside factors altered the normal ratios in the material, adding or subtracting any of the elements involved.

  PROBLEM: The age estimate can be thrown off considerably, if the radioactive element or the daughter element is leached in or leached out of the sample. There are evidences that this could be a significant problem.[63] Simple things such as groundwater movement can carry radioactive material or the daughter element into or out of rock. Rocks must be carefully tested to determine what outside factors might have changed their content.

- **ASSUMPTION:** They assume that the rate of decomposition has always remained constant — *absolutely* constant.[64]

  PROBLEM: Scientific measurements of decay rates have only been conducted since the time of the Curies in the early 1900s. There is little convincing proof that decay rates have been constant over *billions* of years. Furthermore, there *is* evidence that the rate of radioactive decay can change. (See endnote 65.) If the decay rates have ever been higher in

the past, then relatively young rocks would wrongly "date" as being old rocks.

Evolutionist William Stansfield, Ph.D., California Polytech State, has stated:

"It is obvious that radiometric techniques may not be the absolute dating methods that they are claimed to be. Age estimates on a given geological stratum by different radiometric methods are often quite different (sometimes by hundreds of millions of years). There is no absolutely reliable long-term radiological 'clock'."[66]

Evolutionist Frederick B. Jueneman candidly summarizes the situation:

"The age of our globe is presently thought to be some 4.5 billion years, based on radio-decay rates of uranium and thorium. Such 'confirmation' may be shortlived, as nature is not to be discovered quite so easily. There has been in recent years the horrible realization that radio-decay rates are not as constant as previously thought, nor are they immune to environmental influences. And this could mean that the atomic clocks are reset during some global disaster, and events which brought the Mesozoic to a close may not be 65 million years ago, but rather, within the age and memory of man."[67]

What Are the Scientific Indications for a Young Earth?

Few people realize there are age estimation methods which seem to contradict the typical old-age "dates" mentioned in the media. In fact, there are relatively few scientific age estimation systems which have been interpreted as evidence for a billions of years old Earth (*see list in endnote 68*), and many which have been suggested as evidence consistent with the theory that the Earth is much younger. (See list of 102 examples at end of this chapter.)

In the opinion of astrophysicist/geophysicist and Creationist Dr. Harold Slusher[69]:

"There are a number of indicators that seem to indicate an age of no more than 10,000 years, at the very most, for the solar system and the Earth."[70]

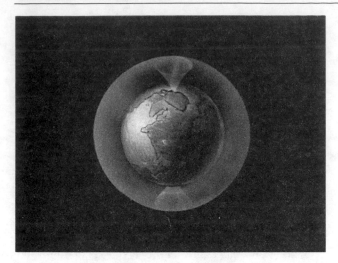

The strength of Earth's magnetic field is decreasing.

Following are some examples accepted by Dr. Slusher and/or others:

Earth's Magnetic Field

Earth is surrounded by an invisible magnetic force which aligns near the North and South Poles. This is the magnetic field that makes directional compasses operate. The needle of the compass points to the North Magnetic Pole. Like all forces of nature, the energy in this dipole magnetic field is decaying (decreasing in strength) due in part to the 2nd Law of Thermodynamics.[71] The strength has dropped 6% since measurements began in 1835.[72]

Dr. Thomas Barnes is a physicist who has studied this in great detail.[73] His conclusion is that the half-life of this magnetic field is approximately 830 to 1400 years.[74]

> **half-life:** the time required for half the amount of a force or substance to be eliminated. For example, 1 ounce of original radioactive material would decay, leaving 1/2 ounce after 1 half-life had elapsed. The remaining 1/2 ounce would be halved to 1/4 ounce after another half-life, and so on.

This means that 830 to 1400 years ago the magnetic field would have been twice as strong as it is today. Another 830 to 1400 years before that, it would have been 4 times as strong, and so on. According to Dr. Barnes:

> "If we went back about 10 thousand years, the Earth's magnetic field would have been as strong as the field in a magnetic star. A magnetic star is like our Sun; it has a

Many age estimating methods have been suggested as evidence for a young Earth.

nuclear power source. Surely our Earth never had a nuclear source like the Sun. Surely our Earth never had a magnetic field stronger than that of a star. That would limit the age of the Earth to 10 thousand years.

Science could definitely say, from the greatest physical evidence (the kind of evidence and physics that we design radar sets with and communications sets) that the Earth's magnetic field cannot be more than about 6 to 15 thousand years old."[75]

Helium in Earth's Atmosphere

Former Nobel Prize nominee Dr. Melvin Cook[76] has studied Earth's natural helium supplies extensively. Eventually, he became convinced that the reason there is so little of this gas in the atmosphere[77] is that the planet is relatively young.

> **radiogenic helium:** helium generated by the decay of uranium atoms. When the radioactive element uranium decomposes into lead, the gas helium is released from the rock into Earth's atmosphere. Helium produced in this way is called "radiogenic helium."[78] It makes up part of the helium found in our atmosphere.

Uranium and thorium deposits throughout the world are steadily producing helium. More helium enters our atmosphere from the Sun and from helium leaking from the Earth's core through the crust.[79] If Earth was actually billions of years old, Dr. Cook believes the atmosphere should now contain a much larger amount of helium, up to a million times more than now exists.

Where is the helium? Evidence indicates that very little of it can escape into space.[80] Dr. Cook and other physicists have said they believe the atmospheric helium indicates Earth's age is less than 10 to 15 thousand years.[81]

Population Growth

The rapid growth of Earth's human population has been an important topic of concern for a number of years. This study has produced information which has been interpreted as evidence of Earth's young age. If people have been living here for a million years or more (as Evolutionists claim), some Creationists wonder: why has there been no global overpopulation problem long before now?

Some say the average world population growth over the centuries has been about 2% per year. One can be generous to the Evolutionists and assume that the growth rate was actually much smaller, perhaps 1/2% per year.

Even at that rate, it would take only 4,000 years to produce today's population beginning from a single original couple. Creationists say this fits well with their theories, since they believe Earth's entire population (save 8 people) was destroyed about 4,000 years ago due to a worldwide flood.

If the Earth is as old as Evolutionists claim, and if humans have been here for more than a million years, then it would seem Earth could potentially have been overpopulated long ago. If the population increased at only 1/2% per year, in 1 million years there could conceivably be trillions of trillions of people today (to be more exact, 10^{2100}).

Even if the population was assumed to have grown at such a *drastically* slower, almost zero rate so that it would have taken a million years to reach the present level, there would have been at least 3,000 billion (3,000,000,000,000) people that have lived on this planet, it is said. Yet, where is the fossil or cultural evidence for such massive numbers? Creationists are confident that humans have been on this planet for only several thousand years.*[82]*

Short-Period Comets

comets: natural objects in space which orbit the Sun (other than planets, their moons, and meteors). As viewed from Earth, a comet has a fuzzy head with a bright center (nucleus) and streaming tail(s) of variable length.*[83]*

There are, also, various facts which have been interpreted as evidence that our entire solar system may be relatively young. One of these is the very rapid breakup of our solar system's short-period comets.

As comets orbit our Sun they disintegrate due to the Sun's powerful gravity, the solar "wind," and internal explosions. If Evolutionists are correct about the age of the solar system, one must ask, why are there *any*

Earth's Moon.

short-period comets left?*[84]* According to Dr. Slusher and various other astronomical researchers, the *maximum* lifetime of a short-period comet is calculated to be about 10 thousand years.*[85]* This presents a problem for Evolutionists because most astronomers believe these comets came into existence at the same time as the solar system itself (some time after the supposed original "big bang").

Evolutionists have devised a theory to deflect criticism on this point. They propose that a gigantic "cloud" of comets is steadily feeding in a new supply. The Evolutionists' explanation for why this "Oort Cloud"*[86]* cannot be seen or measured is that it is too distant to be detected from Earth.

The theory is that comets get "kicked in" to the solar system by gravity or collisions — thus maintaining our solar system's supply of short-period comets. Creationists feel that it is very significant that this theoretical "mother lode" of comets has never been observed or scientifically verified, to date.*[87]* They doubt that it exists.

The Escaping Moon

Due to various factors, including tidal friction, Earth's rotational speed is constantly slowing. This provides evidence to limit the Moon's age to less than 1 billion years (that is, at least 80% lower than the age assigned by Evolutionists).*[88]*

tidal friction: The orbiting Moon exerts a decelerating torque on planet Earth (and vice versa). This braking effect is due to two main factors: (a) Gravitational pull between the Moon and Earth (the Moon's gravity particularly affects the oceans). (b) Earth's rotation speed is greater than the Moon's orbit speed. Thus, Earth's back and forth tidal movements (caused by the Moon) create friction against the rotating planet (especially in shallow waters).*[89]*

The speed at which the Sun is shrinking has been suggested as evidence for a young Earth.

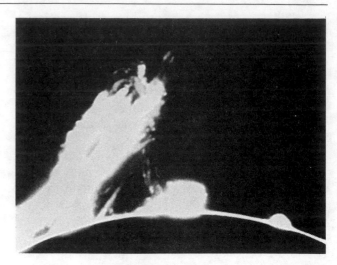

Conservative figures suggest the Sun's diameter is decreasing 1 mile per year (overall, long-term average), but this amount changes year to year due to a 76 to 80 year variation cycle.

The slowing Earth transfers its energy to the Moon. This results in a constant yearly increase in the distance between the Earth and Moon. The deceleration is slowing, but can still be measured.[90]

Extrapolating back in time brings the Moon in contact with Earth in a relatively short period (compared to the "Evolutionary age" of the Earth).[91] Yet, there is no evidence that the Moon was ever extremely close to our planet. In fact, at any distance closer than 11,500 miles, the "Roche Limit," the Earth's powerful tidal forces would break the Moon into small pieces that would orbit Earth much like the rings of Saturn.[92]

Taking this into account, there is as yet no scientifically plausible alternative to support an age of 4 or more billion years for the Moon. Creationists say this phenomenon is strong evidence that the Earth and Moon are not billions of years old.

The Moon's escape is only one of numerous discoveries about the Moon, the planets, and the moons of other planets which have been used to suggest a young Moon and solar system.[93]

Is the Sun Shrinking?

Due to its self-consumption, the Sun is almost surely smaller now than it was at its peak. If the shrinkage rate could be accurately measured and if sufficient solar data could be collected, they could be used to estimate the Sun's age.

How fast is the Sun really shrinking, and how much has the rate varied through the centuries? Evidence to answer these questions is inconclusive, as yet. (See endnote *94*.) But, even at very conservative rates there is still a problem for those who believe in a billions-of-years-old Earth and Sun.

It can be shown that for 99.8% of Earth's supposed *Evolutionary* age[95] it could have been too hot for life

to exist, due to the Sun's greater size. These conservative figures also indicate the Sun could have been twice its present radius only 1 million years ago.[96] 210 million years ago the Sun could have been large enough to touch Earth.[97] Even only 10 million years ago, the Sun could have been too large for life on the planet.

Variations in the rate of shrinkage would, of course, yield substantially different numbers of years. So, caution is needed. Still, the overall implication is clear. The Sun (and thus, also, Earth) may not be nearly as old as assumed.[98] Furthermore, it should be remembered that science has never actually proved the Sun or the Earth are tremendously old. Evolutionist and astrophysicist/geophysicist Dr. John A. Eddy, High Altitude Observatory, Boulder, Colorado:

> "I suspect … that the Sun is 4.5 billion years old. However, given some new and unexpected results to the contrary and some time for frantic readjustment, I suspect that we could live with Bishop Ussher's figure for the age of the Earth and Sun (approximately 6 thousand years). I don't think we have much in the way of observational evidence in astronomy to conflict with that."[99]

Meteorites

meteorite: fallen meteor; a mass of metal or stone from a meteor that has fallen upon Earth, the Moon, or any other body in space.

Every year, many meteorites pierce Earth's atmosphere and are deposited on the ground. Thus, if Earth's strata have indeed been building up over billions of years, it would seem that finding pieces of "fossil" meteorites in the strata should not be too uncommon. Yet, it is – *extremely* so. Meteorites are almost never found in the strata (some say never).[100]

The first Apollo astronauts were surprised to find that the Moon's loose dust layer is thin.

This makes good sense if Creationists are right. They believe the majority of Earth's strata were laid down rapidly, primarily during a worldwide, year-long flood. (See chapter: "The Fossil Record.") Thus, there would be little opportunity for many meteorites to accumulate.

Space Dust

Related to the deposit of meteorites is space dust. The source of this dust is, at least partially, the breakup of comets, meteors and meteorites (as described previously). This interplanetary space dust settles regularly on the planets and has been measured on Earth, the Moon, and Mars.

Dr. Slusher has suggested that this dust is another evidence that Earth and the solar system are young. He he pointed out an obvious contradiction produced by Evolutionists. Their measurements of incoming space dust and their published estimates of the deposition rate[101] did not agree with their billions-of-years-old age for the solar system. Given so much dust and such an enormous amount of time, there should now be a great accumulation of space dust.

In fact, when astronauts first landed on the Moon, many Evolutionists expected a very thick layer of loose dust.[102] Depth estimates ranged from 50 to 180 feet — and even much higher. Sinking deep into this dust was at least one astronaut's greatest fear about landing on the Moon. Thus, large, saucer-shaped feet were provided on the Lunar Lander.

What did astronauts actually discover? The loose dust layer was quite minor. Dr. Slusher and others interpreted this as evidence that the Moon is not billions of years old,[103] and also pointed to low loose meteoritic dust measurements on planets and the rarity of meteoritic material in Earth's oceans.[104]

Is this lack of loose meteoritic dust clear evidence for a young solar system? Probably, but it appears the case is not as clearcut as some thought. Evolutionists now point to new measurements which indicate a very small rate of cosmic dust and meteor inflow to Earth. These, they say, are much more accurate measurements, since they were made from satellites. Conversely, some Creationists wonder why a previous NASA report indicated a very large amount of cosmic dust in the vicinity of the Earth and Moon.[105]

However, if the figures now being used by Evolutionists are accurate, then their previous estimates were tremendously in error,[106] and the evidence for disproving an old age using this *particular* process is weakened.

On the Moon, in particular, the case has been blunted by the discovery of what is said to be meteoritic dust within the subsurface, beneath the surface's thin layer of loose dust. The subsurface is a firm, compacted material called lunar regolith and appears to consist mainly of pulverized Moon rock. But cores drilled into it more than 9 feet[107] appear to show that 1.5% of it is (or could be) meteoritic material[108] uniformly mixed throughout,[109] at least to this depth (and possibly further). Thus there may be much more meteoritic dust on the Moon than is readily apparent at the surface.

However, all Evolutionary theories about the origin of the Moon and the solar system predict a much larger amount of incoming dust in the Moon's early years. In fact, they say that the Sun and the planets were formed from an immense cloud of dust. The very thick layer of dust that would be expected according to these Evolutionary theories is still almost completely missing. As astrophysicist Dr. Donald DeYoung has said,

> "The 'moon dust' problem has not gone away! The absence of lunar dust is an evidence for a more recently created moon than claimed by Evolutionists."[110]

Dating System Implications

Many Creationary scientists are convinced that the billions-of-years calculations of Evolutionists are based, for the most part, on weaker scientific footings than those which yield younger ages.

If Evolution by natural processes from "amoeba" to man is possible, as Evolutionists maintain, it would undoubtedly require billions of years to accomplish. Thus, indications for a young Earth and solar system are bad for Evolutionary theory. If the Earth could be proven to be as young as many Creationists expect, it would be a fatal blow to Evolutionism.

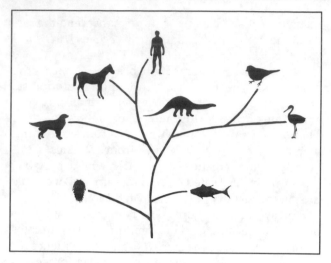

If the universe was conclusively proven to be merely thousands of years old, rather than billions, Evolutionism would appear to be completely incredible.

List of 102 Processes Suggested by Some as Supporting Evidence for an Earth Younger than Billions of Years

Listed in alphabetical order / This list is not necessarily complete. / Inclusion is NOT an indication of the author's opinion of relative validity / Unless otherwise marked, reference details for this section are in endnote *111* and are referenced by A-Z codes after each item.

1. **Aluminum** — rate of influx of aluminum into Earth's oceans from rivers. (F2, S2, Y1)

2. **Antimony** — rate of influx of antimony into Earth's oceans from rivers. (F2, S2, Y1)

3. **Archaeology** — origin of human civilizations. (F2, p. 164 of P2)

4. **Barium** — rate of influx of barium into Earth's oceans from rivers. (F2, S2, Y1)

5. **Bicarbonate** — rate of influx of bicarbonate into Earth's oceans from rivers. (Q2)

6. **Bismuth** — rate of influx of bismuth into Earth's oceans from rivers. (F2, S2, Y1)

7. **Calcium leaching** — rate of leaching of calcium from Earth's continents. (F2, Y3)

8. **Calcium influx** — rate of influx of calcium into Earth's oceans. (F2, Y3)

9. **Carbon-14 production** — the production rate of Carbon-14 is not equal to its disintegration rate. (pp. 159-161 of P2, X2)

10. **Carbon-14 decay** — decay of Carbon-14 in Precambrian wood. (F2)

11. **Carbon-14 in meteorites** — formation of Carbon-14 on meteorites. (Q2)

12. **Carbonates** — rate of influx of carbonates into Earth's oceans. (F2, Y3)

13. **Chlorine leaching** — rate of leaching of chlorine from Earth's continents. (F2, Y3)

14. **Chlorine influx** — rate of influx of chlorine into Earth's oceans. (F2, Y3)

15. **Chromium** — rate of influx of chromium into Earth's oceans from rivers. (F2, S2, Y1)

16. **Cobalt** — rate of influx of cobalt into Earth's oceans from rivers. (F2, S2, Y1)

17. **Comets (short-period)** — existence and decay of numerous short-period comets.

18. **Comets (long-period)** — rate of decay of long-period comets. (F2, L2)

19. **Copper** — rate of influx of copper into Earth's oceans via rivers. (F2, S2, Y1)

20. **Coral** — rate of growth of active coral reefs. (Q2)

21. **Deltas** — rate of growth of river deltas, such as the Mississippi. (F2, p. 163 of P2, V2)

22. **Dust (interstellar)** — extinction of interplanetary dust due to stellar radiation which pushes dust away, but has not yet cleared away the small particles around the sun — same problem also applies to many stars. Also, 3 giant rings of dust circling in solar system. (C2, I1, pp. 55-64 of L2, p. 169 of P2, Q1)

23. **Dust speed** — cosmic dust velocities are dramatically too low if the galaxies are billions of years old. (pp. 169-171 of P2, Q1)

24. **Earth cooling** — rate of cooling of Earth by heat efflux. (F2, P1, S1, pp. 80-85 of X3, Z1, Z2)

25. **Earth to moon distance** — rate of change of Moon's distance from Earth.*[112]*

26. **Erosion** — rate of erosion of Earth's continents. It has been said the continents could be totally eroded 170 to 340 times in less than 3.5 billion years. (D2, F2, p. 163 of P2, U2)

27. **Galaxies** — the lack of proof for the existence of field-galaxies. (p. 69 in C2)

28. **Galaxies** — decay lines of galaxies. (F2, W2)

29. **Galaxy groupings** — "never appear to occur singly".*[113]*

30. **Galaxy mass** — low mass of well-isolated groups or clusters.*[114]*

31. **Galaxy spirals** — spiral-arm structure would be wound up into a near circle.*[115]*

32. **Gas** — expanding interstellar gas. (F2, W1)

33. **Gold** — rate of influx of gold into Earth's oceans from rivers. (F2, S2, Y1)

34. **Helium** — relative rarity in Earth's atmosphere.

35. **Helium in zircons** — in zircon crystals. (D1, H1, K1)

36. **Human population** – rate of growth.

37. **Hydrogen** — hydrogen throughout the universe is being converted into helium without a proven generator of hydrogen to replace it, yet great amounts of hydrogen exist throughout the universe. (p. 177 in P2)

38. **Iron** — rate of influx of iron into Earth's oceans from rivers. (F2, S2, Y1)

39. **Jupiter** — planet is not yet cooled off (Jupiter is said to be radiating more energy than can be accounted for by

radiation received from the sun, gravitational contraction and radioactive decay). (O1)

40. **Lead** — formation of radiogenic lead by neutron capture. (F2, X3)

41. **Lead in zircons** — Lead has been found in zircon crystals in deep granite cores. Due to the high temperature (313°C) of the rock, the lead should have diffused out at a rate of 1% per 300 thousand years. Yet, no loss at all can be detected. Therefore, the supposedly extremely ancient granite may be be younger than 300 thousand years. (D1, J2, K1, N2)

42. **Lead influx** — rate of influx of lead into Earth's oceans from rivers. (F2, S2, Y1)

43. **Lithium** — rate of influx of lithium into Earth's oceans from rivers. (F2, S2, Y1)

44. **Living things** — growth of oldest living part of Earth's biosphere. (B1, pp. 164-165 in P2)

45. **Manganese** — rate of influx of manganese into Earth's oceans from rivers. (F2, S2, Y1)

46. **Magma** — influx of magma and volcanic ejecta from mantle onto Earth's crust. Rates suggest there would be 28-114 times more than exists if Earth is 5 billion years old (20-80 times more in 3.5 billion years). (D2, F2, p. 166 in P2, pp. 156-157 in U1, X1)

47. **Magnesium** — rate of influx of magnesium into Earth's oceans from rivers. (F2, S2, Y1)

48. **Magnetism decay** — of Earth's magnetic field.

49. **Magnetism decay in rocks** — of natural remanent paleomagnetism in Earth rocks. (F2, pp. 280-292 in X3)

50. **Mercury** — rate of influx of the element mercury into Earth's oceans from rivers. (F2, S2, Y1)

51. **Meteorites** — lack of meteorites and meteoritic and cosmic dust accumulation in Earth's strata.

52. **Meteors** not sufficiently sorted by Poynting/Robertson Effect. (pp. 29-35 in C2, I1, R2)

53. **Meteor showers** — maximum life of meteor showers. (F2, L2)

54. **Molybdenum** — rate of influx of molybdenum into Earth's oceans from rivers. (F2, S2, Y1)

55. **Moon rock viscosity** and height of Moon's craters. (pp. 49-53 in C2, G2)

56. **Moon gases** — presence of various inert gases on the Moon's surface, including Argon-36 and Krypton-84. (p. 172 in P2)

57. **Moon of Jupiter (Io)** — existence of volcano on Io. (pp. 43-44 in C2)

58. **Moon of Saturn (Titan)** — existence of escaping methane from Titan. (F2, L2)

59. **Mountain uplift rate** — Despite various erosive forces, it has been said that Earth's mountains are rising at least 100 centimeters per thousand years. Assuming the uniformitarian philosophy of Evolutionists, the mountains might be expected to be much taller if Earth is really old. A mere 55 million years of extrapolation yields mountains more than 5 times higher than Mt. Everest.[116]

60. **Mutation load** — lack of evidence for very large numbers of accumulated mutations which might be expected if life has been evolving for billions of years. (p. 168 in P2)

61. **Nickel** — rate of influx of nickel into Earth's oceans from rivers. (F2, pp. 40-41 in L2, S2)

62. **Ocean floor** — rate of accumulation of calcareous ooze. (F2, p. 164 in P2, Y2)

63. **Oil pressure** — existence of oil gushers and other high pressure entrapments of oil and gas in permeable rock. (F2; p. 159 in P2; pp. 242-248, 253-262 in X3)

64. **Oil seepage** — rate of submarine oil seepage into oceans. (F2, T2)

65. **Oxygen** — present quantity of oxygen in Earth's atmosphere could be generated by plants in 5 thousand years. (p. 178 in P2)

66. **Plutonium** — rate of decay of natural plutonium.[117]

67. **Polonium-218** (half-life 3 minutes) radiohalos found in Earth's granite – suggesting extremely rapid granite solidification in Earth's base rocks. (D1, N2)

68. **Polystrate fossils** – suggesting rapid deposition of the sedimentary strata involved.[118]

69. **Potassium decay** — decay of potassium with entrapped argon. (F2, L1)

70. **Potassium influx** — rate of influx of potassium into Earth's oceans from rivers. (F2, S2, Y1)

71. **Rivers** — meandering serpentine course of many rivers and canyons cut through many layers of strata. (A1)

72. **Rubidium** — rate of influx of rubidium into Earth's oceans from rivers. (F2, S2, Y1)

73. **Saturn's radiation** — planet is not yet cooled off (Saturn is said to be radiating more energy than can be accounted for by radiation received from the sun, gravitational contraction and radioactive decay). (O1)

74. **Saturn's rings** — existence of significant instability despite supposed age. (p. 45 in C2, pp. 65-71 in L2)

75. **Sediments influx** — influx of sediments into Earth's oceans from rivers. It has been said that present rates would yield the oceans' current sediment deposits in just 50 million years. In less than 3.5 billion years, the deposits would be 19 times thicker than the current depth of the ocean. (D2, F2, p. 166 in P2, U2)

76. **Sediments accumulation** — rate of accumulation of sediments for Earth's sedimentary rocks (Morris lists at 20 thousand years maximum). (D2, Q2)

77. **Sediment lithification** — rate of lithification of sediments to form sedimentary rocks (Morris lists at 20 thousand years maximum). (Q2)

78. **Silicon** — rate of influx of silicon into Earth's oceans from rivers. (F2, S2, Y1)

79. **Silver** — rate of influx of silver into Earth's oceans from rivers. (F2, S2, Y1)

80. **Sirius-B** described as red, not white, by ancient astronomers. (p. 67 in C2)

81. **Sodium leaching** — rate of leaching of sodium from Earth's continents. (F2, Y3)

82. **Sodium influx** — rate of influx of sodium into Earth's oceans from rivers. (F2, S2, Y1)

83. **Stars (large)** — existence of very large stars. (p. 161 in P2)

84. **Star cluster breakup** — time for breakup of star clusters, escape of high-velocity stars from globular clusters.*[119]*

85. **Stars** — miscellaneous evidence from the stars. (pp. 59-60 in C2, R2)

86. **Strata unconsolidation** — unconsolidated state of some "deep rocks, even to the Cambrian." (p. 174 in P2)

87. **Strontium formation** — formation of radiogenic strontium by neutron capture. (F2, pp. 38-40 in X3)

88. **Strontium influx** — rate of influx of strontium into Earth's oceans from rivers. (F2, S2, Y1)

89. **Sulfate** — rate of influx of sulfate into Earth's oceans. (F2, Y3)

90. **Sun shrinkage** — evidence of shrinking diameter.

91. **Sun** — Evidence that the sun might not be operating via thermonuclear fusion (lack of neutrinos, temperature, etc.).*[120]*

92. **Thorium-230** isotope found on the Moon. (pp. 44-45 in C2, pp. 177-178 in P2)

93. **Thorium** — rate of influx of thorium into Earth's oceans from rivers. (F2, S2, Y1)

94. **Tin** — rate of influx of tin into Earth's oceans from rivers. (F2, S2, Y1)

95. **Titanium** — rate of influx of titanium into Earth's oceans from rivers. (F2, S2, Y1)

96. **Topsoil** — small average depth of Earth's topsoil worldwide. (p. 174 in P2)

97. **Tungsten** — rate of influx of tungsten into Earth's oceans from rivers. (F2, S2, Y1)

98. **Uranium influx** — rate of influx of uranium into Earth's oceans.*[121]*

99. **Uranium decay** — decay of uranium with initial "radiogenic" lead. (F2, L1)

100. **Uranium-236** isotope found on the Moon. (pp. 44-45 in C2, pp. 177-178 in P2)

101. **Water** — rate of influx of juvenile water into Earth's oceans. (F2, pp. 166-167 in P2, p. 156 in U1)

102. **Zinc** — rate of influx of zinc into Earth's oceans from rivers. (F2, S2, Y1)

THE BOTTOM LINE
on Earth's age

- Some scientific age estimating methods seem to indicate Earth is extremely old. Yet, many more processes apparently indicate it is much younger. Ultimately, both old-age and young-age methods suffer from similar difficulties — extrapolation over the unknown past, questionable assumptions, etc.

- There is no scientific method that can positively prove Earth is very old — or relatively young. Proof of an old Earth would require billions of years of on-site measurements and observations.

The Origin of Life

Earth is filled with myriad life forms of enormous complexity.

Are Evolutionists correct? Could time, chance and natural chemical processes have created life in the beginning? This chapter examines the scientific evidence.

MATERIALISM

Many modern scientists are materialists. That is, they believe physical matter is the only ultimate reality. They suppose that everything in the cosmos, including life, can be explained in terms of interacting matter. Materialists do not accept the existence of spiritual or supernatural forces.

Biologists who believe in materialism are particularly concerned with: (1) proving a purely materialistic origin of life, and (2) proving that life can be created in the laboratory.

life: the quality that distinguishes a living animal or plant from other arrangements of matter, including a dead animal or plant. All known life has cells whose activities are controlled by a DNA/RNA system.

Most scientists are not strict materialists. Biochemist and Creationist Dr. Arthur Wilder-Smith:

"Life rides upon matter, and matter has to be highly organized to carry life. The materialists say that life, since it's made up of atoms, molecules, and chemical reactions, is just simply chemistry and nothing else — and that life originated by chance chemical reactions.

Now, if life consists merely of chemistry, and nothing but chemistry, the best way to understand its real potentialities is to look at some of the chemical substances of life. And we shall see that it is NOT merely a matter of chemistry."[123]

Renowned scientist and Creationist Dr. Louis Pasteur (1822-1895), the father of bacteriology. He developed vaccinations and immunizations which saved millions of lives.

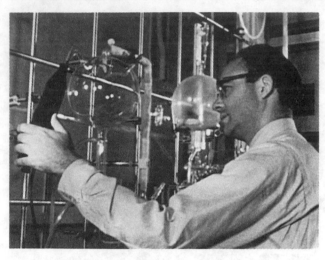

Dr. Miller with his famous apparatus. Scientists have utterly failed at producing life in a test tube. To date, all attempts to prove that life could have evolved on Earth by any natural means have also failed.

Chemicals + Energy — Could They Have Given Birth to the First Life?

It was the famous French scientist and Creationist, Pasteur, who provided the first scientific evidence that living things are not produced from non-living matter.[123] During the Middle Ages, some people thought non-living matter often gave birth to living things (spontaneous generation). Worms, insects, mice, and other creatures were thought to be created by materials in their environment.

> spontaneous generation: the idea that living creatures can be produced naturally from non-living substances.[124] It is important to note that science has never observed such an occurrence.[125]

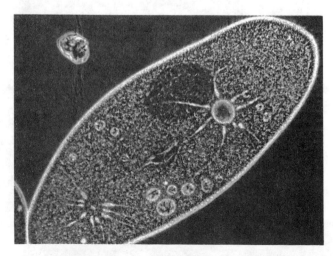

Even the simplest one-celled animal contains mechanisms enormously more complex than any man-made machine.

No one has ever found an organism that never had a parent of some sort. Today, this is one of the best accepted facts in biology. All living things are produced from one or more parents.

Surprisingly, however, many modern people still faithfully believe in a form of "spontaneous generation." Materialists assume life arose spontaneously somewhere in ancient Earth's water supply — water which contained absolutely no life, just minerals and chemical substances used by living things.[126]

Because oxygen in the atmosphere would destroy all possibility of life arising by natural processes, materialists assume the atmosphere had no oxygen. They also assume it contained certain necessary ingredients, including ammonia, nitrogen, hydrogen, water vapor and methane.[127] However, it is well known that mixing these ingredients does not create life. Therefore, materialists theorize something else must be needed — perhaps a bolt of energy.[128]

Science Tries to Create Life

Dr. Stanley Miller and Dr. Sidney Fox were two of the first scientists to attempt laboratory experiments aimed at trying to prove that life could arise spontaneously. They designed a pyrex apparatus containing methane, ammonia, and water vapor, but no oxygen. Through this mixture they passed electric sparks to simulate lightning strikes. [129]

What was the result? No life was produced, of course, but the electricity did combine some atoms to form amino acids.

> amino acids: compounds that are the simplest units out of which proteins[130] can be assembled.

Did the Miller/Fox experiment prove that life could arise in some ancient sea struck by lightning? No, it seems to substantially weaken the case.[131] The mixture of amino acids and other simple chemicals produced are not right for producing life. All known life uses amino acids which are exclusively of the "left-handed" form.

> left-handed molecules: a term used to refer to the "stereochemistry"[132] of a molecule's construction; An amino acid can be chemically "left-handed" or "right-handed" in its orientation. These two forms are identical in their atoms, but opposite in their 3-dimensional arrangement. They are mirror images of each other.

No known life can use any combination of both "right-handed" and "left-handed" amino acids. Adding even one "right-handed" amino acid to a chain of

> *All living things come into existence from parents.*

"left-handed" amino acids can destroy the entire chain![133] When amino acids are synthesized in the laboratory, there is always a *50%* mixture of the two forms. Only through highly advanced, intelligently controlled processes can these two forms be separated.

Even if this overwhelming obstacle did not exist, many more major problems remain for the Evolution of life. There are numerous reasons why the amino acids would disintegrate or never form in the first place.[134] Furthermore, life requires much more than amino acids. One necessity is proteins.

> **proteins:** extremely complex chemicals (molecules) constructed of amino acids; found in all animals and plants.

One chemist has calculated the immense odds against amino acids ever combining to form the necessary proteins *by undirected means*. He estimated the probability to be more than 10^{67} to 1 *against* even a *small* protein forming — by time and chance, in an ideal mixture of chemicals, in an ideal atmosphere, and given up to 100 billion years (an age 10 to 20 times greater than the supposed age of the Earth).[135] Mathematicians generally agree that, statistically, any odds beyond 1 in 10^{50} have a zero probability of ever happening ("and even that gives it the benefit of the doubt!").[136]

Various highly qualified researchers feel they have scientifically proved, beyond question, that even the simplest known form of life could *never* have begun without first being designed and assembled by an outside, highly intelligent being.[137]

> **molecule:** a chemical combination of atoms.

What has chemist Dr. Wilder-Smith concluded is the bottom line on this issue?

> "It is *emphatically* the case that life could NOT arise spontaneously in a primeval soup of this kind."[138]

DNA MOLECULES AND THE OVERWHELMING ODDS AGAINST EVOLUTION

Within each cell there is an area called the nucleus which contains the all-important chromosomes.[139] Chromosomes are microscopically small, rod-shaped structures which carry the genes. Within the chromosomes is an even smaller structure, discovered in the 1950s, called DNA.[140] This is one of the most important chemical substances in the human body — or in any other living thing.

DNA is a super-molecule which stores coded hereditary information. It consists of two long "chains" of chemical "building blocks" paired together. In humans, the strands of DNA are almost 2

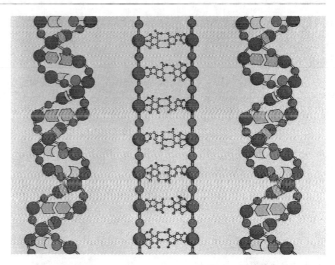

What are the chances of evolving the DNA molecule crucial to all life by natural processes? Without an outside controlling designer of some kind, it appears to be practically impossible (and some say that is an understatement).

yards long, yet less than a trillionth of an inch thick.[141]

In function, DNA is somewhat like a computer program on a floppy disk. It stores and transfers encoded information and instructions. However, DNA is millions of times more highly advanced than any computer program. For example, the DNA of a human stores enough information code to fill 1,000 books — each with 500 pages of very small, closely-printed type.[142] The code is so sophisticated that it can routinely construct an entire adult human, starting with just a single, microscopic cell (the fertilized egg). Even the DNA of a single bacterium is composed of 3 million units,[143] all aligned in a very precise, meaningful sequence.

Many scientists are convinced that cells containing such a complex code and such intricate chemistry could never have come into being by pure, undirected chemistry.[144] No matter how chemicals are mixed, they do not create DNA spirals or any intelligent code whatsoever. Only DNA reproduces DNA.

Distinguished chemist and physicist Dr. John Grebe[145] used the following illustration to represent the type of insurmountable odds against the Evolution of the enormously complex DNA molecule:

> "The 15,000 or more atoms of the individual sub-assemblies [of a single DNA molecule], if left to chance as required by the evolutionary theory, would go together in any of 10^{87} different ways."[146]

Evolutionists claim the universe is about 10 or 20 billion years old.[147] Yet, there are less than 10^{17} seconds in 20 billion years. Therefore, even if a trial and error combination occurred every second from the beginning to today, the odds still appear hope-

Human DNA stores an immensely complex code long enough to fill 1,000 books — each with 500 pages of small, closely printed type.

Evolutionist Michael Denton:

"The complexity of the simplest known type of cell is so great that it is impossible to accept that such an object could have been thrown together by some kind of freakish, vastly improbable event. Such an occurrence would be indistinguishable from a miracle."[151]

Famous Evolutionist Sir Fred Hoyle[152] is in agreement with Creationists on this point. He has reportedly said that supposing the first cell originated by chance is like believing a tornado could sweep through a junkyard filled with airplane parts and form a Boeing 747.[153]

Most Evolutionary origin-of-life researchers now agree with Hoyle: life could not have originated by chance or by any known natural processes.[154] Many are searching for some theoretical force within matter that might push matter toward the assembly of greater complexity. Creationists say this is doomed to failure, since it contradicts the 2nd Law of Thermodynamics. (See chapter: "The Origin of the Universe")

It is important to note that the information transmitted by DNA is not written on or within the molecules themselves. It is transmitted by the intelligently-organized pattern of their arrangement.[155] Molecules have no intelligence. And, like a computer disk, DNA has no intelligence. The complex, purposeful codes of this "master program" could only have originated outside itself. In the case of a computer program, the original codes were put there by an intelligent being, a programmer. Likewise, for DNA it seems logial that intelligence must have come first, *before* the existence of DNA.

Dr. Wilder-Smith is an honored scientist who is certainly well-informed on modern biology and biochemistry. What is his considered opinion as to the

lessly high against the natural assembly of this single molecule.[148]

Chemist Dr. Grebe:

"That organic evolution could account for the complex forms of life in the past and the present has long since been abandoned by men who grasp the importance of the DNA genetic code."[149]

Researcher and mathematician I.L. Cohen:

"At that moment, when the the DNA/RNA system became understood, the debate between Evolutionists and Creationists should have come to a screeching halt. ... the implications of the DNA/RNA were obvious and clear. ...Mathematically speaking, based on probability concepts, there is no possibility that Evolution was the mechanism that created the approximately 6,000,000 species of plants and animals we recognize today."[150]

> *A*t that moment, when the RNA/DNA system became understood, the debate between Evolutionists and Creationists should have come to a screeching halt.
>
> *I.L. Cohen*

10^{87} Combinations (see previous Grebe quotation) =

1,000,000,000,000,000,000,000,000,000,000,000,000,000,000,000,000,000,000,000,000,000,000,000,000,000,000,000,000,000,000

(minus) 10^{17} Seconds 100,000,000,000,000,000

Remaining "odds" = 1 in —

999,999,999,999,999,999,999,999,999,999,999,999,999,999,999,999,999,999,999,999,000,000,000,000,000,000

If this is true, some Creationists might conversely suggest that the "odds" are, at least
999,999,999,999,999,999,999,999,999,999,999,999,999,999,999,999,999,999,999,999,000,000,000,000,000,000
to 1 in favor of the position that an intelligent designer *was* responsible for making this extremely complex molecule.

source of the DNA codes found in each wondrous plant and animal?

> "...an attempt to explain the formation of the genetic code from the chemical components of DNA ...is comparable to the assumption that the text of a book originates from the paper molecules on which the sentences appear, and not from any external source of information."[156]

> "As a scientist, I am convinced that the pure chemistry of a cell is not enough to explain the workings of a cell, although the workings are chemical. The chemical workings of the cell are controlled by information which does not reside in the atoms and molecules of that cell.

> There is an author which transcends the material and the matter of which these strands are made. The author first of all conceived the information necessary to make a cell, then wrote it down, and then fixed in it a mechanism of reading it and realizing it in practice — so that the cell builds itself from the information...."[157]

One need only look carefully at any living creature to gain some concept of its enormous complexity. If you have a pet, consider the complexities that must be involved — enabling that "package of matter" to move about, play, remember, show signs of affection, eat, and reproduce!

If that is not enough to boggle your mind, imagine being given the task of constructing a similar living pet from carbon, calcium, hydrogen, oxygen, etc. — the animal's basic constituent parts.

If you have ever held a beloved pet in your hands, completely limp and dead, you may have some comprehension of the helplessness of even the most intelligent and sophisticated scientist when it comes to the overwhelming problem of trying to create life.

In contrast, the natural world does not have the advantages people bring to the problem. In nature, there are only matter, energy, time, chance and the

Imagine being given the task of constructing any living animal from scratch, using carbon, calcium, water, etc. It boggles the mind.

physical laws — no guiding force, no purpose, and no goal.

Yet, even with all of modern man's accumulated knowledge, advanced tools, and experience, we are still absolutely overwhelmed at the complexities. This is despite the fact that we are certainly not starting from absolute zero in this problem; there are millions of actual living examples of life to scrutinize.

The Incredible Complexity of Man

All living things are extremely complex, even the tiniest single-celled animals and bacteria.[158] However, none surpasses the overall complexity of the human being. Not only is each person constructed of *trillions* of molecules and cells, but the human brain alone is filled with billions of cells forming many trillions of connections.[159] The design of the human brain is truly awesome and beyond our understanding. Every cubic inch of the human brain contains at least 100 million nerve cells interconnected by 10 thousand miles of fibers.

It has been said that man's 3 pound brain is the *most* complex and orderly arrangement of matter in the entire universe![160] Far more complicated than any computer,[161] the human brain is capable of storing and creatively manipulating seemingly infinite amounts of information. Its capabilities and potential stagger the imagination. The more we use it the better it becomes.

The brain capabilities of even the smallest insects are mind-boggling. The tiny speck of a brain found in a little ant, butterfly or bee enable them not only to see, smell, taste and move, but even to fly with great precision. Butterflies routinely navigate enormous distances. Bees and ants carry on complex social organizations, building projects, and communications processes. These miniature brains put our computers and avionics to shame, in comparison.

The marvels of the bodies of both animals and man are evidently endless. Dr. A.E. Wilder-Smith makes this thought-provoking and humbling statement:

> "When one considers that the entire chemical information to construct a man, elephant, frog, or an orchid was compressed into two minuscule reproductive cells [sperm and egg nuclei], one can only be astounded.

> In addition to this all the information is available on the genes to *repair* the body (not only to construct it) when it is injured. *If one were to request an engineer to accomplish this feat of information miniaturization, one would be considered fit for the psychiatric clinic.*"

It is certainly true that a machine carefully made by a craftsman reflects the existence of its creator. It would be foolish to suggest that time and chance could

At the moment of conception, the DNA code goes to work — using nutrients to build an entire human body, brain and personality from a single fertilized egg cell. All the instructions are in the code.

Not only does life contain tremendous diversity, but great beauty as well. The intricacies are overwhelming.

make a typewriter or a microwave oven, or that the individual parts could form *themselves* into these complex mechanisms due to the physical properties of matter. Yet, life is far, *far* more complex than any man-made machine.

The more scientists study life, the more they become deeply impressed. Nature is full of intricate design and beauty. In contrast to man-made objects, which look increasingly crude in finish and detail the closer they are viewed (i.e., through powerful microscopes), the closer life is examined the more complex and wondrous it appears.*[162]*

Planet Earth is filled with myriad forms of life, each with enormous levels of complexity. Materialists believe life in all its amazing forms consists merely of atoms and molecules. They believe these atoms and molecules formed *themselves* into millions of intricate animals and plants. Creationists maintain this view is illogical in the extreme. They point out that there is an enormous difference between producing a building block by natural means and producing an entire 80-story building from those building blocks. Buildings require builders; master programs require programmers. Creationists are scientifically convinced that the real world could never come into being without some form of highly intelligent and powerful designer.

(For those who may be interested, Dr. Wilder-Smith's personal conclusions as to the source of teleonomy in nature are noted in endnote *163*.)

THE BOTTOM LINE
on the origin of life

- During all recorded human history, there has *never* been a substantiated case of a living thing being produced from anything other than *another* living thing.

- As yet, Evolutionism has not produced a scientifically credible explanation for the origin of such immense complexities as DNA, the human brain, and many elements of the cosmos.

- It is highly premature for materialists to claim that *all* living things evolved into existence when science has yet to discover how *even one* protein molecule could actually have come into existence by natural processes.

- There is no scientific proof that life did (or ever could) evolve into existence from non-living matter. Further, there is substantial evidence that spontaneous generation is impossible. Only DNA is known to produce DNA; no chemical interaction of molecules has even come close to producing this ultra-complex code which is so essential to all known life.

The Origin of Species

Evolutionists represent life's ancestry with a single "tree."
Creationists say there have clearly been many "trees" —
each basic kind of animal separately created with genetics allowing diversification within each kind.

Evolutionism represents life's ancestry with a single "tree." Creationists say there were many "trees" — each basic kind of animal separately created with inherent genetics resulting in growing diversity within each. Are Evolutionists correct, is there clear biological proof that a single-celled animal could eventually evolve into man, given enough time? What light does science and everyday experience shed on this question?

species: an official category in the biological classification system; sometimes defined as an inter breeding pool of genes — or as a plant or animal population consisting of individuals which breed with one another and produce fertile offspring. The term "species" is actually somewhat indefinite. As one expert has said, "A species is what a competent systematist considers to be a species."

Creationists believe a creator designed various basic kinds of animals (e.g., the dog, the giraffe, the horse, etc.) out of the basic chemical elements.[164] They conclude a unique set of complex coded information was incorporated within each type of creature, enabling the reproduction of more creatures of like kind. Unique codes would prevent the possibility of later production of new and completely different kinds of creatures. That is, fish would never be able to produce frogs. Lizards would never give birth to birds.

> *From the claims made for neo-Darwinism one could easily get the impression that it has made great progress towards explaining Evolution, mostly leaving the details to be cleared up. In fact, quite the reverse is true.*
>
> *Peter Saunders (University of London) and Mae-Wan Ho (Open University)*

Designed to Diversify

Creationists believe these genetic codes were designed to allow interesting and useful diversity within each kind (within limits). Thus, different varieties of cows, parrots, cats, and the like have developed through centuries of selective breeding and natural selection. Thus, basic kinds have been able to survive, despite changing climates and food sources.

Creationists conclude, for example, that all of today's great variety of dogs would not have existed at the time of the original Creation. Poodles, for instance, are a relatively recent development. They were selectively bred for certain features. Breeding enthusiasts ultimately limited the genes for coat type to those for very curly hair that does not shed.

All characteristics of today's poodle were resident within the DNA code of the original dogs which had genes for a great variety of coat types. By eliminating certain characteristics in favor of others, Creationists assume it was thus possible to obtain a vast variety of dog types, including Saint Bernards, Shelties, Chihuahuas, and probably even wolves.

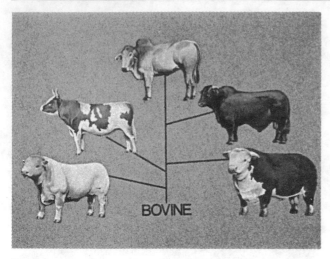

The original genetic design of the first cows allowed for diversification.

An early portrait of former theology student Charles Darwin, 4 years after his famous voyage on the H.M.S. Beagle to South America.

A "Tree" or a "Forest"?

Evolutionists maintain that the history of life should be thought of as a great Evolutionary tree with many branches, all ultimately connected to a base representing the first living creature(s) — the common ancestor(s) of all life.

In contrast, Creationists believe life's history can better be represented diagrammatically by a *forest* of trees. Each tree is representative of a different baramin. On each tree there may be numerous branches, representing the genetic variety possible within each kind. (See sample list in endnote *165*.)

baramin: from the Hebrew roots — "bara" (created) and "min" (kind); all organisms that are descended from a single created population. The word "baramins" *[166]* has been suggested by Creationists as a modern name for the basic created types of living things. Creationists believe that a definite boundary was established between the various baramins, and that this boundary has made possible the classification of living things into distinct groups. Creationists conclude that "baramin" is not exactly equivalent to any single category in modern (Evolutionistic) taxonomy, such as the terms: "species," "genus," "family," or "order." They maintain that new species can arise, but new baramin cannot.*[167]*

Man has long known it is impossible to breed substantially different kinds of animals. If a cat is mated with a dog, one doesn't get a creature that is half-cat and half-dog; one gets nothing. Modern science has established that the coded information involved in the DNA molecules does not allow reproduction to take place in such cases.

Many Creationists suggest that Genesis explains this when it says the creator made separate original "kinds." *[168]* It is assumed that the creator designed each kind to remain separate throughout time, rather than to have all eventually blend. Abundant variations would be possible within each kind, but none between kinds.

The Theories of Charles Darwin

Charles Darwin, a former theology student turned materialist,*[169]* was a catalyst for the popularization of Evolutionism. The first edition of his book *The Origin of Species* was published in 1859.*[170]* It was a sellout on the first day.*[171]*

Finches of the South American islands of Galapagos were used as an example in Darwin's theory. Did Darwin interpret the evidence correctly?

What did it say that created such a stir? Basically, Darwin suggested possible scientifically-explainable means for modern animals to have come into existence through natural processes — without the aid of a creator. Darwin and his followers preached a belief in progress, development to ever higher stages, with perfection the ultimate goal.*[172]*

On the Galapagos Islands, Darwin observed finches of various types. He assumed that a single population of finches had originally come to the island and later diversified into new "species." He further assumed these variations supported his contention that whole new kinds of animals could eventually be produced by such a process. He promoted belief in the idea that life could use small changes to develop upwards, ultimately all the way to man.*[173]*

Based on the ideas of Darwin and on the refinements of latter-day Evolutionists, many teach that wherever energy and matter exist they will eventually form life, given suitable conditions. Once life has been formed, they say, nature will automatically cause it to evolve into the highest forms possible in the given environment. As has already been shown, there are serious problems with this belief. (See chapters on

"The Origin of the Universe" and "The Origin of Life," and endnote *174*.)

Creationists believe these finches are probably all in the same baramin, and maintain that the Galapagos finches provide no evidence of Evolution. (See endnotes *175* and *176*).

Darwin's book set out to prove that life undergoes small variations which are connected with or caused by the environment. By the 6th edition of his book, Darwin, like Lamarck (the 18th century French naturalist) came to the conclusion that such small changes must be inheritable.*[177]*

In a crude sense, the theory was: if giraffes experienced too much competition for food so that they had to stretch their necks ever higher to reach the topmost leaves of trees, then, ultimately — if all generations stretched their necks — the necks of descendents would get longer and longer.

This concept is sometimes called Lamarckianism and has been amply disproved through practical experience. Parents who exercise with weights every day do not automatically pass the development of large muscles on to their children. Having a leg amputated does not cause a man to father legless children, even if every father in every generation was so unfortunate as to have his leg amputated. The parents' DNA sex cells are not affected by any such things. Unfortunately, Darwin knew nothing of the tremendously important DNA/RNA system within each living thing.

The following section reveals a related discovery made at the time of Darwin which destroyed Darwin's theories of Evolutionary heredity. Unfortunately, it received no public attention for 35 years.*[178]*

Geneticist and botanist Gregor Mendel

Mendel experimented heavily with the breeding of garden peas and discovered that mathematical laws govern the heredity of all living things.

A mutant cow with six "legs." Such animals obviously have great difficulty surviving, even when assisted by man. Mutations are degradations in a finely-tuned code.

The Important Discoveries of Mendel

Gregor Mendel (1822-1884) was the careful researcher and Creationist who developed the science of heredity on a sound mathematical basis. In Czechoslovakia, he spent many years conducting careful experiments and maintaining detailed records.

science of heredity: studies the transmission of physical characteristics from parent to child; synonymous with the "science of genetics."

Mendel used pea plants to discover why, for example, 2 plants with red flowers can yield a yellow-flowered offspring. He proved that both "parent" plants carry a hidden (recessive) gene for yellow. Thus, the production of the yellow flower does not mean there was a change in the plants themselves. The code for a yellow flower was not new; it was there all the time, stored in the flowers' DNA. The two red-flowered plants did not somehow produce a yellow flower out of nowhere. The physical characteristics of any creature correspond to well-defined mathematical laws.

On the basis of these laws, one can accurately predict how different qualities will be inherited by later generations. The particular traits of any individual plant or animal are the result of the latent code in its DNA. Traits can be lost or modified, but the appearance of totally new structures is not possible.[179]

Creationary geneticists say these laws firmly establish why baramins can never change into radically different kinds of creatures. The DNA codes are repeatedly duplicated with extreme accuracy.[180] Creationists believe this precision and the laws of genetics have strongly proved that animals and plants cannot evolve; truly *new* structures cannot form.

Mendel's genetic laws disproved Darwin's Evolutionary model of heredity. Later Evolutionists (neo-Darwinists) turned to mutations as a possible mechanism for significant change.

> *The mass of evidence shows that all, or almost all, known mutations are unmistakably pathological and the few remaining ones are highly suspect.*
> *Evolutionist C.P. Martin*

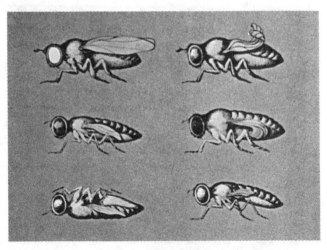

Mutant fruit flies. Mutations are harmful losses of coded information.

Mutations: "Magic Wands" or Menance?

mutation: in nature, a very rare, sudden, random alteration in the DNA code; mutations are mistakes — accidental, random rearrangements of the programmed code.

Mutations became the new supposed "magic wand" to overcome the barriers between the different types of plants and animals.*[181]* To put it simply, Evolutionists commonly thought that: "Amoeba" + MUTATIONS + Time + Energy + Chance can equal man. This formula reminds some scientists of the fairy tale in which a frog turns into a prince. Evolution says, in effect, the same thing — but the process takes longer.

macro-mutation: a theoretical and extremely large mutational change; the sudden appearance of a major new type of structure. No such mutation has been scientifically observed or been proven to have ever occurred.*[182]*

Why do mutations occur? One cause is radiation. The effects of atomic bombs and nuclear generator accidents have made people justifiably wary of radiation. Radiation can produce bizarre, malforming mutations. Even without such weapons and accidents, Earth's inhabitants are presently exposed to radiation from the sun and the stars, plus radiation from various Earth minerals.

Scientists have used x-ray radiation to deliberately cause mutations in African violets and fruit flies so that they could study the effects. Fruit flies reproduce very quickly. Therefore, a single scientist can observe the effects over a host of generations.

What have scientists found? Do mutations improve living things? Millions of dollars in research have proved that they do not. Most mutated animals would easily die in nature because mutations are almost invariably damaging in one way or another.*[183]*

Random rearrangements of information always result in loss of information. Therefore, when mutations produce random rearrangements in the complex information stored in DNA, the result is loss, not improvement.

Natural Selection

Darwin elevated the concept of "survival of the fittest" to the place of Creator.*[184]* Natural selection was supposed to produce ever higher forms of animals.*[185]* In a sense, Darwinists believed: "Amoeba" + Time + Energy + Chance + NATURAL SELECTION = Man.

Later research established that natural selection is *not* capable of creating anything truly new.*[186]* Natural selection is actually a conservation process in nature. Each living thing is faced with a struggle to

What natural process (or combination of processes), if any, can explain the existence of all the diverse and complex creatures which exist on Earth?

survive. This struggle generally weeds out the weak or ill-suited individuals. Those stronger or better suited will survive and produce offspring. Thus, it is only the genes of the survivors that will be passed on. In time, their characteristics will be in the majority of the population.

This pervading effect has nothing to do with the arrival of new basic types; it has to do with types *already* in existence. Natural selection works to prevent a species or baramin from deteriorating and from retaining disadvantageous characteristics.*[187]*

Mutations + Natural Selection

Within a species or baramin, natural selection prevents degeneration due to harmful changes in the DNA of individuals (mutations). Mutations are almost always lethal. If not immediately, they at least reduce the survival capacity of the type of creature so that it eventually becomes extinct. Survival of the fittest weeds out the mistakes. Many Evolutionists agree that Evolution by means of mutations is simply not plausible.*[188]*

What would happen in the highly unlikely event that a good mutation somehow did pop up in an individual? Could natural selection cause Evolution by maintaining this mutation in the population and additionally preserving other good mutations, eventually resulting in a new type of animal? The answer appears to be an emphatic no.*[189]*

There is no scientific proof that natural selection can cause a species to drift upwards; its sole function appears to be to prevent a drift downwards.*[190]* For instance, natural selection does make sure that good earthworms are produced, but not earthworms that are half something else — half-snake or half-amphibian or anything else — because that would have a disadvantage according to Darwin's own theory. Dr. Wilder-Smith explains:

> "The whole theory is dependent upon the idea that you won't get, by chance, a complete new organ produced at once — but you will get small changes. But, those small changes up to something better will be a disadvantage to the species until they are complete. And, as they never are complete, natural selection prevents the drift upwards just as effectively as it prevents the drift downwards. That being the case, we can account for the fact that basic kinds of animals have remained constant through all these years by this feedback mechanism."[191]

Eyes and Brains

It is even more difficult to imagine that such highly complex structures as eyes and brains could evolve. Darwin himself admitted this.[192] Not only is there no known process to fuel such Evolution, but an eye that is only partially evolved and does not work could easily be a detriment to the creature. Natural selection (ultimately death) would remove the creature from the gene pool of good earthworms.[193]

Darwin thought natural selection, the struggle for life, and survival of the fittest would cause a slow, irresistible Evolution upward from one species to another, all the way to apes and man. However, Darwin was wrong; natural selection itself prevents this.[194]

Creationists seem justified in their belief that the genetic laws stabilize basic kinds of animals within boundaries.[195] Never has anyone documented the development of a species that is truly more complex.[196] Evolutionists have been unable to prove that any Evolution (macro-evolution) is going on today. Creationists believe that the laws and discoveries of genetics provide considerably stronger scientific support for the theories of Creationism than they do for Evolutionism.[197]

---

*N*o one has ever produced a species by mechanisms of natural selection. No one has ever gotten near it...

Evolutionist Dr. Colin Patterson

THE BOTTOM LINE
on the origin of species

- Science has discovered no scientific proof that animals or plants can truly evolve.

- The best established facts of genetics, biology, and botany studies do not favor Evolutionism.

The Origin of Mankind

Are humans specially created beings, as surveys indicate most people believe?
Or are we simply highly-advanced animals which evolved through eons of survival of the fittest?

This chapter critically examines evidence used to support the theory that man is a descendent of animals. Each of the most famous suggested "links" in the Evolutionary ladder of man is discussed.

missing links: If there is a chain of descent linking man with the primates, it should be possible to find at least some of the chain's links in the fossil record. The fossils should reveal transitional creatures bridging the chasm between ape-like animals and man, as the creatures became progressively more human-like. Creationists do not believe these links are missing; they believe they simply never existed. Evolutionists assume they existed, although many admit that no unquestionable evidence of such creatures has been found, to date.[198] Evolutionists claim these links are now missing, some forever, with others waiting to be discovered in the fossils.

Ramapithecus

Ramapithecus has been widely represented as one of the creatures from which man evolved. This idea has been promoted through illustrations showing *Ramapithecus* routinely walking almost as upright as man. Most Evolutionary experts now concede this is not correct, and that in fact *Ramapithecus* was merely an extinct ape.[199]

Australopithecus

Australopithecus is another African ape[200] and probably the best known supposed candidate for the "missing link." However, evidence of misinterpreta-

Ramapithecus Australopithecus Homo Habilis Sianthropus Pithecanthropus Hesperopithecus Eoanthropus Neanderthalensis

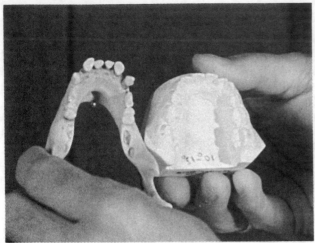

Jaw arch angle is often used to try to distinguish between human and ape skulls. Yet, orthodontists know people can have very parallel arches, as in this comparison (chimpanzee to *Homo sapiens*).

tion due to over-eagerness on the part of evolutionists is becoming increasingly evident.

Jaws of Apes and Men

Evolutionists have frequently emphasized similarities between the jaws of these apes and the angulation of human jaws. Creationist Dr. John Cuozzo is an expert on human jaws and teeth, and has long studied the question of human origins. After collecting and analyzing casts of numerous australopithecine jaws and comparing them in detail with those of humans, he made an interesting discovery. Jaw angulation can be an unreliable indicator of relative humanness and should not be the determining factor in deciding whether a fossil jaw is human, ape, or "missing link."[201]

Australopithecine Bones

After years of study of the australopithecine evidence, Malcolm Bowden,[202] like many others, is certain these animals are not a "missing link" but simply another variety of extinct ape.[203]

"A number of precise measurements were made on the australopithecine bones. They were compared by computer with those of apes — and with human beings (*Homo sapiens*). Each time, the measurements came out so very much closer to those of apes than they did to those of human beings. And, in fact, Dr. Oxnard [an Evolutionist] — who did this experiment and made these measure-

ments — came to the conclusion that he doubted if there was any link with the australopithecines and *Homo sapiens*."[204]

This conclusion seems to be supported by the work of Sir Solly Zuckerman (an Evolutionist). He carried out a number of examinations, tests and measurements of these australopithecine bones.[205] Lord Zuckerman concluded that the australopithecine link is based not on hard facts, but on speculation.

One individual australopithecine skeleton was named "Lucy" by Evolutionist Donald Johanson.[206]

> **"Lucy":** a particular *Australopithecus* skeleton which Donald Johanson named after a girl mentioned in a Beatles song ("Lucy in the sky with diamonds..."); *Australopithecus afarensis*.

Various Evolutionists, including Richard Leakey,[207] have concluded there is no good evidence that "Lucy" was a "missing link."[208] Current evidence seems to indicate *Australopithecus* was an extinct variety of ape, and nothing more.[209] Various Evolutionary publications have said the skeleton of "Lucy" is very similar to that of modern pygmy chimpanzees.[210]

The weight of evidence seems to indicate that Australopithecus, Homo Habilis , and Sinanthropus are merely extinct varieties of apes, and nothing more.

Homo Habilis

Homo habilis was touted as a link between *Australopithecus* and *Homo erectus* — and a link between apes and man. Current conclusions indicate it was simply an ape — another australopithecine (similar to a small chimpanzee or an orangutan).[211]

> *Homo erectus*: an assemblage of bones of a large type of extinct ape; this classification includes "Peking Man" and "Java Man."

Sinanthropus

"Peking Man" (designated *Sinanthropus pekinensis* - 1927 and *Homo erectus* — 1940) is another widely publicized "missing link." Researchers found these very ape-like remains about 25 miles from Peking, China, in the 1920s and 30s. The evidence included skulls (mainly fragments) and teeth, but almost no limb bones. In only 5 instances were the skulls complete enough to determine even so much as the brain capacity. After their discovery and description, the original bones were mysteriously "lost" sometime between 1941 and 1945. They have never been recovered.[212]

Mr. and Mrs. "Nebraska Man" as depicted in a 1922 newspaper. Later, this proved to be an embarrassing mistake.

The jaw of an orangutan was combined with human bones to produce the "Piltdown Man" — a long-lived hoax which fooled many Evolutionary scientists who wanted to believe a true "missing link" had finally been found.

Today, the evidence consists merely of "casts" (of unproven accuracy)*[213]* and 2 teeth.

One of the more complete skulls was Number 11.*[214]* Evolutionists commissioned reconstructions from it, named it "Nellie," and brought it before the Press. Few people realize, however, that:

- Clear evidence was found of another presence at this site — true human beings who were mining limestone here, who transported thousands of quartz stones here, and who left tools and built fires. Fossil remains of 10 humans were found at this site.

- Almost every modern expert agrees that each *Sinanthropus* had been killed and eaten by hunters. Each skull was bashed inward in a manner that would allow the brain to be taken out. Since there were no bodies, and considering other evidence at the site, the circumstantial evidence seems to agree

with the theory that hunters brought severed ape heads to the site to extract the brains for food.

After studying all the evidence in great depth, Bowden and various other researchers have come to the conclusion that the hunters were human beings, and *Sinanthropus* was a variety of ape they ate (evidently to extinction).*[215]* As Bowden explains:

"When these men went out on forays into the forests to find meat, they would kill antelope, deer, and whatever else was there. They would cut out the meat and throw the remains onto the fire. Now, if they caught a monkey, monkey's meat is too tough to eat. So, they would lop off its head, bring it back and cook it. When it was cooked, they would smash open the skull to get at the brains inside which were a delicacy [and still are in some parts of the world]."

The discoverer of "Java Man" ultimately said the skull cap was probably from a large gibbon-like ape, such as this.

Artist's impression of the "Piltdown Man."

Then, they would toss the broken pieces of skull on the fire, mixed up with the other animal bones, which is where they were found. And perhaps only several hundred years later, the 'experts' came along and found these bones of apes. They put them together in a reconstruction and claimed that they found another missing link, 'Peking Man'."[216]

Perhaps "Peking Man" was simply a now-extinct variety of ape, once hunted and eaten in China by humans.

"Java Man"

"Java Man" is scientifically referred to as *Pithecanthropus erectus* — 1894 ("erect ape-man"). It is said to be a variety of *Homo erectus*. This assemblage of bones consists mainly of a skull cap (found in 1891) and a thigh bone (found about a year later). Eugene Dubois found these bones when he went to the island of Java to discover the "missing link" and prove Evolution. Later research has shown the legbone is almost unquestionably from a modern-type human.[217] The skull cap, however, is very ape-like and may have nothing to do with the legbone. The skull cap was found about 46 feet away from the leg. Eventually Dubois himself said the skull cap was probably from a gibbon-like ape.[218]

Evidently, "Java Man" was simply another big mistake — the misleading combination of an ape's skull cap with the thigh bone of a human.

> *Students of fossil primates have not been distinguished for caution... The record is so astonishing that it is legitimate to ask whether much science is... in this field at all.*
> Evolutionist Lord Solly Zuckerman

"Nebraska Man"

Soon after its discovery, "Nebraska Man" was officially designated *Hesperopithecus haroldcooki*.[219] Various leading Evolutionists,[220] including the eminent Henry F. Osborn,[221] initially publicized it as a genuine missing link. The evidence was used against Creationism in the famous Scopes "Monkey Trial" in Dayton, Tennessee.[222]

A vivid reconstruction was commissioned, based on the only evidence — a single tooth found in Nebraska and a few supposed tools.[223] Later excavations uncovered the rest of the remains. The tooth was *not* that of an animal-like man — or even of an ape. The creature was actually a type of wild pig, living now only in Paraguay.[224]

"Piltdown Man"

Reconstructions of Piltdown Man (*Eoanthropus dawsoni*) were based on skull fragments found in a gravel pit at Piltdown, East Sussex, England. For almost 40 years, this find was used as a classic proof that man had evolved from ape-like animals. Not until the 1940s was it proven to be entirely a hoax. Piltdown Man was a half-baked fraud consisting of the altered, combined bones of an orangutan ape and a modern human.[225] People, unfortunately including hundreds of scientists, believed in it, not because it was truly convincing evidence, but because they *wanted* to believe.

Neanderthals

Neanderthal Man was based on remains first found in the Neanderthal Valley of western Germany. For many years scientists accepted Neanderthal Man as a subhuman "missing link." Hundreds of museums and textbooks promoted it as such. The sad truth is that Neanderthals were 100% human all along, and (according to a leading Evolutionist) they were very similar to northwest Europeans.[226]

Neanderthal brain capacity was actually somewhat larger than the norm today.[227] These people appear robust and strongly built. However, Neanderthals generally suffered from various debilitating diseases which left disfigurement in their bones — rickets, arthritis, syphilis, etc.[228]

The sometimes heavy brow ridges are features that develop to some extent even today among native peoples that do a great deal of tough chewing as young-

Animals and plants listed in order of chromosome numbers. There is no reasonable ascending Evolutionary order.

Creationists believe that man and ape are separate creations. They believe apes and men have always coexisted.

Reconstructions of supposed "missing links" are based on very little scientific proof and lots of imagination.

sters (e.g., Eskimos that chew blubber or leather). Unusually strong muscles develop which mold the soft growing bone at the brows.[229]

Neanderthals were definitely not the ancestors of humankind. They were just a coexistent variety of people, perhaps a "race," with certain skeletal characteristics.

Did man evolve from animals? If he did, there appears to be no proof of it in the fossil record.[230]

Molecules of Apes and Men

Since results have been so poor in finding fossil evidence that man evolved either from apes[231] or from ape-like animals, Evolutionists have turned to other means — molecular taxonomy. Evolutionary anthropologists have used molecular taxonomy to compare the internal chemistry of humans and apes in an attempt to prove common ancestry.

> **molecular taxonomy:** "taxonomy" = "biological classification;" molecular taxonomy is a study which seeks to build an Evolutionary "tree" based on similarities or differences in animal chemistry. Molecular taxonomists attempt to classify living things according to their presumed Evolutionary relationships based on similarities in molecules.

It is known that the chromosome banding and some of the blood proteins of humans and chimpanzees are quite similar. Evolutionists have claimed this as proof that people and chimps had common ancestors. Does this fact *prove* common ancestry? No, it is only circumstantial evidence.

Creationists believe there are better ways to interpret these similarities.[232] Rather than being evidence of common descent, similarities in internal construction would be expected, they say, if both chimps and man were created by the same designer.

Indeed, it would be logical for a designer to use similar construction in structures designed to serve like functions, rather than "reinventing the wheel" each time, so to speak.

What has the latest scientific research revealed? There is no convincing evidence of an Evolutionary development. Even Evolutionists are now rejecting the claim that the blood, DNA, or other chemical factors indicate a definite Evolutionary relationship between man, chimp, or gorilla. (See endnote 233.)

> **chromosome numbers:** Each type of plant and animal has a particular number of chromosomes in each body cell. Humans have 46 chromosomes.

The Great Gap Between People and Apes

It is important to understand that although apes and people do resemble each other in some obvious ways, there are also substantial differences.[234]

It is obvious that man is gifted with tremendous creativity, inventiveness, and technical genius. What animal can create symphonies, novels, inspiring motion pictures, or wondrous buildings? Plainly, these qualities form a great gap between all animals and man. Man is undeniably unique.

If anything is related to Evolution, it would seem natural for it to be the number of chromosomes in each creature — the more the genetic material, the higher the Evolution. However, these numbers seem to show no Evolutionary pattern whatsoever.[235]

Although Evolutionists once frequently claimed that research in molecular biology would yield devastating evidence against Creationism, the opposite has often been the case. The family tree that was expected to be found in the sequences of chemical units in proteins and in DNA just simply is not there.[236]

Molecular biologist Michael Denton asserts:

"There is little doubt that if this molecular evidence had been available one century ago, it would have been seized upon with devastating effect by the opponents of evolution theory like Agassiz [a biologist from Harvard who opposed Darwin], and the idea of organic evolution might never have been accepted."[237]

Has Man Always Been Man? Have Apes Always Been Apes?

Not only is there no evidence that man is evolving,[238] but there is increasing fossil and archaeological evidence which suggests that human beings and all of the extinct apes could have lived at the same time[239] — side by side. (See list in endnote 240.)

Professor emeritus Dr. Wilbert Rusch[241] has studied this question for many years:

"As we find more fossils, we find man consistently appearing PARALLEL with all of his supposed ancestors. The concept of man developing from these animals is simply very dubious and cannot be held. Instead, we have parallel development — a record of man consistently existing as far back as we go in the fossil record."[242]

Use of Artistic Freedom in Reconstructions

Scientists acknowledge that the "origin of man" reconstructions commonly shown in books and museums are based upon very little evidence and a large amount of imagination.[243] Despite millions of dollars in research, it is said that all the bones of the most important supposed ape links could be placed on a single table or in a single coffin.[244]

Not only have heads and bodies often been reconstructed on the basis of just a few bone fragments or teeth, but human-like faces have been added to ape bodies (and vice versa) without sufficient scientific proof for such reconstructions. Much fantasy has been involved in these murals and busts.

It is impossible to tell how much hair a person had by looking at bones. Yet almost all illustrations of Neanderthals have shown them as covered in long thick body hair.[245] Likewise, even a complete skull cannot tell the artist how much fat was under the skin or exactly where it was deposited. Nor can it provide evidence of the exact shape of the nose, the eyes, the lips, or the ears.[246] Yet, these are the very features that make such major differences in appearance.

It is well known that when artists have been shown ape-like bones identified by "experts" as ancestors of man, the resulting reconstructions have had a rather human appearance — making them seem to fit very nicely into the Evolutionary theory. (See endnotes 247 and 248.)

> *If you were to spend your life picking up bones and finding little fragments of head and little fragments of jaw, there's a very strong desire there to exaggerate the importance of those fragments...*
>
> *Evolutionist Greg Kirby*

THE BOTTOM LINE
on the origin of man

- There is no scientific proof that modern man is evolving.

- There is no scientific proof that man evolved from ape-like ancestors, or from any other animal.

- Creationists maintain that man has always been man, and apes have always been apes. There is no proof that this is wrong.

The Fossil Record

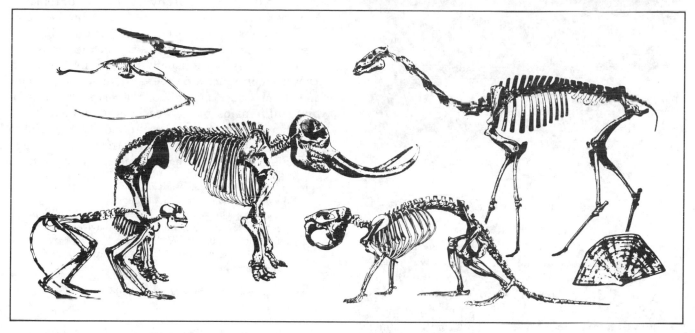

Fossil discoveries were once relatively rare. Now, they are abundant, adding greatly to human knowledge of the past.

T he strata beneath Earth's cities, parks and wilderness are filled with vast numbers of dead animals and plants — some petrified, some carbonized, some almost totally dissolved, and others merely decayed. What is the origin and meaning of this vast graveyard? Evolutionists and Creationists interpret these remains in markedly different ways.

Many Evolutionists claim that fossils are the world's *best* evidence of Evolution. Other Evolutionists say such statements greatly overstate the facts.

Creationists maintain that the fossil record provides superb evidence against Evolutionism, showing that animals have not evolved, but merely diversified within basic, separate types. Creationists do not view fossils as remnants of great spans of history. Rather, they believe much of the fossil record is a solemn reminder of a great death event — a multifaceted, worldwide catastrophe involving flooding, earthquakes, volcanic eruptions, etc. In various cultures, this is traditionally known as the flood of Noah.

Which of these two radically different views of the fossil record best fits the evidence? This chapter discusses: the strata, key fossils claimed as evidence for Evolutionism, the origin of coal, the Grand Canyon, and a global flood as described by Creationists.

Interpreting the Strata's Organization and Disorganization

There is a somewhat erratic tendency for fossils to be found in specific groupings. Marine animals are frequently found buried together — certain reptiles and dinosaurs together — mammals together — etc. These general groupings are sometimes called "geologic systems." [249] These groupings are occasionally found in a certain vertical order within the sediments. This order is the so-called Geologic Column — an

Strata in the Grand Canyon, U.S.A.

Few people realize that there is no radioactive dating method for directly determining the absolute age of dinosaur bones.

idealized grouping of the generalized systems into a single, vertically-stacked series. This idea was developed partially in an attempt to sort out some kind of order in the chaotic layers of strata.[250]

Evolutionists interpret these grouping in terms of the Evolutionary model. They believe there was once an age of fishes, a later age of reptiles, and ultimately an age of mammals and man.

Creationists insist that the evidence is grossly insufficient to prove this view. They believe the little order that does exist is primarily due to burial of successive ecological zones during and after a worldwide flood.[251]

The "Geologic Column" is actually more of a concept than a reality.[252] Eighty to eighty-five percent of Earth's land surface does *not* have even 3 of the 10 "geologic periods" appearing in the correct consecutive order required by Evolutionism.[253] Even the walls of the Grand Canyon include only about 5 of these "periods."[254] All rock systems include gaps in the sequence expected by Evolutionists. It is common to find layers in orders which contradict the "proper" Evolutionary sequence.[255]

Dating the "Geologic Periods"

How do Evolutionists date most fossils? How, for example, do they determine the age of a dinosaur bone? Creationists suspect that most dinosaurs did not become extinct until about 3 or 4 thousand years

> *A circular argument arises: Interpret the fossil record in terms of a particular theory of evolution, inspect the interpretation, and note that it confirms the theory. Well, it would, wouldn't it?*
>
> *Evolutionist Tom Kemp*

ago.[256] Evolutionists claim extinction was complete some 60 or 70 million years ago.

It is important to understand that no one has scientifically proven the age of any fossil dinosaur remains. Few fossils are assigned a "date" based on the radioactive age estimation systems.[257] If anything, the case is stronger for a recent death of the dinosaurs, since their fossils are usually not heavily fossilized. They contain much original bony material, proteins and amino acids. The millions-of-years estimates for dinosaur remains and other fossils are quite theoretical. They are based on the assumption that Evolution with its "geologic periods" is correct.[258] The age estimate is assigned using the "index fossil" method.

index fossil: a term used primarily by Evolutionists to identify fossils thought to be unique representatives of a particular and distinct period of geologic history;[259] Some trilobites, for instance, are thought to have only existed during the Cambrian period. Therefore, if a rock is found to contain one of these, it is automatically "dated" as Cambrian.

paleontologist: a person who scientifically studies fossil animals and plants.

It is not uncommon for paleontologists who believe in Evolutionism to date the fossils by the rock layer in which they are found — and the rock layer by the fossils.[260] To assign a "date" to a dinosaur bone, they would first determine what layer of rock (or system of rock) the fossil was found in. Next, they would look up the layer in a geology book or chart. The paleontologist would then say the bone was, for instance, 100 million years old, based on the assigned 100 million year old "age" of the rock.

How did the geologists come up with that age? "The rock must be at least 100 million years old, because it contains this type of dinosaur."

It is not difficult to see that this is circular reasoning. The fossil is "dated" by the strata, and the strata are "dated" by the fossil. From time to time, Evolutionists recognize this blind spot, but such admissions are rare.

Of course, Evolutionists *must* postulate that most dinosaur bones are millions of years old. This is part of their origins model. Evolution requires huge time spans to yield even the remotest possibility of producing the tremendous changes necessary to develop dinosaurs, birds, mammals, and man.

Sometimes there is circular reasoning involved in the radioactive age estimation systems, as well. A particular "date" produced by an age estimation system may be considered accurate simply because it is the age which was *expected* (based on the above circular reasoning about the strata and the fossil),[261] or because it was the date researchers *wanted*, based on their personal theories. Alternately, when a radioactive system yields an age estimate which does not at all match what an Evolutionary researcher wants, it may be rejected.[262]

Macroevolution and the Fossil Record

Evolutionary theory states that animals have evolved ever higher throughout time, producing radically different creatures with complex and unique features. One group of the fishes produced amphibians, which in turn produced many varieties of amphibians, one group of which produced the reptiles. A group of reptiles produced the dinosaurs, another group the mammals, and another group the birds.

If this scenario is true, it would seem logical to expect numerous clear evidences in the fossil record. According to Evolutionism:

- The original life forms were quite simple and eventually became increasingly complex through thousands of generations. (The fossil record should substantiate this claim.)[263]
- Life eventually evolved all types of new animals, including all the Families known today.

It would seem there should be substantial evidence of clear Evolutionary ancestors in the fossil record — of the transitions between invertebrates (animals without backbones), vertebrates (animals with back-

There is no proof for the existence of billions of supposed Evolutionary transitional stages in the animal world. If macroevolution abounded in the past, why is there little or no fossil evidence of it?

bones), fish, amphibians, reptiles, mammals, birds, etc. In fact, one might expect to find evidence of *billions* of transitional forms in the fossil record.

The Origin of Flight

One series of Evolutionary steps which might reasonably be expected to be recorded in the fossil record is the development of flight. In fact, one would think such documentation would be easy to find. There are, after all, a number of completely different creatures with flying ability, and the unfolding of such an important capability would clearly require new physical features.

The search for evidence of the origin of flight has been quite disappointing to Evolutionists. No convincing transitional forms have been found to fill the gap between creatures that can fly and those that

Artist's impression of *Archaeopteryx*, perching and in-flight. The feathers indicate a strong flier.

Three living birds have claws on their wings.

The ability to fly involves numerous complex body parts and functions — and a specialized brain to control them.

cannot. Appearing abruptly in the fossil record with complete, fully-functional wings are: birds, bats,[264] flying reptiles (pterosaurs), and flying insects.[265]

ARCHAEOPTERYX: A "Missing Link?"

Archaeopteryx is an extinct, flying bird[266] which had wing claws and teeth. Evolutionists have widely promoted this animal as a definite transitional form between dinosaurs and birds. On the other hand, Creationists (and even some Evolutionists) maintain there are significant problems with this claim.[267]

> *We have to admit that there is nothing in the geological records that runs contrary to the view of conservative creationists...*
>
> *Evolutionist Edmund Ambrose*

Horses come in many different sizes. This specimen is a full-grown adult. Relative smallness, alone, cannot be a reliable evidence of macroevolution.

- Some biologists say the teeth and wing-claws of *Archaeopteryx* are not conclusive details in distinguishing reptiles from birds. Some reptiles have teeth, and some do not. Some fossil birds had teeth, and some did not.[268] The claws on the wings are not a distinguishing factor, either. Some living birds have them, such as the ostrich, the touraco,[269] and the hoatzin.[270] There is no question that these are 100% birds.[271]

- Most importantly, this creature had feathers. Feather impressions found with *Archaeopteryx* indicate they were fully-developed and functional. There is no evidence of reptilian scales developing into feathers.[272] No animal except a bird has ever been known to have feathers.[273]

- The wings of *Archaeopteryx* are said to be fully-developed and completely functional, and the bones were hollow, just as in other birds.[274]

- True, *Archaeopteryx* did have a breastbone that was "shallow." However, some living birds, also, have very small breastbones.[275] And, on the other hand, *Archaeopteryx* did have an extremely robust furcula which is interpreted by many as evidence that it was a strong flier,[276] and therefore was a *bird* — not an unfinished transitional dinosaur evolving *into* a bird.[277]

furcula: the bone where the muscles attach which give the power stroke in flight.

- Bones and further evidences of other birds[278] (which their Evolutionist discoverers have said were essentially identical with those commonly living today) appear to have been found in formations which Evolutionists estimate are as "old" as or "older" than *Archaeopteryx*. The inference is that the *Archaeopteryx* specimens could not have been any

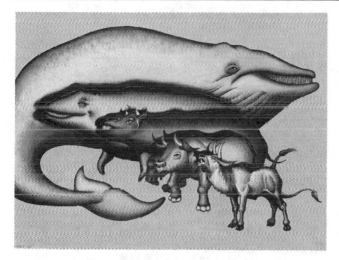

Evolutionary theory forces evolutionists to assume that whales evolved from a land-dwelling animal similar to a cow.

The fossil record simply provides evidence that some types of horses have now become extinct. There is no good evidence of macroevolution.

sort of "missing link." *Archaeopteryx* was too late, if birds already existed.

Do Fossil Horses Prove Macroevolution?

Besides *Archaeopteryx*, the other main group of fossils promoted most widely as evidence for Evolution is a series of fossil horses of varying sizes. These horses also vary in their number of toes and ribs. Some Evolutionists have claimed these absolutely prove that modern one-toed horses macroevolved from a very small mammal which had multiple toes.[279]

Many professors have taught this theory as fact, including biologist and paleontologist Dr. Gary Parker.[280] However, after detailed study, he rejected the theory completely and no longer teaches it. He and many others have concluded that the museum exhibits and textbook illustrations showing horses evolving are misleading and contrived. They do not represent good science. (See endnote *281*.) Dr. Parker:

"More detailed information has now forced us to abandon the idea that horses have truly evolved. We find that the size difference between the fossil horses is not crucial. It is now possible to breed extremely small horses.

What about the so-called 'dawn horse?' We now know that it was not a horse at all. Instead it was a rock badger or a coney — what scientists would call a hyrax. It was the ancestor NOT of the horses, but of the coneys that still live on Earth today.

What about the 'in-between forms' that show how the toe number was gradually reduced? Some living Shire horses have been known to have more than one toe per foot. Also, all of the supposed 'in-between forms' are found buried in the same geological formations, which indicates they lived at the same time and could not have been the ancestors of one another.

Instead, it's more like a scene we might see around an African waterhole, where animals of many sizes and shapes — animals with a few toes or with many toes — all lived together at the same time."[282]

Paleontologist and Evolutionist Dr. Niles Eldredge, American Museum of Natural History:

"I admit that an awful lot of that [fantasy] has gotten into the textbooks as though it were true. For instance, the most famous example *still on exhibit downstairs* [American Museum of Natural History] is the exhibit on horse evolution prepared perhaps fifty years ago. That has been *presented as literal truth in textbook after textbook*. Now, I think that *that is lamentable*, particularly because the people who propose these kinds of stories themselves may be aware of the *speculative nature* of some of the stuff. But by the time it filters down to the textbooks, we've got science as *truth* and we've got a problem."[283]

Is There, or Is There Not, Substantial Fossil Evidence of Macroevolution?

Has clear evidence of macroevolution been found in the fossil record? Well-known paleontologists at prestigious Evolutionist institutions, including Harvard, the American Museum of Natural History, etc., have said it is questionable whether *any* proof of Evolution has ever truly been seen in the rocks. (See endnotes concerning: Plants,[284] fish,[285] amphibians,[286] reptiles,[287] mammals,[288] and the entire animal and plant world[289].)

Renowned fossil experts, such as British paleontologist Colin Patterson (an Evolutionist), have stated that *no* true Evolutionary transitional forms have ever been revealed in the fossil record.[290]

Darwin said that the world's fossils provided perhaps the most serious objection to his theory.[291] However, he believed this situation would change as fossil collections expanded. Since Darwin's time, millions of dollars have been spent by museums, universities, governments, and individual researchers to find evidence of Evolution in the fossil record. Many tons of new fossils have been unearthed and closely examined. There is no longer any lack of fossils. For some time now, there have been more specimens than scientists and museums can handle.[292]

Evolutionists have been keenly disappointed to find that the result is the same as in Darwin's day. There is still no proof of Evolution (true macroevolution). (See endnote 293 and 289 through 294 for quotations and references.)

What Does the Fossil Record Actually Show?

- The fossils clearly record the fact that millions of animals and plants have lived and died on this planet.

- They reveal that some varieties and types have become extinct. The Earth is becoming increasingly impoverished of its formerly greater diversity of animals and plants.

- Most fossils are *not* of extinct animals. Quite to the contrary, most fossils are very similar (if not totally identical) to creatures living today. It is said there are many more *living* species of animals than there are types known *only* as fossils.[294]

If Evolution is true, some wonder why the case is not just the reverse. Why are not millions of times more extinct types found than living species?

Biochemist and author Dr. Duane Gish[295] has debated a large number of well-informed Evolutionists on these points. It is his conclusion that:

> Although "the fossil record is often cited by Evolutionists as support for the theory of Evolution, actually, the fossil record is an embarrassment to the theory of Evolution. It provides support for the concept of direct special Creation."[296]

If the Creationist model is correct, the fossil record should:

- Begin with the abrupt appearance of very complex forms of life.

- There should be no evidence of Evolutionary ancestors for each basic type of animal and plant. Creationists feel the fossil record agrees with this *exceedingly well.*[297]

Fossil horseshoe crab (left).

Living horseshoe crab (right)
As is common among fossils, there is little difference.

How Did Most Animals and Plants Become Fossilized?

Fossilization is a rare and unusual occurrence, not an everyday event. According to the best available evidence, animals and plants cannot become fossils unless they are buried relatively quickly and deeply in appropriate materials.[298]

The usual animal or plant that dies in a forest does not become a fossil, and neither does the average creature that dies in a sea or lake. Under most normal conditions, a dead creature floats and disintegrates. The body is destroyed by predators, bacteria and the elements.

What conditions would be most ideal for the kind of massive fossil formations found in the sediments? Creationists believe it would be a violent, global flood catastrophe.

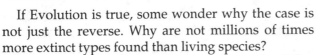

*R**apid burial is a key factor in the formation of fossils. This fact is often ignored by promoters of Evolutionism.*

Fossilization almost always requires rapid burial. Dinosaur remains worldwide are associated with water-laid sediment.

Worldwide Evidence of Rapid, Catastrophic Burial and Erosion

Traditionally, Evolutionists have claimed that most of Earth's strata were laid down *slowly* over millions of years. Yet, the fossils contained within these sediments clearly speak of rapid burial.*[299]* Increasingly, Evolutionists are joining Creationists as believers in catastrophism.

Humankind actually lives upon a vast fossil graveyard, filled with evidence of catastrophe. The outer layers of the planet contain vast quantities of fossils bearing testimony of rapid burials on an immense scale.

Enormous deposits of intact fossil fish can be found, buried suddenly by overwhelming quantities of mud and sand.*[300]* Whole dinosaurs have been found quickly buried in sediments and thus preserved for modern examination. Some sites contain huge deposits of diverse animals. All were evidently swept together by masses of water and mud.

Coal: Its Catastrophic Origin

Coal is a rock which contains a large amount of carbon. It may primarily be the product of vast amounts of dead plants. Although once thought to take millions of years to form, it is now known that coal can form (and does form) quite rapidly. Scientists now produce both coal and oil in the laboratory, in small quantities.*[301]*

There is no proof that coal seams are being created in modern swamps or bogs — or anywhere in nature

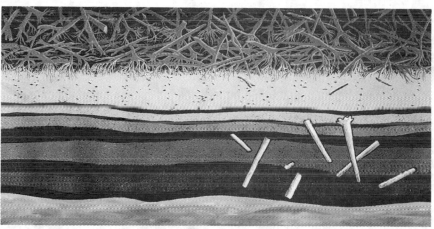

Artist's reconstruction of the formation of coal layers with buried logs, based on the findings of Dr. Austin.

today. Therefore, what caused Earth's vast coal deposits? Creationists are certain they were mostly formed in connection with a worldwide flood.

Geologist and coal formation specialist Dr. Steven Austin*[302]* has studied this question extensively.*[303]* He, and many others, are now convinced that the plants that formed coal did not grow at the sites where the coal is found. They believe the plants were transported from other locations by flood water.

This fits well with the fact that coal deposits are always found in sediments deposited by water and are commonly associated with huge masses of marine fossils.

Dr. Austin has concluded that various coal layers in the United States consist of a surprising main ingredient — tree bark.*[304]* His theory is that these bark sheets and fragments were deposited beneath huge, floating masses of trees — forests uprooted and swept away by massive flooding. As the trees floated in the waves, abrading against each other, a large amount of

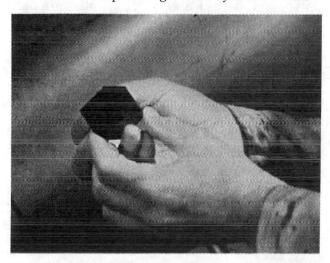

Coal does not take a long time to form. It can be produced in laboratories. The main requirement is heat, not pressure or long periods of time.

Mass graves of fossils are found throughout the world. Most, if not all, are part of muddy sediments laid by water.

Canyonlands, Utah, U.S.A.
Creationists believe this and other canyons could easily have been
produced as a result of a worldwide flood and its aftereffects.

Huge buoyant mat of uprooted trees, plants and other debris
floating on floodwaters — as described by Dr. Austin.

bark would be soaked off and ground off the trees. These bark fragments would then sink to the sea bottom. Layers of these fragments would then be buried beneath the muddy sediments of the flood. Tree bark is currently being deposited in this manner in Spirit Lake on Mount Saint Helens (Washington, U.S.A.) underneath a huge log mat created by the volcanic destruction of a large forest.

Polystrate Fossils

Occasionally, whole trees have sunk to the bottom and

> *The fossil record does not support any long-age concept... The record only makes sense if the world's strata were laid down fairly recently.*
>
> Creationist Albert Mehlert

been buried. As a result of this flood deposition, fossil tree trunks can sometimes be found buried at various angles in these sediments. Some logs are found buried amidst various layers of coal and mud — extending through one layer after another.[305] These vertical tree trunk fossils are another indication that the layers were laid down *quickly* under flood conditions, not over slow eons in some peat bog.

Rapid Strata Formation and Erosion

There is now scientific evidence that other great layers of strata were deposited quickly. Examples are found throughout the world. For instance, geologist Dr. Art Chadwick[306] has reported evidence that the layers of the Grand Canyon could have been accumulated in a short time. After much research of a 500 foot layer in the canyon, he came to the conclusion that it was not deposited slowly over millions of years in a large lake or shallow sea, as Evolutionists had claimed. Instead, it was apparently laid down very quickly and violently under deep water.

Chadwick believes the layer may have been produced by a process involving turbidity currents, or something similar.

turbidity currents: mass movements of sediment in deep water which can occur at very high speeds. They lay down huge masses of sediment in a matter of hours or minutes. Moving at speeds of up to 60 miles per hour, the sediment can be deposited in areas up to 100 thousand square miles.

Legends and mythologies of tribes and peoples worldwide tell of a
time when the entire Earth was devastated by a massive flood
catastrophe.

Such discoveries are revolutionizing ideas on rates of sedimentation and the depths of water in which sediments were deposited.*[307]* As Dr. Chadwick states:

> "We can accumulate great quantities of sediment in a given area very rapidly. This has changed our whole thinking about the processes that came to lay these layers here in the Grand Canyon."*[308]*

> **sedimentary rocks:** rocks deposited by water (or sometimes wind). They consist of material derived from pre-existing materials (e.g., rocks, sand, lime, mud, organic materials). Most of Earth's crust is covered with such sediments.

Not only is there evidence that various layers in the Canyon formed quickly, but many Creationists now believe the entire Grand Canyon, itself, was produced rapidly. Recent research has revealed increasing indications that the bulk of the canyon was not carved by the slow-paced erosion of the Colorado River, but rather by violent, fast-working flood conditions*[309]* which rapidly eroded through sediments which show evidence of having been still soft.*[310]* Most Creationists conclude that much of the Grand Canyon was carved in the after-effects of a great worldwide flood (the Genesis flood of Noah).

Creationists believe this was the greatest of all floods, a catastrophe of truly worldwide proportions.*[311]* They assert that most of Earth's geologic depositions, including the great coal layers, were created as a result of this year long flood and its dramatic aftereffects which reverberated throughout the world for hundreds of years.*[312]* Indeed, much of Earth's geology does testify to catastrophe and to rapid deposition by water. (See endnote *313*.) Further credence is lent by the fact that a universal flood destruction is found in the legends of almost all ancient peoples around the world. (See endnote *314*.)

Creationist reconstruction of the giant barge called Noah's Ark based on the description in Genesis. (From the Creationist motion picture "The World That Perished.")

THE BOTTOM LINE
on the fossil record

- All the different kinds of animals appear abruptly and fully functional in the strata with no proof of macroevolutionary ancestors. At the very least, this is a strong indication that not all life evolved from a common ancestor.

- There is no scientific proof that life has evolved.

- Although scientists will continue to discover new varieties of fossil animals and plants, it is generally agreed that the millions of fossils already discovered and the sediments already explored provide a generally reliable indication of which way the evidence is going. That is, there will continue to be little or no fossil evidence found to support Evolutionism.

- Most fossil animals and plants were buried in water-laid sediments.

- There is no scientific proof that the fossils, the coal, or the Earth are billions of years old.

- There is increasing evidence that many sedimentary rocks, which some thought took thousands or millions of years to accumulate, almost certainly were deposited in only months, days, or hours.

- In almost all cases, the very existence of the fossils, in the types and numbers discovered, strongly indicates catastrophic conditions were involved in the burial and preservation of these animal and plant remains. Without such conditions, there seems to be no plausible way to explain their existence.

Conclusions About Origins

To the surprise of many, evidence from almost every field of science has caused the case for Evolutionism to steadily weaken through the years. Physicist and mathematician Wolfgang Smith[315] recently stated his view of the present situation:

"The salient fact is this: *if by evolution we mean macroevolution* (as we henceforth shall), *then it can be said with the utmost rigor that the doctrine is totally bereft of scientific sanction.* Now, to be sure, given the multitude of extravagant claims about evolution promulgated by evolutionists with an air of scientific infallibility, this may indeed sound strange.

And yet the fact remains that there exists to this day not a shred of *bona fide* scientific evidence in support of the thesis that macroevolutionary transformations have ever occurred." [316]

Dr. Michael Denton (non-Creationist):

"Ultimately the Darwinian theory of evolution is no more nor less than the great cosmogonic myth of the twentieth century." [317]

The public is almost totally unaware of the substantial scientific problems with Darwinism and all forms of Evolutionism. Students have generally been taught Evolution as if it were an established fact (not a theoretical model of origins), or else that it is a concept with no possible alternative. Yet, there are many in the higher echelons of science, who are convinced that the Evolutionism is *not* well-supported by fact. (See endnote *318.*)

REFERENCE SECTION

The Origin of the Universe

MANY SCIENTISTS DO NOT ACCEPT EVOLUTIONISM

1

☐ Researcher and lecturer David Watson notes the current trend that is disturbing the confidence of those that had thought Evolutionism was the accepted scientific consensus:

"*...a tidal wave of new books... threaten to shatter that confidence — titles like **Darwin Retried** (1971), Macbeth; **The Neck of the Giraffe: Where Darwin Went Wrong** (1982), Hitching; **The Great Evolution Mystery** (1983), Taylor; **The Bone Peddlers: Selling Evolution** (1984), Fix; **Darwin Was Wrong — A Study in Probabilities (1984)**, Cohen; **Darwinism: The Refutation of a Myth** (1987), Lovtrup; and **Adam and Evolution** (1984), Pitman. Not one of these books was written from a Christian-apologetic point of view: they are concerned only with scientific truth* — as was Sir Ernst Chaim when he called (E)volution 'a fairy tale'.*"

[David C.C. Watson, "Book Reviews," *Creation Research Society Quarterly*, Vol. 25, No. 4 (P.O. Box 14016, Terre Haute, Indiana 47803: March 1989), p. 200 (emphasis added).]

PARTIAL LIST OF CREATIONIST SCIENTISTS (PAST AND PRESENT)

- **600+ voting scientists of the Creation Research Society** (voting membership requires at least an earned master's degree in a recognized area of science) (Membership Secretary, Creation Research Society, P.O. Box 14016, Terre Haute, Indiana 47803).
- **The 150 Ph.D. scientists and 300 other scientists with masters degrees in science or engineering who are members of the Korea Association of Creation Research.** The President of KACR is the distinguished scientist and Professor Young-Gil Kim of the Korea Advanced Institute of Science and Technology. Ph.D. in Materials Science, Rensselaer Polytechnic Institute / highly distinguished / inventor of various important high-tech alloys.)
- **Louis Agassiz** (helped develop the study of glacial geology and of ichthyology)
- **Charles Babbage** (helped develop science of computers / developed actuarial tables and the calculating machine)
- **Francis Bacon** (developed the Scientific Method)
- **Robert Boyle** (helped develop sciences of chemistry and gas dynamics)
- **David Brewster** (helped develop science of optical mineralogy)
- **Georges Cuvier** (helped develop sciences of comparative anatomy and vertebrate paleontology)
- **Humphry Davy** (helped develop science of thermokinetics)
- **Henri Fabre** (helped develop science of insect entomology)
- **Michael Faraday** (helped develop science of electromagnetics / developed the Field Theory / invented the electric generator)

- **Ambrose Fleming** (helped develop science of electronics / invented thermionic valve)
- **Joseph Henry** (invented the electric motor and the galvanometer / discovered self-induction)
- **William Herschel** (helped develop science of galactic astronomy / discovered double stars / developed the Global Star Catalog)
- **James P. Joule** (developed reversible thermodynamics)
- **Johann Kepler** (helped develop science of physical astronomy / developed the Ephemeris Tables)
- **Carolus Linnaeus** (helped develop sciences of taxonomy and systematic biology / developed the Classification System)
- **Joseph Lister** (helped develop science of antiseptic surgery)
- **Matthew Maury** (helped develop science of oceanography/hydrography)
- **James Clerk Maxwell** (helped develop the science of electrodynamics)
- **Gregor Mendel** (founded the modern science of genetics)
- **Samuel F.B. Morse** (invented the telegraph)
- **Isaac Newton** (helped develop science of dynamics and the discipline of calculus / father of the Law of Gravity / invented the reflecting telescope)
- **Blaise Pascal** (helped develop science of hydrostatics / invented the barometer)
- **Louis Pasteur** (helped develop science of bacteriology / discovered the Law of Biogenesis / invented fermentation control / developed vaccinations and immunizations)
- **William Ramsay** (helped develop the science of isotopic chemistry / discovered inert gases)
- **John Ray** (helped develop science of biology and natural science)
- **Lord Rayleigh** (helped develop science of dimensional analysis)
- **Bernhard Riemann** (helped develop non-Euclidean geometry)
- **James Simpson** (helped develop the field of gynecology / developed the use of chloroform)
- **Nicholas Steno** (helped develop the science of stratigraphy)
  - **George Stokes** (helped develop science of fluid mechanics)
  - **William Thompson** (Lord Kelvin) (helped develop sciences of thermodynamics and energetics / invented the Absolute Temperature Scale / developed the Trans-Atlantic Cable)
  - **Leonardo da Vinci** (helped develop science of hydraulics)
  - **Rudolf Virchow** (helped develop science of pathology)
  - **John Woodward** (helped develop the science of paleontology)
  - **Also see Creationists mentioned in endnote references and quotations (see index), including:** Aardsma, Austin, Barnes, Benton, Bowden, Byl, Chadwick, Cook, DeYoung, Gentry, Gish, Grebe, Howe, Kaufmann, Klotz, Lester, Marsh, Morris, Parker, Rusch, Slusher, Thaxton, Vardiman, White, Wilder Smith, Williams, etc.
  - **A more thorough list of current Creationist scientists is not provided** due to fears of job discrimination and persecution in today's atmosphere of limited academic freedom in Evolutionist-controlled institutions.

> *T*he only competing explanation for the order we all see in the biological world is the notion of *Special Creation.*
> Niles Eldredge, Ph.D., paleontologist and Evolutionist, American Museum of Natural History

SUGGESTED SOURCES FOR FURTHER INFORMATION ON SCIENTISTS WHO ACCEPT CREATIONISM

☐ Paul A. Bartz, "Religious Bigots Expel Scientific Giants from Classroom!: Kepler, Pasteur and Maxwell Replaced with Darwin, Huxley," *Bible-Science Newsletter*, Vol. 27, No. 3 (P.O. Box

32457, Minneapolis, Minnesota 55432, Phone 612-635-0614: Bible-Science Association, March 1989), pp. 3, 14.

☐ Henry M. Morris, *A History of Modern Creationism* (Santee, California: Master Books, 1984) (surveys the origin and history of the Creation Research Society, the Institute for Creation Research, and various other Creationist organizations in the U.S. and overseas).

☐ Henry M. Morris, *Men of Science — Men of God* (San Diego: Creation-Life Publishers, 1982), 128 pp. (includes biographies and of 65 prominent "Bible-believing" scientists of the past).

2

☐ Larry Hatfield, "Educators Against Darwin," *Science Digest Special* (Winter 1979), pp. 94-96.

3

☐ **Arthur Ernest Wilder-Smith**: Chemist / Lecturer / Creationist / Ph.D. in physical organic chemistry at University of Reading, England (1941) / Dr.es.Sc. in pharmacological sciences from Eidgenossische Technische Hochschule (Swiss Federal Institute of Technology) in Zurich / D.Sc. in pharmacological sciences from University of Geneva (1964) / F.R.I.C. (Fellow of the Royal Institute of Chemistry) / Professorships held at numerous institutions including: University of Illinois Medical School Center (Visiting Full Professor of Pharmacology, 1959-61, received 3 "Golden Apple" awards for the best course of lectures), University of Geneva School of Medicine, University of Bergen (Norway) School of Medicine, Hacettepe University (Ankara, Turkey) Medical School, etc. / Former Director of Research for a Swiss pharmaceutical company / Presented the 1986 Huxley Memorial Lecture at the invitation of the University of Oxford / Author or co-author of over 70 scientific publications and more than 30 books published in 17 languages / Dr. Wilder-Smith is also a NATO three-star general.

4

☐ Arthur E. Wilder-Smith in Willem J.J. Glashouwer and Paul S. Taylor, writers, *The Origin of the Universe* (Mesa, Arizona: Eden Films and Standard Media, 1983) (a Creationist motion picture).

5

☐ Evolutionist and paleontologist Niles Eldredge, Ph.D., of the American Museum of Natural History:

"Indeed, the only competing explanation for the order we all see in the biological world — is the notion of Special Creation."

[Niles Eldredge, *Time Frames: The Rethinking of Darwinian Evolution and the Theory of Punctuated Equilibria* (New York: Simon and Schuster, 1985), p. 29.]

BOTH EVOLUTIONISM AND CREATIONISM ARE OUTSIDE ULTIMATE SCIENTIFIC PROOF OR DISPROOF

6

☐ Creationist Luther Sunderland:

"Using purely scientific techniques, it is impossible for us to evaluate theories about pre-recorded history with the same degree of confidence that theories on currently operating processes can be studied." (p. 153)

[Luther D. Sunderland, "Is Darwinism Testable Science?", in Luther D. Sunderland, *Darwin's Enigma: Fossils and Other Problems*, 4th edition (Santee, California: Master Books, 1988), pp. 26-39.]

☐ Evolutionist Dr. Colin Patterson:

"We must ask first whether the theory of evolution by natural selection is scientific or pseudoscientific (metaphysical) ... Taking the first part of the theory, that evolution has occurred, it says that the history of life is a single process of species-splitting and progression. This process must be unique and unrepeatable, like the history of England. This part of the theory is therefore a historical theory, about unique events, and <u>unique events are, by definition, not part of science, for they are unrepeatable and so not subject to test.</u>"

[Colin Patterson, *Evolution* (London: British Museum of Natural History, 1978), pp. 145-146 (emphasis added).]

☐ To be considered a scientific "fact," an observation must pass 2 tests, explains geologist Kenneth Currie, Ph.D, Geological Survey of Canada (Ottawa):

"First, it must be <u>repeatable</u>, that is the same concatenation of circumstances always produces the same result. Second, it must be impersonal, that is, the same set of circumstances yields the same observation to different observers or to a suitably adjusted machine."

[Kenneth L. Currie, "Uniformity, Uniformitarianism, and the Foundations of Science," in Paul A. Zimmerman, *Rock Strata and the Bible Record* (St. Louis: Concordia Publishing House, 1970), pp. 40-51 (quote from p. 40, emphasis added).]

☐ Geneticist and Creationist John Klotz, Ph.D.

"The glory of modern science is the experimental method, the carefully worked out system of test and control which guarantees objective evidence. No Russian needs to believe what American scientists say; he can test their findings in his own laboratory. The history of science is replete with instances of frauds who have been exposed as such because they could not demonstrate to others their reported findings. Yet there are some fields in which little experimentation is possible: some areas of astronomy, for example, for only to a limited degree can the scientific method be applied in dealing with the broader aspects of this subject. For that reason astronomy is largely descriptive and theoretical. Another of these areas in which experimentation is of limited applicability is the area under consideration, paleontology. <u>It is not possible to apply to the past the rigid tests which can be applied to phenomena on our time level. Consequently a study of the past does not give the degree of validity and reliability that a study of phenomena on our time level yields</u> ... Scientists cannot speak with certainty of the past ... This fact has often been overlooked, and the consequence is that <u>many people assign to scientific statements regarding the past a higher degree of reliability and validity then is justified</u>."

[John W. Klotz, "Assumptions in Science and Paleontology," in Paul A. Zimmerman, editor, *Rock Strata and the Bible Record* (St. Louis: Concordia Publishing House, 1970), pp. 24-39 (quote from pp. 24-25) (emphasis added).]

John W. Klotz: Creationist / Biologist and Geneticist / Ph.D in Biology from the University of Pittsburgh / Former Professor of Biology and Chairman of the Division of Natural Science, Concordia Senior College, Fort Wayne, Indiana / Chief Academic Officer, Concordia Seminary, St. Louis / Member of the Editorial Board of the Creation Research Society Quarterly.

7

☐ **agnostic:** "I do not know" (gnostic = "I know"); Agnostics believe it is not possible to know for certain whether or not a god exists. Generally, they strongly doubt the existence of god. This term was coined by Evolutionist Thomas H. Huxley to describe his own belief.

☐ **atheist:** Atheists take a more definite position and say there is no god.

☐ **theist:** Theists accept the existence of a god. Many Evolutionists are theists, and all Creationists are theists.

☐ According to polls, the most common of these beliefs appear to be Creationism and theistic Evolutionism, in terms of general popularity in North American society as a whole. Least common seems to be atheistic Evolutionism.

8

☐ Ruling out the possibility of a supernatural force marks a very fundamental difference between Creationists and some Evolutionists. Both agnostic and atheistic Evolutionists approach evidence with the viewpoint (or presupposition) that there is *no* creator. That is their bias. Convinced Creationists approach evidence from the viewpoint that there *is* a creator god. This is their bias. Starting with these two different presuppositions, Evolutionists and Creationists often look at evidence in differing ways and produce contrasting interpretations.

9

☐ The well-known British biologist, agnostic, and Evolutionist Sir Julian Huxley once provided this definition of Evolution:

"Evolution in the extended sense can be defined as a directional and essentially irreversible process occurring in time, which in its course gives rise to an increase of variety and an increasingly high level of organization in its products. Our present knowledge indeed forces us to the view that the whole of reality is evolution — a single process of self-transformation."

[Julian Huxley, "Evolution and Genetics," in James Roy Newman, editor, *What is Science?* (New York, New York: Simon and Schuster, Inc., 1955), p. 278 (emphasis is Huxley's).]

THE NATURE OF SCIENCE AND SCIENTISTS

10

☐ Biologist, geneticist and Creationist John Klotz, Ph.D.:

"It might also be pointed out that scientists are not quite as objective as they say they are. It is simply not possible for the scientist to detach himself completely from the theories and hypotheses which he espouses. This is particularly true when they are different or new. He finds considerable pride of authorship and an intense personal loyalty to ideas which he has developed. For this reason there is a great deal of subjectivity in science."

[John W. Klotz, "Assumptions in Science and Paleontology," in Paul A. Zimmerman, editor, *Rock Strata and the Bible Record* (St. Louis: Concordia Publishing House, 1970), pp. 24-39 (quote from p. 25, emphasis added).]

11

☐ *New Scientist* magazine:

"And scientists ... are emotional human beings who carry with them a generous dose of subjectivity into the supposedly objective search for The Truth."

[Roger Lewin, "Bones of Contention," *New Scientist*, Vol. 119, No. 1624 (August 4, 1988), p. 53 (emphasis added).]

12

☐ Russell T. Arndts, "The Logic of Evolutionary Reasoning,"*Contrast: The Creation Evolution Controversy*, Vol. 8, No. 2 (2911 E. 42nd St., Minneapolis, Minnesota 55406: March-April 1989), pp. 1-2, 4 (discusses assumptions and human bias involved in the Evolutionary theory).

☐ *"If you want to impress people with how good your science is, if you want to get tenure in a modern university, if you want to get a research grant, you can't afford to come and say, 'Well I think this MIGHT be the case BUT there are all sorts of indications here that it MIGHT NOT be the case and it's all sort of confused.' People always tend in science, as elsewhere, to sharpen up and clean up a story ... Of course, it's not a fraud, it is part of the general atmosphere in which you're not actually saying to people, tell the truth, tell the whole truth and let it all out."* (Leon Kamin of Northeastern University, p. 14)

"It doesn't take much to take a little bit of the data, change it the way you want it to look and then publish it — and it's impossible to detect that." (Dr. Bruce Dan, Senior Editor of the Journal of the American Medical Association, p. 1)

"The 1980s have witnessed a flurry of scientific fraud and misconduct cases including a number of cases as yet unresolved." (Narrator, p. 1)

"After the initial inquiry by this committee into this subject (scientific fraud and misconduct in connection with scientific research), the committee has had growing reason to believe that we are only seeing the tip of a very unfortunate, dangerous, and important iceberg." (John Dingell, Chairman of Congressional House Subcommittee on Oversight and Investigations, p. 2)

"Yet one recent study has alleged science's quality control mechanisms can't even be counted on to catch simple sloppiness, let alone a clever fraud." (Narrator, p. 10)

["Do Scientists Cheat?", *NOVA*, Television program #1517 (125 Western Avenue, Boston, Mass. 02134: WGBH Transcripts, Broadcast October 25, 1988), 31 pp. (emphasis added).]

☐ Timothy M. Beardsley, "Truth or Consequences?: How Should Institutions Handle Charges of Fraud?", *Scientific American*, Vol. 259, No. 2 (August 1988), p. 24.

☐ Kenneth A. Ham and Paul S. Taylor, *The Genesis Solution* (Grand Rapids, Michigan: Baker Books, 1988), pp. 10-22.

☐ Michael J. Mahoney, "Self-Deception in Science," paper presented at the annual meeting of the American Association for the Advancement of Science (Philadelphia. May 28, 1986), also published in *Origins Research*, Vol. 11, No. 1 (Colorado Springs, Colorado 80937-8069: Students for Origins Research, Spring-Summer 1988), pp. 1-2, 6-7, 10.

> *I* have little hesitation in saying that a sickly pall now hangs over the big bang theory.
> Sir Fred Hoyle, astronomer, cosmologist, and mathematician, Cambridge University

☐ Roger Lewin, *Bones of Contention: Controversies in the Search for Human Origins* (New York: Simon & Schuster, 1987), 348 pp. (challenges the notion that science is synonymous with cool, objective reasoning / documents the personal side of great controversies in paleoanthropology).

☐ Daniel Goleman, *Vital Lies, Simple Truths: The Psychology of Self-Deception* (New York: Simon & Schuster, 1985).

☐ Jerry Bergman, *The Criterion: Religious Discrimination in America* (6245 South Newton Avenue, Richfield, Minnesota 55423: Onesimus Publishing, 1984), 80 pp. (discusses evidence of widespread job discrimination against scientists who seriously question Evolution / reviews evidence of lack of academic freedom).

☐ D. Faust, *The Limits of Scientific Judgment* (Minneapolis: University of Minnesota Press, 1984).

☐ Wolfgang Smith, *Cosmos & Transcendence: Breaking Through the Barrier of Scientistic Belief* (P.O. Box 424, Rockford, Illinois 61105: Tan Books and Publishers, Inc., 1984), 168 pp. (*"Presents an insider's critique of the scientific world-view based upon the sharp but *oft-overlooked distinction between scientific truth and scientistic faith ... demonstrates that major tenets promulgated in the name of Science are not in fact scientific truths but rather scientistic speculations — for which there is no evidence at all.").*

☐ William Broad and Nicholas Wade, *Betrayers of the Truth: Fraud and Deceit in the Halls of Science* (New York: Simon & Schuster, 1982), 256 pp. (shows that science is often much more than a dispassionate quest for truth / examines the kinds of pressures that can lead scientists to stray from the pursuit of truth / documents cases of scientific fraud / challenges the conventional view of science).

☐ J.V. Bradley, "Overconfidence in Ignorant Experts," *Bulletin of the Psychonomic Society*, Vol. 17 (1981), pp. 82-84.

☐ Karin D. Knorr-Detina, *The Manufacture of Knowledge: An Essay on the Constructivist and Contextual Nature of Science* (New York: Pergamon Press, 1981).

☐ Randy L. Wysong, "Can Laymen Question?" and "Methodology," in Randy L. Wysong, *The Creation-Evolution Controversy* (Midland, Michigan: Inquiry Press, 1976), pp. 17-54.

☐ Stephen I. Abramowitz, Beverly Gomes, Christine V. Abramowitz, "Publish or Politic: Referee Bias in Manuscript Review," *Journal of Applied Social Psychology*, Vol. 5, No. 3 (July-September 1975), pp. 187-200.

☐ Ian I. Mitroff, *The Subjective Side of Science* (New York: American Elsevier Publishing Co., 1974).

13

☐ Robert A. Nisbet, "A Presuppositional Approach to the Four View Model of Biological Origins," *Origins Research*, Vol. 11, No. 2 (Fall-Winter 1988), pp. 1, 14-16 (discusses some of the presuppositions and assumptions of scientists who believe in either Evolutionism, theistic Evolutionism, or Creationism).

14

☐ In admonishment to fellow paleontologists, Evolutionist Dr. Robert Martin, Senior Research Fellow at the Zoological Society of London:

"So even the fossil evidence on which theories depend is open to subjective interpretation."

[Robert Martin, "Man Is Not an Onion," *New Scientist*, Vol. 75, No. 1063 pp. 283-285 (quote from p. 285 — emphasis added).]

15

☐ Biologist and Creationist John Klotz, Ph.D.:

"It is clear that much of the structure of modern Evolutionary paleontology rests upon assumptions which are by their very nature not capable of verification ... There is no disagreement with many of the observations of paleontology, but there may be disagreement with the interpretations which are placed on these observations."

[John W. Klotz in Paul A. Zimmerman, editor, *Rock Strata and the Bible Record* (St. Louis: Concordia Publishing House, 1970), p. 39 (emphasis added).]

BIG BANG THEORY

16

☐ **cosmogony**: composed of the Greek words "kosmos" (universe and everything in it) plus "gonos" from the word "gignomai" meaning "come to be", "originate", "become".

17

☐ Harold S. Slusher, *The Origin of the Universe*, revised edition (P.O. Box 2667, El Cajon, California 92021: Institute for Creation Research, 1980), 90 pp. (p. 17 — *"The red shift is probably the single most important observational fact on which modern cosmology is based."*).

18

☐ Astrophysicist Dr. Harold Slusher contends that whether or not the galaxies are moving apart is not really that important to Creationists:

"...the fact of galaxies moving apart can be explained by many other states of matter and energy than a primeval atom that exploded. For that matter, the alleged explosion produces radiation and high-speed elementary particles, not galaxies. Galaxies moving apart have nothing whatever to do with the expanding motion of debris from an explosion."

[Harold S. Slusher, *The Origin of the Universe*, revised edition (P.O. Box 2667, El Cajon, California 92021: Institute for Creation Research, 1980), p. 24.]

19

☐ Mathematician John Byl on the redshift of distant galaxies:

"If the red shifts of distant galaxies are accepted as reflective of actual radial motion ... then the most distant galaxies are receding from us at close to the speed of light. For a universe age of 6000 years this implies that, assuming the speeds to be constant, the most distant galaxies must be at a distance of at least 6000 light years. Otherwise we get a singularity after creation. Taking into account the travel time for light, it follows that the most distant galaxies currently observed must have been at least 3000 light years distant at the time of light emission. Note that in this model the red shift is proportional not to the actual distance, but to the apparent distance. Hence, upon extrapolation into the past, we do not obtain a big-bang situation where all the material was at one point at one time. It should be possible to test this case by observing the variation of the apparent distances of distant galaxies. If they really are fairly close then their apparent magnitudes should decrease significantly over a relatively short timespan." (Creationist John Byl, Ph.D., Professor of Mathematics and Head of the Department of Mathematical Sciences at Trinity Western University in Canada)

[John Byl, "On Small Curved-Space Models of the Universe," *Creation Research Society Quarterly*, Vol. 25, No. 3 (P.O. Box 14016, Terre Haute, Indiana 47803: December 1988), p. 139 (emphasis added.]

☐ Vincent A. Ettari, "Critical Thoughts and Conjectures Concerning the Doppler Effect and the Concept of an Expanding Universe," *Creation Research Society Quarterly*, Vol. 25, No. 3 (P.O. Box 14016, Terre Haute, Indiana 47803: December 1988), 145 pp.

☐ Harold S. Slusher, *The Origin of the Universe*, revised edition (P.O. Box 2667, El Cajon, California 92021: Institute for Creation Research, 1980), 90 pp. (p. 25 — The *"Doppler shift interpretation of the red shift of the galaxies ... leads to tremendously large magnitudes of the velocities of recession. The speeds in some cases approach the speed of light."*).

20

☐ Evolutionist and astronomer Geoffrey Burbridge, Ph.D., former president of the Astronomical Society of the Pacific, former director of the Kitt Peak National Observatory, Professor of Physics at the University of California, San Diego:

"Evidence of this kind exists. If it is accepted, it means:

(1) That at least some quasars do not lie at so-called cosmological distances.

(2) That at least some parts of the redshift of quasars are due to some effect other than the expansion of the universe.

(3) That quasars are physically related to bright, comparatively nearby galaxies.

... The large redshifts, if they are not associated with the expansion of the universe, must either be gravitational in

origin, or due to local motions, or there must be an explanation which so far has eluded us..." (p. 137-138)

"The fairest way to deal with the problem is not to fall back on authority (what eminent authorities believe or don't believe) but to examine the evidence for oneself." (p. 140)

[Geoffrey Burbridge, "Quasars in the Balance," *Mercury*, Vol. 17, No. 5 (a publication of the Astronomical Society of the Pacific, Sept.-Oct. 1988), pp. 136-141 (emphasis added).]

21

☐ Halton Arp, *Quasars, Redshifts and Controversies* (Berkeley, California: Interstellar Media, 1987), 198 pp.

☐ Geoffrey Burbridge, "Redshift Rift," *Science 81*, Vol. 2, No. 10 (December 1981), p. 18.

☐ William Kaufmann III, "The Most Feared Astronomer on Earth," *Science Digest*, Vol. 89, No. 6 (July 1981), p. 81.

☐ Geoffrey Burbridge, "Evidence for Non-Cosmological Redshifts — QSOs Near Bright Galaxies and Other Phenomena," in G.O. Abell and P.J.E. Peebles, editors, *Objects of High Redshift*, Symposium No. 92 of the International Astronomical Union held in Los Angeles, August 28-31, 1979 (Dodrecht, Holland and Boston, U.S.A.: D. Reidel Publishing Co., 1980), pp. 99-105 (technical).

☐ Harold S. Slusher, *Age of the Cosmos*, ICR Technical Monograph No. 9 (P.O. Box 2667, El Cajon, California 92021: Institute for Creation Research, 1980), p. 15.

☐ Fred Hoyle and J.V. Narlikar, "On the Nature of Mass," *Nature*, Vol. 233 (Sept. 1971), pp. 41-44.

22

☐ Also, see: Harold S. Slusher, *The Origin of the Universe*, revised edition (P.O. Box 2667, El Cajon, California 92021: Institute for Creation Research, 1980), p. 20 [p. 20 — W.G. Tifft *"reported that the red shifts of a group a galaxies in the center of the Coma Cluster separated into three distinct bands ... with a confidence level of 99% ... (but) the galaxies in each of the three groups are uniformly distributed about the cluster's central region."*]

23

☐ G.O. Abell and P.J.E. Peebles, editors, *Objects of High Redshift*, Symposium No. 92 of the International Astronomical Union held in Los Angeles, August 28-31, 1979 (Dodrecht, Holland and Boston, Mass.: D. Reidel Publishing Co., 1980), 340 pp.

☐ D.A. Hanes, "Is the Universe Expanding?" *Nature*, Vol. 289, No. 5800 (1981), pp. 745-746.

24

☐ "An Object with a Blue Shift in Telescopes and Observatories," *Science Bulletin* (Garden City, New Jersey: Nelson Doubleday, 1970).

☐ G.O. Abell and P.J.E. Peebles, editors, *Objects of High Redshift*, Symposium No. 92 of the International Astronomical Union held in Los Angeles, August 28-31, 1979 (Dodrecht, Holland and Boston, U.S.A.: D. Reidel Publishing Co., 1980), 340 pp.

25

☐ Vincent A. Ettari, "Critical Thoughts and Conjectures Concerning the Doppler Effect and the Concept of an Expanding Universe," *Creation Research Society Quarterly*, Vol. 25, No. 3 (P.O. Box 14016, Terre Haute, Indiana 47803: December 1988), pp. 142-143.

☐ Michael Zeilik, *Astronomy: The Evolving Universe*, 2nd edition (New York: Harper and Row, 1982), 623 pp., see p. 456.

☐ Donald B. DeYoung and John C. Whitcomb, "The Origin of the Universe," *Creation Research Society Quarterly*, Vol. 18, No. 2 (P.O. Box 14016, Terre Haute, Indiana 47803: September 1981), p. 84-85.

☐ Harold S. Slusher, *The Origin of the Universe*, revised edition (P.O. Box 2667, El Cajon, California 92021: Institute for Creation Research, 1980), pp. 18-19.

☐ G.F.R. Ellis, "Is the Universe Expanding?", *General Relativity and Gravitation*, Vol. 9, No. 2 (February 1978), pp. 87-94.

26

☐ Paul A. La Violette, "Is the Universe Really Expanding?", *The Astrophysical Journal*, Vol. 301 (February 15, 1986), pp. 544-553.

☐ Harold S. Slusher, *The Origin of the Universe*, revised edition (P.O. Box 2667, El Cajon, California 92021: Institute for Creation Research, 1980), p. 18.

☐ D.F. Crawford, "Photon Decay in Curved Space-Time," *Nature*, Vol. 277 (1979), pp. 633-635.

☐ J.C. Pecker, A.P. Roberts and J.P. Vigier, "Non-Velocity Redshifts and Photon-Photon Interactions," *Nature*, Vol. 237, No. 5232 (May 26, 1972), pp. 227-229 (collisions of photons would reduce their speed and generate a redshift in a dense cloud of colliding photons — redness would increase with cloud's heat).

There is no recorded experiment in the history of science that contradicts the second law or its corollaries...
G. Hatspoulous and E. Gyftopoulos, physicists

SUGGESTED SOURCES FOR OTHER COMMENTS ON PROBLEMS WITH THE DOPPLER EXPLANATION FOR THE REDSHIFT

☐ Vincent A. Ettari, "Critical Thoughts and Conjectures Concerning the Doppler Effect and the Concept of an Expanding Universe," *Creation Research Society Quarterly*, Vol. 25, No. 3 (P.O. Box 14016, Terre Haute, Indiana 47803: December 1988), pp. 140-146 (evidence for "misinterpretation of these red shifts").

☐ James B. Hovis, "A Reinterpretation of the Stellar Radial Doppler Red Shift," *Contrast: The Creation Evolution Controversy*, Vol. 3, No. 6 (P.O. Box 32457, Minneapolis, Minnesota 55432, Phone 612-635-0614: November-December 1984), pp. 1-2, 4.

☐ Evolutionist Geoffrey Burbridge:

"It seems to me that examples of this kind make an almost overwhelming case for the reality of large non-cosmological rodshifts. (p. 101) "I believe that however much many astronomers wish to disregard the evidence by insisting that the statistical arguments are not very good, or by taking the approach that absence of understanding is an argument against the existence of the effect, it is there and many basic ideas have to be revised. A revolution is upon us whether or not we like it." (p. 103)

[Geoffrey Burbridge, "Evidence for Non-Cosmological Redshifts — QSOs Near Bright Galaxies and Other Phenomena," in G.O. Abell and P.J.E. Peebles, editors, *Objects of High Redshift*, Symposium No. 92 of the International Astronomical

Union held in Los Angeles, August 28-31, 1979 (Dodrecht, Holland and Boston, U.S.A.: D. Reidel Publishing Co., 1980), pp. 99-105 (technical).]

SUGGESTED SOURCES FOR FURTHER EVIDENCE AGAINST THE "BIG BANG" THEORY

27

☐ Donald B. DeYoung, *Astronomy and the Bible: Questions and Answers* (Grand Rapids, Michigan: Baker Book House, 1989), 144 pp. (pp. 89-90 includes a list of some "missing links" in the theory).

☐ Hermann Schneider, "Did the Universe Start Out Structured?" *Creation Research Society Quarterly*, Vol. 21, No. 3 (P.O. Box 14016, Terre Haute, Indiana 47803: December 1984), pp. 119-123.

☐ G. Russell Akridge, "The Expanding Universe Theory Is Internally Inconsistent," *Creation Research Society Quarterly*, Vol. 19, No. 1 (P.O. Box 14016, Terre Haute, Indiana 47803: June 1982), pp. 56-59.

☐ Gerardus D. Bouw, "Cosmic Space and Time," *Creation Research Society Quarterly*, Vol. 19, No. 1 (P.O. Box 14016, Terre Haute, Indiana 47803: June 1982), pp. 28-32.

☐ Donald B. DeYoung and John C. Whitcomb, "The Origin of the Universe," *Creation Research Society Quarterly*, Vol. 18, No. 2 (P.O. Box 14016, Terre Haute, Indiana 47803: September 1981), pp. 84-90.

☐ Harold S. Slusher, *The Origin of the Universe*, 2nd edition (P.O. Box 2667, El Cajon, California 92021: Institute for Creation Research, 1980), 90 pp.

SUGGESTED SOURCES FOR EVIDENCE IN CONTRADICTION TO EVOLUTIONARY THEORIES FOR THE ORIGIN OF THE SOLAR SYSTEM, GALAXIES, ETC.

☐ George Mulfinger, editor, *Design and Origins in Astronomy* (5093 Williamsport Drive, Norcross, Georgia 30092: Creation Research Society Books, 1984), 150 pp.

☐ Walter T. Brown, Jr., "The Scientific Case for Creation: 116 Categories of Evidence," *Bible-Science Newsletter*, Vol. 22, No. 7 (P.O. Box 32457, Minneapolis, Minnesota 55432, Phone 612-635-0614: Bible-Science Association, July 1984), pp. 1-2 (Suggests problems with Evolutionary theories for the origin of the solar system, including: 2 planets rotate "backwards" / 6 moons revolve "backward" / 4 planets have moons going in 2 different directions / low hydrogen and helium of 4 planets / "wrong" angular momentum for Sun / strong tidal force of Sun / etc.).

☐ Henry M. Morris, *The Biblical Basis for Modern Science* (Grand Rapids, Michigan: Baker Book House, 1984), pp. 155-176.

☐ John C. Whitcomb, Jr., *The Bible and Astronomy* (Winona Lake, Indiana: BMH Books, 1984), 32 pp.

☐ Harold S. Slusher, *Origin of the Universe* (P.O. Box 2667, El Cajon, California 92021: Institute for Creation Research, 1980), 90 pp.

☐ John C. Whitcomb, Jr. and Donald B. DeYoung, *The Moon: Its Creation, Form, and Significance* (Winona Lake, Indiana: BMH Books, 1978), 180 pp.

☐ John C. Whitcomb, Jr., *Origin of the Solar System* (Winona Lake, Indiana: BMH Books, 1964), 34 pp.

☐ Evolutionist J. Trefil:

"*The problem of explaining the existence of galaxies has proved to be one of the thorniest in cosmology. By all rights,*

they just shouldn't be there, yet there they sit. It's hard to convey the depth of frustration that this simple fact induced among scientists."

James Trefil, The Dark Side of the Universe (New York: Charles Scribner's Sons, 1988), p. 55.

28

☐ Evolutionist Sir Fred Hoyle, famous British astronomer and cosmologist:

"*As a result of all this, the main efforts of investigators have been in papering over holes in the big bang theory, to build up an idea that has become ever more complex and cumbersome... I have little hesitation in saying that a sickly pall now hangs over the big bang theory. When a pattern of facts become set against a theory, experience shows that the theory rarely recovers.*"

[Fred Hoyle, "The Big Bang Under Attack," *Science Digest*, Vol. 92 (May 1984), p. 84 (emphasis added).]

☐ "*The time asymmetry of the universe is expressed by the second law of thermodynamics, that entropy increases with time as order is transformed into disorder. The mystery is not that an ordered state should become disordered but that the early universe was in a highly ordered state. (p. 39, D. Page)*

"*There is no mechanism known as yet that would allow the universe to begin in an arbitrary state and then evolve to its present highly-ordered state.*" (p. 40, D. Page, physicist at Pennsylvania State University, Evolutionist)

[Don A. Page, "Inflation Does Not Explain Time Asymmetry," *Nature*, Vol. 304 (July 7, 1983).]

CONCERNING ORDERLINESS IN THE COSMOS

29

☐ Evolutionist and professor H.J. Lipson, F.R.S.:

"*I think however that we must go further than this and admit that the only accepted explanation is Creation. I know that this is anathema to physicists, as indeed it is to me, but we must not reject a theory that we do not like if the experimental evidence supports it.*"

[H.J. Lipson, "A Physicist Looks at Evolution," *Physics Bulletin*, Vol. 31 (1980), p. 138 (emphasis added).]

☐ Evolutionist W. Penfield, O.M. Litt.B., M.D., F.R.S.:

"*The wonder is ... that there should be a universe at all, with its laws and plan and apparent purpose.*"

[Wilder Penfield, *The Mystery of the Mind* (Princeton, New Jersey: Princeton University Press, 1975), p. 73.]

☐ Sir James Jeans:

"*A scientific study of the universe has suggested a conclusion which may be summed up... in the statement that the universe appears to have been designed by a pure mathematician.*"

[Sir James Jeans, *The Mysterious Universe* (New York: Macmillan Co., 1932 / Cambridge, England: University Press, 1932), p. 140 (emphasis added).]

☐ James Prescott Joule (1818-1889) was one of the brilliant scientists responsible for defining the laws of thermodynamics. He made this interesting statement:

"*When we consider our own frames, 'fearfully and wonderfully made,' we observe in the motion of our limbs a continual conversion of heat into living force (kinetic energy), which may be either converted back again into heat or employed in producing an attraction through space (potential energy), as when a man ascends a mountain. Indeed the phenomena of nature, whether mechanical, chemical or vital, consist almost entirely in a continual conversion of attraction through space, living force, and heat into one another. Thus it is that order is maintained in the universe — nothing is deranged, nothing ever lost, but the entire machinery, complicated as it is, works smoothly and harmoniously. And though, as in the awful vision of Ezekiel, 'wheel may be in middle of wheel,' and every thing may appear complicated and involved in the apparent confusion and intricacy of an almost endless variety of causes, effects, conversions, and arrangements, yet is the most perfect regularity preserved...*"

[James P. Joule in an 1847 lecture in Manchester, quoted in Arnold B. Arons, *Development of Concepts of Physics...* (Reading, Massachusetts: Addison-Wesley Publishing Company, 1965), p. 429 (emphasis added).]

OTHER SOURCES OF INTEREST CONCERNING DESIGN IN NATURE

☐ Henry M. Morris and Gary E. Parker, *What Is Creation Science?*, Revised and Expanded Version (San Diego: Creation-Life Publishers, 1987), pp. 33-36, 43-46, 52-54, 56-57, 63-71, 91, 182, 188-190.

☐ Ron Cottrell, *The Remarkable Spaceship Earth* (Denver: Accent Books, 1982) (layman level discussion of evidence that Earth is the product of a designer).

☐ Fred J. Meldau, *Why We Believe in Creation Not in Evolution* (Denver: Christian Victory Publishing Co., 1959), pp. 349.

☐ Also see index, concerning "design."

2ND LAW OF THERMODYNAMICS

30

☐ Heat is the name of energy when it is moved from one area to another. [Allen L. King, *Thermophysics* (San Francisco: W.H. Freeman & Company, 1962), p. 5.]

☐ Heat is transferred by virtue of a temperature difference. Work is energy transferred by virtue of a force.

31

☐ Emmett L. Williams, editor, *Thermodynamics and the Development of Order* (5093 Williamsport Drive, Norcross, Georgia 30092: Creation Research Society Books, 1981), p. 18.

32

☐ Lord Kelvin as quoted in A.W. Smith and J.N. Cooper, *Elements of Physics*, 8th edition (New York, New York: McGraw-Hill Publishing, 1972), p. 241.

☐ Emmett Williams (1981), p. 19 (endnote above).

☐ World-renowned Evolutionist and avid anti-Creationist Isaac Asimov confirms that:

"*Another way of stating the second law then is, 'The universe is constantly getting more disorderly!' Viewed that way we can see the second law all about us. We have to work hard to straighten a room, but left to itself it becomes a mess again very quickly and very easily. Even if we never enter it, it becomes dusty and musty. How difficult to maintain houses, and machinery, and our own bodies in perfect working order: how easy to let them deteriorate. In fact, all we have to do is nothing, and everything deteriorates, collapses, breaks*

down, wears out, all by itself — and that is what the second law is all about."

[Isaac Asimov, "In the Game of Energy and Thermodynamics You Can't Even Break Even", *Smithsonian Institution Journal* (June 1970), p. 6 (emphasis added).]

☐ Technically and most succinctly, the 2nd Law of Thermodynamics says that:

"*The total amount of entropy in nature is increasing.*"

[S. Gasstone, *Textbook of Physical Chemistry* (New York: D. Van Nostrand Company, 1946.]

33

☐ R.B. Lindsay, "Physics — To What Extent Is It Deterministic?" *American Scientist*, Vol. 56, No. 2 (1968), pp. 100-111.

34

☐ Creationist Emmett Williams, Ph.D.:

"*Obviously evolution involves transformation, and natural transformations require energy. Such a description of evolution as given above (refers to Huxley quote, see index) would require tremendous quantities of energy and many energy transformations. The process of evolution requires energy in various forms, and thermodynamics is the study of energy movement and transformation. The two fields are clearly related. Scientific laws that govern thermodynamics must also govern evolution.*"

[Emmett L. Williams, editor, *Thermodynamics and the Development of Order* (5093 Williamsport Drive, Norcross, Georgia 30092: Creation Research Society Books, 1981), p. 10.]

☐ **Emmett L. Williams, Jr.:** Creationist / Ph.D. in Metallurgical Engineering from Clemson University / Formerly served as Development Specialist with Union Carbide Nuclear Corporation and as Metallurgical Consultant for several industrial firms / Currently on staff of Continental Telephone Laboratories, Norcross, Georgia / Former Professor of Physics at Bob Jones University / Former editor of the *Creation Research Society Quarterly*.

HAS THE 2ND LAW OF THERMODYNAMICS EVER BEEN CIRCUMVENTED?

35

☐ No, says expert Frank A. Greco:

"*An answer can readily be given to the question, 'Has the second law of thermodynamics been circumvented?' NOT YET.*"

[Frank Greco, "On the Second Law of Thermodynamics," *American Laboratory*, Vol. 14 (October 1982), p. 80-88 (emphasis added).]

☐ No experimental evidence disproves it, say physicists G.N. Hatspoulous and E.P. Gyftopoulos:

"*There is no recorded experiment in the history of science that contradicts the second law or its corollaries...*"

[E.B. Stuart, B. Gal-Or, and A.J. Brainard, editors, *Deductive Quantum Thermodynamics in a Critical Review of Thermodynamics* (Baltimore: Mono Book Corporation, 1970), p. 78 (emphasis added).]

> *O*f all the statements that have been made with respect to theories on the origin of life, the statement that the Second Law of Thermodynamics poses no problem for an evolutionary origin of life is the most absurd...
> Duane Gish, Ph.D., biochemist

☐ *"Of all the statements that have been made with respect to theories on the origin of life, the statement that the Second Law of Thermodynamics poses no problem for an evolutionary origin of life is the most absurd... The operation of natural processes on which the Second Law of Thermodynamics is based is alone sufficient, therefore, to preclude the spontaneous evolutionary origin of the immense biological order required for the origin of life."* (Duane Gish, Ph.D. in biochemistry from University of California at Berkeley)

[Duane Gish, "A Consistent Christian-Scientific View of the Origin of Life," *Creation Research Society Quarterly*, Vol. 15, No. 4 (P.O. Box 14016, Terre Haute, Indiana 47803: March 1979), pp. 199, 186.]

☐ Emmett Williams, Ph.D, Creationist:

"It is probably no exaggeration to claim that the laws of thermodynamics represent some of the best science we have today. While the utterances in some fields (such as astronomy) seem to change almost daily, the science of thermodynamics has been noteworthy for its stability. In many decades of careful observations, not a single departure from any of these laws has ever been noted."

[Emmett L. Williams, editor, *Thermodynamics and the Development of Order* (5093 Williamsport Drive, Norcross, Georgia 30092: Creation Research Society Books, 1981), pp. 7-8.]

☐ Also, see: Charles B. Thaxton, Walter L. Bradley, and Roger L. Olsen, *The Mystery of Life's Origin: Reassessing Current Theories* (New York: Philosophical Library, 1984), pp. 113-165.

36

☐ In the context of this discussion, "order" means "arrangedness", not necessarily "uniformity". That is, adaption of the parts to the whole, and of the whole to some plan.

[Harold L. Armstrong, "Thermodynamics, Energy, Matter, and Form, *Creation Research Society Quarterly*, Vol. 15, No. 2 (P.O. Box 14016, Terre Haute, Indiana 47803: September 1978), pp. 119-121, and Vol. 15, No. 3 (December 1978), pp. 167-168, 174.]

37

☐ The well-known chemist and Evolutionist Sidney Fox confirms this belief in increasing complexity:

"Evolution, however, has put together the smallest components; it has proceeded from the simple to the complex."

[Sidney W. Fox, "Chemical Origins of Cells - 2," *Chemical and Engineering News*, Vol. 49 (December 6, 1971), p. 46.]

FOR FURTHER EVIDENCE THAT THE 2ND LAW IS A MAJOR PROBLEM FOR EVOLUTION — and for rebuttal arguments against claims this law is wrongly applied as evidence against evolution — and for discussions of why the 2nd law is not contradicted by growth, living systems, crystal formation, etc., see:

38

☐ "Creationist Interpretations of Chemical Organization in Time and Space," *Creation Research Society Quarterly*, Vol. 22, No. 4 (P.O. Box 14016, Terre Haute, Indiana 47803: March 1986), pp. 157-158.

☐ Charles B. Thaxton, Walter L. Bradley, and Roger L. Olsen, *The Mystery of Life's Origin: Reassessing Current Theories* (New York: Philosophical Library, 1984).

☐ Henry M. Morris, *The Biblical Basis for Modern Science* (Grand Rapids, Michigan: Baker Book House, 1984), pp. 185-215.

☐ Henry M. Morris, "Creation and the Laws of Science," in Henry M. Morris and Gary E. Parker, *What Is Creation Science?* (San Diego: CLP Publishers, 1982), pp. 153-188.

☐ Emmett L. Williams, editor, *Thermodynamics and the Development of Order* (Norcross, Georgia: Creation Research Society Books, 1981).

☐ Harold S. Slusher, *The Origin of the Universe*, revised edition (P.O. Box 2667, El Cajon, California 92021: Institute for Creation Research, 1980), pp. 3-10.

☐ Arthur E. Wilder-Smith, *The Creation of Life* (Wheaton, Illinois: Harold Shaw Publishers, 1970).

☐ Arthur E. Wilder-Smith, *Man's Origin, Man's Destiny* (Wheaton, Illinois: Harold Shaw Publishers, 1968).

SOURCES OF INTEREST FOR AN EXPLANATION OF WHY THE FORMATION OF CRYSTALS AND SNOWFLAKES OR THE GROWTH OF HUMAN BEINGS ARE NOT CONTRADICTIONS OF THE 2ND LAW

☐ Walter L. Bradley, "No Relevance to the Origin of Life," *Origins Research*, Vol. 10, No. 1 (1987), pp. 13-14 (addresses some arguments raised by Dr. John W. Patterson and Francis Arduini, etc., shows that the basic arguments used by Evolutionists against the 2nd Law have no relevance to the origin of life).

☐ Robert A. Gange, "Commentary on the Patterson/Walter Exchange," *Origins Research*, Vol. 10, No. 1 (1987), pp. 14-16 .

☐ Tracy Waters, "A Reply to John Patterson's Scientific Arguments," *Origins Research*, Vol. 9, No. 2 (1986), pp. 8-9.

☐ Jerry Kelley, "Thermodynamics and Probability," *Origins Research*, Vol. 9, No. 2 (1986), pp. 11-13.

☐ Jerry Kelley, "On the Nature of Order," *Origins Research*, Vol. 9, No. 2 (1986), pp. 14-15.

☐ Dudley J. Benton, "Thermodynamics, Snowflakes, and Zygotes," *Creation Research Society Quarterly*, Vol. 23, No. 2 (P.O. Box 14016, Terre Haute, Indiana 47803: September 1986), p. 86.

☐ Robert A. Gange, *Origins and Destiny* (Waco, Texas: Word Books, 1986) (contains an explanation of The New Generalized Second Law of Thermodynamics and the information content in biological systems).

☐ David A. Kaufmann, "Human Growth and Development, and Thermo II," *Creation Research Society Quarterly*, Vol. 20, No. 1 (P.O. Box 14016, Terre Haute, Indiana 47803: June 1983), pp. 24-28.

☐ Emmett L. Williams, editor, *Thermodynamics and the Development of Order* (Norcross, Georgia: Creation Research Society Books, 1981), pp. 91-110.

☐ Harold L. Armstrong, "Evolutionistic Defense Against Thermodynamics Disproved," *Creation Research Society Quarterly*, Vol. 16, No. 4 (P.O. Box 14016, Terre Haute, Indiana 47803: March 1980), pp. 226-227, 206, and Vol. 17, No. 1 (June 1980), pp. 72-73, 59.

☐ Duane T. Gish, "A Consistent Christian-Scientific View of the Origin of Life," *Creation Research Society Quarterly*, Vol. 15, No. 4 (P.O. Box 14016, Terre Haute, Indiana 47803: March 1979), pp. 185-203, especially pp. 200-201.

☐ J. Coppedge, *Evolution: Possible or Impossible* (Grand Rapids, Michigan: Zondervan, 1973).

☐ Hubert P. Yockey, "A Calculation of the Probability of Spontaneous Biogenesis By Information Theory," *Journal of Theoretical Biology*, Vol. 67 (1977), pp. 377-398.

☐ Duane T. Gish, *Speculations and Experiments Related to Theories on the Origin of Life* (P.O. Box 2667, El Cajon, California 92021: Institute for Creation Research, 1972).

39

☐ The 2nd Law of Thermodynamics is just as valid for open systems as it is for closed systems, says John Ross, Harvard University:

"...there are no known violations of the second law of thermodynamics. Ordinarily the second law is stated for isolated systems, but the second law applies equally well to open systems."

[John Ross, letter in *Chemical and Engineering News*, Vol. 58 (July 7, 1980), p. 40.]

TELEONOMY

40

☐ Arthur E. Wilder-Smith in Willem J.J. Glashouwer and Paul S. Taylor, writers, *The Origin of the Universe* (Mesa, Arizona: Eden Films and Standard Media, 1983) (a Creationist motion picture).

41

☐ Ernst Mayr, Ph.D., Evolutionist:

"Living organisms, however, differ from inanimate matter by the degree of complexity of their systems and by the possession of a genetic program... The genetic instructions packaged in an embryo direct the formation of an adult, whether it be a tree, a fish, or a human. The process is goal-directed, but from the instructions in the genetic program, not from the outside. Nothing like it exists in the inanimate world."

[Ernst Mayr in Roger Lewin, "Biology Is Not Postage Stamp Collecting," *Science*, Vol. 216, No. 4547 (May 14, 1982), pp. 718-720 (quote from p. 719, emphasis added).]

42

☐ Dr. Henry Morris has proposed this comprehensive definition of the 2nd Law of Thermodynamics in accordance with this concept:

"In any ordered system, open or closed, there exists a tendency for that system to decay to a state of disorder, which tendency can only be suspended or reversed by an external source of ordering energy directed by an informational program and transformed through an ingestion-storage-converter mechanism into the specific work required to build up the complex structure of that system.

If either the information program or the converter mechanism is not available to that 'open' system, it will not increase in order, no matter how much external energy surrounds it. The system will decay in accordance with the Second Law of Thermodynamics."

[Henry M. Morris, "Entropy and Open Systems," *Acts and Facts*, Vol. 5 (P.O. Box 2667, El Cajon, California 92021: Institute for Creation Research, October 1976).]

43

☐ A.E. Wilder-Smith in Willem J.J. Glashouwer and Paul S. Taylor, writers, *The Origin of the Universe* (Mesa, Arizona: Eden Films and Standard Media, 1983) (Creationist film/video).

It is possible (and, given the Flood, probable) that materials which give radiocarbon dates of tens of thousands of radiocarbon years could have true ages of many fewer calendar years.
Gerald Aardsma, Ph.D., physicist and C-14 dating specialist

44

☐ ORDER OF CREATION IN THE CHRISTIAN AND JEWISH BIBLICAL RECORDS (BOOK OF GENESIS, CHAPTERS 1 AND 2):
- Watery, formless planet Earth suspended in the darkness of space.
- Light.
- Separation of light from the darkness — and the first indication that the planet is rotating (day and night cycle produced).
- Formation of Earth's atmosphere, separating the water into two parts: (a) oceanic and subterranean water, (b) atmospheric water.
- Dry land and oceans.
- System to water the entire land surface using subterranean waters (?-springs or mist, or both).
- Vegetation, seed bearing plants, trees that bear fruit.
- Sun and Moon — complete with established orbits so as to mark passage of time (months, seasons, and years).
- Stars.
- Water creatures of all kinds. (All that had "the breath of life" were vegetarian.)
- Birds (all vegetarian).
- Land animals (all vegetarian): (a) creatures that move close to the ground (small animals), (b) large animals, and (c) animals of use to man as livestock.
- Man.
- The garden of Eden.
- Woman.

The Earth, A Young Planet?

45

☐ See list in endnote on "List of Processes Suggested By Some As Evidence for a Multiple Billions-of-Years-Old Earth."

46

☐ These pre-1911 "dates" were based on Evolutionary, uniformitarian presuppositions. Evolutionists have since attempted to lend increased credibility to these assumed dates by use of radiometric dating (which, of course, is also based on uniformitarian presuppositions — as shall be shown).

CARBON-14 DATING

47

☐ Carbon-14 dating is also called the "radiocarbon" method.

48

☐ With minor exceptions.

49

☐ Not all organic remains are useful for Carbon-14 dating, since the technique requires samples which have not been contaminated by other carbonates while alive.

[Willard F. Libby, *Radiocarbon Dating* (Chicago: University of Chicago Press, 6th revised edition, 1965), p. 11.]

☐ Thus, Carbon-14 dating is OK for wood, but often not valid for some freshwater clams, for example.

50

☐ **Willard Frank Libby:** Evolutionist / Ph.D. University of California (1933) / Sc.D. Wesleyan University (1955) / Former

Professor of Chemistry at University of California in Los Angeles / Author of *Radiocarbon Dating*.

51

☐ Cosmic rays strike the nuclei of air molecules, liberating neutrons which are absorbed by Nitrogen-14.

52

☐ There are roughly a trillion Carbon-12 atoms per Carbon-14 atom in living things.

53

☐ It is interesting to note that radiocarbon dating evidence has refuted various Evolutionary views of human history – for instance, mistaken notions concerning a so-called "mesolithic" period. Evolutionist Colin Renfrew, Professor of Archaeology at the University of Southampton:

"An interesting consequence of radiocarbon dating has been to limit the scope of the term 'mesolithic'. Formerly this was seen as representing a worldwide epoch in man's existence, in which man lived the life of the fisherman and the hunter of small game, after the end of the final glaciation of the last ice age, yet before the inception of farming. We can now see that in the Near East he was already beginning to specialize in the exploitation of some of the plants and animals that were later domesticated <u>before</u> *the end of the ice age... Rather than appearing as a universal stage of evolution, this mesolithic way of life appears as one possible, localized mode of adjustment to the new environmental conditions."*

[Colin Renfrew, *Before Civilization* (New York: Alfred A. Knopf Publishers, 1973), p. 63.]

SOME ASSUMPTIONS OF CARBON-14 AGE ESTIMATION CALCULATIONS

54

☐ **GLOBAL EQUILIBRIUM** — Assumes that an equilibrium has been reached between the global rate of production of Carbon-14 and the global rate of Carbon-14 decay, and assumes that this complete balance has remained generally constant for at least 20 to 30 thousand years.

[R.H. Brown, "Can We Believe Radiocarbon Dates?", *Creation Research Society Quarterly*, Vol. 12, No. 1 (P.O. Box 14016, Terre Haute, Indiana 47803: June 1975), pp. 66-68; Melvin A. Cook, *Prehistory and Earth Models* (London: Max Parrish, 1966).]

☐ **CONTAMINATION** — Frequently assumes that the plant or animal remains were not contaminated after death by Carbon-14 atoms from other materials of different ages.

[Willard F. Libby, *Radiocarbon Dating* (Chicago: University of Chicago Press, 1955), p. 10.]

☐ **COSMIC RAYS** — Assumes cosmic ray intensity has not changed significantly for at least the last 20 thousand years.

[See: S.A. Korff, "Effects of Cosmic Radiation on Terrestrial Isotope Distribution," *Transactions of the American Geophysical Union*, Vol. 35 (February 1954), pp. 105+; Willard F. Libby, *Radiocarbon Dating* (Chicago: University of Chicago Press, 1955), p. 8.]

☐ **MAGNETIC FIELD** — Assumes that the intensity of Earth's magnetic field has not varied significantly during the span of time being dated.

[See: Robert E. Lee, "Radiocarbon: Ages in Error," *Anthropological Journal of Canada*, Vol. 19, No. 3 (1981), pp. 9-29, and Harold S. Slusher, *Critique of Radiometric Dating* (San Diego: CLP Publishers, 1973), p. 38.] (Also see index: "magnetic field.")

☐ **OCEAN DEPTHS** — Generally assumes there have been only small variations in ocean depths during the time span being dated.

[Willard F. Libby, *Radiocarbon Dating* (Chicago: University of Chicago Press, 1955), pp. 19-31.]

☐ **OCEAN TEMPERATURE** — Assumes only minor ocean temperature variations during the time span.

[Willard F. Libby, *Radiocarbon Dating* (Chicago: University of Chicago Press, 1955), p. 31.]

☐ **DECAY RATE** — Assumes the Carbon-14 decay rate has never varied significantly during the time span.

[P.A. Catacosinos, "Do Decay Rates Vary?", *Geotimes*, Vol. 20 (1975), p. 11; Donald B. DeYoung, "The Precision of Nuclear Decay Rates," *Creation Research Society Quarterly*, Vol. 12, No. 1 (P.O. Box 14016, Terre Haute, Indiana 47803: March 1976), pp. 38-41; Edward S. Deevey, Jr., "Radiocarbon Dating," *Scientific American*, Vol. 186 (February 1952), pp. 24-28; also see correction letter, Edward S. Deevey, Jr., "Letters," *Scientific American*, (Vol. 186), February 1952), p. 2.]

OTHER SUGGESTED SOURCES OF INFORMATION ON THE ASSUMPTIONS OF CARBON-14 AGE ESTIMATIONS

55

☐ Ian T. Taylor, *In the Minds of Men* (Toronto: TFE Publishing, 1984), p. 317-320.

☐ Weston W. Fields, *Unformed and Unfilled: The Gap Theory* (Phillipsburg, New Jersey: Presbyterian and Reformed Publishing Company, 1978), pp. 219-220.

☐ A.J. White, "Radiocarbon Dating," *Creation Research Society Quarterly*, Vol. 9 (P.O. Box 14016, Terre Haute, Indiana 47803: December 1972), pp. 155-158.

☐ J.L. Kulp, "The Carbon-14 Method of Age Determination," *Scientific Monthly*, Vol. 75 (November 1952), pp. 261+.

56

☐ Creationists say that conventional Carbon-14 age estimating techniques ignore the possibility of a worldwide flood. Creationists say that the calculated age estimates are far too old when involving objects older than about 4 or 5 thousand years (the assumed time of the Flood). Many Creationists believe that radiocarbon is a valid age estimation method which is likely to be of increasing usefulness as they work out the proper way to convert from measured Carbon-14 content to true calendar age.

☐ *"<u>Comparison of ancient, historically dated artifacts (from Egypt, for example) with their radiocarbon "date" has revealed that radiocarbon years and calendar years are not the same even for the last 5,000 calendar years. (The two are in rough agreement for the last 2,000 years, however.</u> Since no reliable historically dated artifacts exist which are older than 5,000 years, it has not been possible to determine the relationship of radiocarbon years to calendar years for objects which yield dates of tens of thousands of radiocarbon years. Thus, <u>it is possible (and, given the Flood, probable) that materials which give radiocarbon dates of tens of thousands of radiocarbon years could have true ages of many fewer calendar years.</u>"*

(Physicist and radiocarbon dating specialist Gerald Aardsma, Ph.D. from University of Toronto, doing research in accelerator mass spectrometry for radiocarbon dating, Chairman of the Astro/Geophysics Department of the Institute for Creation Research Graduate School) [Gerald E. Aardsma, Personal correspondence to Paul S. Taylor (December 28, 1988) (emphasis added).]

CALIBRATION OF CARBON-14 WITH TREE-RINGS

57

☐ Tree-rings have been used in an attempt to check and correct (calibrate) the Carbon-14 system, but many Creationists (and some Evolutionists) have reservations about their true accuracy. Many Creationists believe the tree rings of bristlecone pines are being misinterpreted when used to support dates of almost 8 thousand years.

☐ Physicist and Carbon-14 dating specialist Gerald E. Aardsma, Ph.D. stresses that an accurate calibration table using tree rings can only be correct if the rings are accurately assigned to each of their true calendar years, which is a difficult problem. Additionally, Evolutionists are using some circular reasoning in producing their calibration table:

> "Long tree ring chronologies are rare (there are only two that I am aware of which are of sufficient length to be of interest to radiocarbon) and difficult to construct. They have been slowly built up by matching ring patterns between trees of different ages, both living and dead, from a given locality. As one might expect, the farther back the tree ring chronology extends, the more difficult it becomes to locate ancient tree specimens with which to extend the chronology. To alleviate this problem it seems, from the published literature, to be a common practice to first radiocarbon date a large number of potential tree specimens and then select those with appropriate radiocarbon age for incorporation into the tree ring chronology. Such a procedure introduces a bias into the construction of the tree ring chronology for the earliest millennia which could possibly obscure any unexpected radiocarbon behavior. It is not clear to what extent this circular process has influenced the final tree-ring calibrations of radiocarbon... Creationists are clearly justified in maintaining a high degree of skepticism.

[Gerald E. Aardsma, Personal correspondence to the author (December 28, 1988).]

☐ **Gerald E. Aardsma:** Creationist / Nuclear Physicist / Ph.D. in Nuclear Physics from University of Toronto / Chairman of Astro-Geophysics Department, Institute for Creation Research.

☐ Henry M. Morris, *The Biblical Basis for Modern Science* (Grand Rapids, Michigan: Baker Book House, 1984), pp. 448-454 (Shows that both radiocarbon dating and tree ring dating are extremely erratic and unreliable.).

☐ Walter E. Lammerts, "Are the Bristle-Cone Pine Trees Really So Old?," *Creation Research Society Quarterly*, Vol. 20, No. 2 (P.O. Box 14016, Terre Haute, Indiana: 47803: September 1983), pp. 108-115.

☐ P. A. Morrow and C. LaMarche Valmore, Jr., "Tree Ring Evidence for Chronic Insect Suppression of Productivity in Subalpine Eucalyptus," *Science*, Vol. 201, No. 4362 (1978), pp. 1244-1246 (Shows that insects can affect tree ring growth).

☐ D.J. Tyler, "Radiocarbon Calibration — Revisited," *Creation Research Society Quarterly*, Vol. 15, No. 1 (P.O. Box 14016, Terre Haute, Indiana 47803: June 1978), pp. 16-23.

☐ D.J. Tyler, "The Crisis in Radiocarbon Calibration," *Creation Research Society Quarterly*, Vol. 14 (P.O. Box 14016, Terre Haute, Indiana 47803: 1977), pp. 92-99.

☐ Harold S. Gladwin, "Dendrochronology, Radiocarbon, and Bristlecones," *Anthropological Journal of Canada*, Vol. 14, No. 4 (1976), pp. 2-7, and *Creation Research Society Quarterly*, Vol. 15, No. 1 (P.O. Box 14016, Terre Haute, Indiana 47803: June 1978), pp. 24-26 (Says that the bristlecone is "even more undependable than the junipers" — growing no rings during dry years, growing rings in relation to local weather, etc.).

☐ Elizabeth K. Ralph and Henry M. Michael, "Twenty-five Years of Radiocarbon Dating," *American Scientist*, Vol. 62 (September/October 1974), p. 556 (Questions the trustworthiness of bristlecone pine dating).

☐ Sidney A. Clementson, "A Critical Examination of Radiocarbon Dating in the Light of Dendrochronological Data," *Creation Research Society Quarterly*, Vol. 10, No. 4 (P.O. Box 14016, Terre Haute, Indiana 47803: March 1974), pp. 229-236.

☐ L.M. Libby and H.R. Lukens, "Production of Radiocarbon in Tree Rings by Lightning Bolts," *Journal of Geophysical Research*, Vol 78, No. 26 (September 10, 1973), pp. 5902-5903.

EXAMPLES OF OCCASIONAL WRONG "DATES" OBTAINED WITH CARBON-14

58

☐ **SNAILS IN ARTESIAN SPRINGS** — "The Carbon-14 contents of the shells of the snails of *Melanoides tuberculatus* living today in artesian springs in southern Nevada indicate an apparent age of 27,000 years."

[Alan C. Riggs, *Science*, Vol. 224 (April 6, 1984), pp. 58-61.]

☐ **FRESHWATER CLAMS** — Shell from a live clam "dated" thousands of years old.

[Melvin A. Cook, "Carbon-14 and the 'Age' of the Atmosphere," *Creation Research Society Quarterly*, Vol. 7, No. 1 (P.O. Box 14016, Terre Haute, Indiana 47803: June 1970), p. 55; M.S. Kieth and G.M. Anderson, "Radiocarbon Dating: Fictitious Results with Mollusk Shells," *Science*, Vol. 141 (August 16, 1963), p. 634.]

Note: The factor that throws off Carbon-14 dating of these freshwater clams is that the water in which they live is rich with carbon atoms from dissolved limestone. Thus, unlike land animals, much of their carbon content originates in limestone rather than in the air.

☐ **SEALS** — Dried seal carcasses less than 30 years old "dated" as old as 4,600 years, and a freshly killed seal "dated" at 1300 years old. [W. Dort, Jr., "Mummified Seals of Southern Victoria Land," *Antarctic Journal of the United States*, Vol. 6 (1971), p. 210+ (Also, "when the blood of a seal freshly killed at McMurdo Sound in the Antarctic was tested by Carbon-14, it showed the seal had died 1,300 years ago.")].

☐ **PEAT** — 15 thousand year difference on a single block of soil [K.M. Goh, P.J. Tonkin, and T.A. Rafter, "Implications of Improved Radiocarbon Dates of Timaru Peats on Quaternary Loess Stratigraphy," *New Zealand Journal of Geology and Geophysics*, Vol. 21, No. 4 (1978), pp. 463-466, especially p. 464].

☐ **FRACTIONATION** — A minor factor involved in some wrong dates is called fractionation. Not all plants absorb the standard

---

*T*he best physical evidence that the earth is young is a dwindling resource that evolutionists refuse to admit is dwindling. ...the magnetic energy in the field of the earth's dipole magnet. ...To deny that it is a dwindling resource is phony physics.

Thomas Barnes, Ph.D., physicist

---

ratio of radioactive carbon. Thus, at death these plants and the animals which eat them have abnormally low levels of Carbon-14. And when their remains are dated, they, therefore, give the false impression of being very old. But this error can evidently be mostly corrected for by measuring the Carbon-13 content, which is now reportedly being done in most radiocarbon labs.

ARTICLES QUESTIONING THE ACCURACY OF CARBON-14 AGE ESTIMATES GREATER THAN 4 TO 5 THOUSAND YEARS AND/OR CREATIONIST CLAIMS THAT C-14 MAY PROVIDE SUPPORTING EVIDENCE FOR A YOUNG EARTH

59

☐ Robert H. Brown, "Implications of C-14 Age Vs. Depth Profile Characteristics," *Origins*, Vol. 15, No. 1 (Loma Linda, California: Geoscience Research Institute, Loma Linda University, 1988), pp. 19-29 (p. 19 — *"The radiocarbon age of organic material in sediments would be expected to increase in linear relationship with depth of sediment if geologic and geochemical processes have always had the same characteristics as in recent times. The available data on C-14 age profiles indicate that the characteristic relationship is non-linear in a direction which suggests that the C-14/C-12 ratio was less in the past than it is now. / p. 28 — "provide increased credibility for the conclusion offered in my 1975 treatment, viz., that C-14 ages in the prehistoric range should be expected to be progressively in excess of the real time involved."*).

☐ Robert H. Brown, "The Upper Limit of C-14 Age?", *Origins*, Vol. 15, No. 1 (Loma Linda, California: Geoscience Research Institute, Loma Linda University, 1988), pp. 39-43 (Using Accelerator Mass Spectrometry and state-of-the-art techniques, independent labs have "dated" samples which should be too old to "date" according to Evolutionist expectations. Yet, the resulting age estimates have been in the "40 thousand year range," using a system that Evolutionists expected to be accurate to 70 thousand years. / p. 42 of this article suggests an active carbon exchange inventory for the pre-Flood world of 25-40 times the present value.).

☐ Robert H. Brown, "C-14 Depth Profiles as Indicators of Trends of Climate and C-14/C-12 Ratio," *Radiocarbon*, Vol. 28, No. 2A (1986), pp. 350-357.

☐ Melvin A. Cook, "Nonequilibrium Radiocarbon Dating Substantiated," in *Proceedings of the First International Conference on Creationism*, Vol. II (362 Ashland, Pittsburgh, PA 15228: Creation Science Fellowship, 1986), pp. 59-68.

☐ Stan F. Vaninger, "Archaeology and the Antiquity of Ancient Civilization: A Conflict with Biblical Chronology?," *Creation Research Society Quarterly*, Vol. 22, No. 2 (P.O. Box 14016, Terre Haute, Indiana 47803: September 1985), pp. 64-67.

☐ Henry M. Morris, *The Biblical Basis for Modern Science* (Grand Rapids, Michigan: Baker Book House, 1984), p. 265.

☐ David A. Johannsen, "Radiocarbon...," *Origins Research*, Vol. 3, No. 1 (Colorado Springs, Colorado 80937-8069: Students for Origins Research, 1980), pp. 4-8 (shows how short-age chronologists have recalibrated the long-age dates of Carbon-14 and shows how these dates are consistent with the young earth model / includes examination of bristlecone pine dates).

☐ Robert H. Brown, "The Interpretation of C-14 Dates," *Origins*, Vol. 7 (Loma Linda, California: Geoscience Research Institute, Loma Linda University, 1980), pp. 9-11.

☐ Robert H. Brown, "The Interpretation of C-14 Dates," *Origins*, Vol. 6, No. 1 (Loma Linda, California: Geoscience Research Institute, Loma Linda University, 1979), pp. 30-44 (Evidence

that Earth's pre-Flood biosphere carbon would significantly affect C-14 dates).

☐ Donald B. DeYoung, "Creationist Predictions Involving C-14 Dating," *Creation Research Society Quarterly*, Vol. 16, No. 2 (P.O. Box 14016, Terre Haute, Indiana 47803: September 1979), p. 142.

☐ Robert H. Brown, "C-14 Age Profiles for Ancient Sediments and Peat Bogs," *Origins*, Vol. 2 (Loma Linda, California: Geoscience Research Institute, Loma Linda University, 1975), pp. 6-18.

☐ Donald B. DeYoung, "Geochemistry of the Stable Isotopes," *Creation Research Society Quarterly*, Vol. 11, No. 1 (P.O. Box 14016, Terre Haute, Indiana 47803: June 1974), p. 34.

☐ Ronald D. Long, "The Bible, Radiocarbon Dating and Ancient Egypt," *Creation Research Society Quarterly*, Vol. 10, No. 1 (P.O. Box 14016, Terre Haute, Indiana 47803: June 1973), pp. 19-30.

☐ R. Hefferlin, "A Mathematical Formulation of a Creationist-Flood Interpretation of Radiocarbon Dating," *Creation Research Society Quarterly*, Vol. 8 (P.O. Box 14016, Terre Haute, Indiana 47803: 1972), pp. 68-71.

☐ A.J. White, "Radiocarbon Dating," *Creation Research Society Quarterly*, Vol. 9, No. 3 (P.O. Box 14016, Terre Haute, Indiana 47803: December 1972), pp. 155-158.

☐ Robert H. Brown, "Radiocarbon Dating," in Walter E. Lammerts, editor, *Why Not Creation?* (Grand Rapids, Michigan: Baker Book House, 1970), pp. 80-89, and *Creation Research Society Quarterly*, Vol. 5, No. 2 (P.O. Box 14016, Terre Haute, Indiana 47803: September 1968), pp. 65-68.

☐ Walter E. Lammerts, "Radiocarbon and Potassium-Argon Dating in the Light of New Discoveries in Cosmic Rays," in Walter E. Lammerts, editor, *Why Not Creation?* (Grand Rapids, Michigan: Baker Book House, 1970), 101-105, and *Creation Research Society Quarterly*, Vol. 6, No. 1 (P.O. Box 14016, Terre Haute, Indiana 47803: June 1969), pp. 71-73.

☐ R.L. Whitelaw, "Radiocarbon Confirms Biblical Creation (and So Does Potassium-Argon)," in Walter E. Lammerts, editor, *Why Not Creation?* (Grand Rapids, Michigan: Baker Book House, 1970), pp. 90-100, and *Creation Research Society Quarterly*, Vol. 5, No. 2 (P.O. Box 14016, Terre Haute, Indiana 47803: September 1968), pp. 78-83.

☐ Melvin A. Cook, "Carbon-14 and the Age of the Atmosphere," *Creation Research Society Quarterly*, Vol. 7, No. 1 (P.O. Box 14016, Terre Haute, Indiana 47803: June 1970), pp. 53-56.

☐ Robert L. Whitelaw, "Time, Life and History in the Light of 15,000 Radiocarbon Dates," *Creation Research Society Quarterly*, Vol. 7, No. 1 (P.O. Box 14016, Terre Haute, Indiana 47803: June 1970), pp. 56-71.

☐ Melvin A. Cook, "Radiological Dating and Some Pertinent Applications of Historical Interest: Do Radiological Clocks Need Repair?," *Creation Research Society Quarterly*, Vol. 5, No. 2 (P.O. Box 14016, Terre Haute, IN 47803: September 1968), pp. 69-77.

☐ H.L. Armstrong, "An Attempt to Correct for the Effects of the Flood in Determining Dates by Radioactive Carbon," *Creation Research Society Quarterly*, Vol. 2, No. 4 (P.O. Box 14016, Terre Haute, Indiana 47803: 1966), pp. 28-30.

☐ John C. Whitcomb, Jr. and Henry M. Morris, *The Genesis Flood* (Nutley, New Jersey: Presbyterian and Reformed Publishing Company, 1961).

INACCURATE AGE ESTIMATES

60

☐ The uranium-lead dating method has produced so many anomalous readings that it has fallen into disrepute, even among Evolutionists.

- "It should be noted that dates (absolute dates) obtained by different methods (radioactive dating methods) _commonly show some discrepancies_... As the Committee on the Measurement of Geological Time said in 1950, '_These figures (i.e. dates) are, as railway timetables say, subject to change without notice._'" (p. 378)

  [D.G.A. Whitten and J.R.V. Brooks, _The Penguin Dictionary of Geology_ (Middlesex, England: Penguin Books, 1972), 520 pp. (emphasis added).]

- Robert H. Brown, "Graveyard Clocks: Do They Really Tell Time?", _Signs of the Times_ (June 1982), pp. 8-9.

- John Woodmorappe, "Radiometric Geochronology Reappraised," _Creation Research Society Quarterly_, Vol. 16 (P.O. Box 14016, Terre Haute, IN 47803: September 1979), pp. 102-129.

- Randy L. Wysong, _The Creation-Evolution Controversy_ (Midland, Michigan: Inquiry Press, 1976), pp. 154-156.

61

- John G. Funkhouser, et al., "The Problems of Dating Volcanic Rocks by the Potassium-Argon Methods," _Bulletin Volcanologique_, Vol. 29 (1966), p. 709.

- John G. Funkhouser and John J. Naughton, "Radiogenic Helium and Argon in Ultramafic Inclusions from Hawaii," _Journal of Geophysical Research_, Vol. 73, No. 14 (July 15, 1968), pp. 4601-4607 (especially p. 4606) (volcanic eruption of 1800 on Hualalai Island, Hawaii, produced rocks which falsely "dated" 160 million to 3 billion years).

- C. Noble and John J. Naughton, "Deep-Ocean Basalts: Inert Gas Content and Uncertainties in Age Dating," _Science_, Vol. 162 (October 11, 1968), p. 265.

- William Laughlin, "Excess Radiogenic Argon in Pegmatite Minerals," _Journal of Geophysical Research_, Vol. 74, No. 27 (December 15, 1969), p. 6684.

- Sidney P. Clementson, "A Critical Examination of Radioactive Dating of Rocks," _Creation Research Society Quarterly_, Vol. 7, No. 3 (P.O. Box 14016, Terre Haute, Indiana 47803: December 1970), pp. 137-141.

62

- Radiochronologists must make certain basic assumptions about the rocks they "date", assumptions about their total past environment, formation, and radioactive decay rates. However, Creationist Dr. Duane Gish claims:

  "_Radiochronologists must resort to indirect methods which involve certain basic assumptions. Not only is there no way to verify the validity of these assumptions, but inherent in these assumptions are factors that assure that the ages so derived, whether accurate or not, will always range in the millions to billions of years_ (excluding the carbon-14 method, which is useful for dating samples only a few thousand years old)."

  [Duane T. Gish, _Evolution: The Fossils Say No!_, 3rd edition (San Diego: CLP Publishers, 1979), p. 63 (emphasis added).]

- Also, see: Henry M. Morris, editor, _Scientific Creationism_, new edition (Santee, California: Master Books, March 1987).

**T**he likelihood of the formation of life from inanimate matter is one to a number with 40,000 noughts after it... It is big enough to bury Darwin and the whole theory of evolution. ...if the beginnings of life were not random, they must therefore have been the product of purposeful intelligence.

Sir Fred Hoyle, astronomer, cosmologist, and mathematician, Cambridge University

- Physicist Donald DeYoung, Ph.D.:

  "_The different methods of radiometric dating, when checked against each other, often are in approximate agreement. If the results are misinterpreted as to age, as proposed here, then a common unknown factor (a measurement or an assumption which is defective) may be perturbing all the age values to a longer apparent age than actual. Another explanation in some isolated cases of dating conclusions may be a 'tracking phenomenon.' By this is meant, a tendency of reported scientific measurements to cluster about an incorrect value. Researchers are often reluctant to report findings too far different from previous results in their published findings. This clustering effect shows up in reports of nuclear half-life determinations, and it may also rule the 4.5 billion year assumed history of the earth and moon._"

  [John C. Whitcomb and Donald B. DeYoung, _The Moon: Its Creation, Form and Significance_ (Winona Lake, Indiana: BMH Books, 1978), p. 102 (emphasis added).]

- **Donald B. DeYoung**: Creationist / Physicist, specializing in solid-state and nuclear science, as well as astronomy / Ph.D. in physics from Iowa State University / M.S. from Michigan Tech University / Associate Professor of Physics and Astronomy at Grace College in Winona Lake, Indiana / Published articles in _The Journal of Chemistry and Physics of Solids_, _The Journal of Chemical Physics_, and _Creation Research Society Quarterly_ / Editor of the _Creation Research Society Quarterly_ (began March 1989).

63

- U.S. Geological Survey:

  "_...As much as 90 percent of the total radioactive elements of some granites could be removed by leaching the granulated rock with weak acid... as much as 40 percent of the uranium in most fresh-appearing igneous rocks is readily leachable._"

  [M.R. Klepper and D.G. Wyant, _Notes on the Geology of Uranium_, U.S. Geological Survey Bulletin No. 1046-F (1957), p. 93 (emphasis added).]

SOURCE FOR FURTHER INFORMATION ON THE PROBLEM OF LEACHING

- John C. Whitcomb, Jr. and Henry M. Morris, _The Genesis Flood_ (Philadelphia: Presbyterian and Reformed Publishing Company, 1961), pp. 335-340.

64

- This most basic assumption is evidenced in the statement of Evolutionists Dott and Batten:

  "_Neither heating nor cooling, changes in pressure, nor changes in chemical state can affect in any detectable way the average rate of spontaneous decay. Because the rate cannot be artificially changed in the laboratory, it is assumed that it always has been uniform_ for a given isotope."

  [R.H. Dott and R.L. Batten, _Evolution of the Earth_ (New York: McGraw Hill, 1971), p. 99 (emphasis added).]

WITHOUT AN ABSOLUTELY CONSTANT DECAY RATE, RADIOACTIVE AGE ESTIMATIONS WOULD NOT BE RELIABLE. YET, RATE CHANGES ARE BEING DOCUMENTED BY VARIOUS SPECIALISTS, INCLUDING EVOLUTIONISTS.

Researchers have pointed out various reasons why small changes in decay rates in modern laboratory work could tend to be overlooked.

65

☐ Theodore W. Rybka, "Consequences of Time Dependent Nuclear Decay Indices on Half Lives," ICR Impact Series, No. 106, *Acts & Facts* (P.O. Box 2667, El Cajon, California 92021: Institute for Creation Research, April 1982).

☐ *Geochimica et Cosmochimica Acta*, Vol. 35 (1971), pp. 261-288, and Vol. 36 (1972), p. 1167. (Includes data indicating that different radioactive dating methods used on volcanic rock on Reunion Island in the Indian Ocean gave results varying from 100 thousand to 4.4 billion years. Results from different methods were contradictory.)

☐ Donald B. DeYoung, "A Variable Constant," *Creation Research Society Quarterly*, Vol. 16, No. 2 (P.O. Box 14016, Terre Haute, Indiana 47803: September 1979), p. 142.

☐ K.P. Dostal, M. Nagel, and D. Pabst, "Variations in Nuclear Decay Rates," *Zeitschrift fur Naturforschung* (Vol. 32a, April 1977), pp. 345-361.

☐ P.A. Catacosinos, "Do Decay Rates Vary?", *Geotimes*, Vol. 20, No. 4 (1975), p. 11.

☐ Donald B. DeYoung, "The Precision of Nuclear Decay Rates", *Creation Research Society Quarterly*, Vol. 12, No. 2 (P.O. Box 14016, Terre Haute, Indiana 47803: March 1976), pp. 38-41. (Lists half-life decay variation in 20 radioactive isotopes, including Carbon-14, and variations up to 5%).

☐ J. Anderson and G. Spangler, "Radiometric Dating: Is the 'Decay Constant' Constant?", *Pensee*, Vol. 4 (Fall 1974), p. 34.

☐ Harold L. Armstrong, "Decay Constant: Really Constant?", *Creation Research Society Quarterly*, Vol. 11, No. 1 (P.O. Box 14016, Terre Haute, Indiana 47803: June 1974).

☐ W.K. Hensley, W.A. Basset, and J.R. Huizenga, "Pressure Dependence on the Radioactive Decay Constant of Beryllium-7," *Science*, Vol. 181 (September 21, 1973). (Documents that the radioactive decay rate of Beryllium-7 varies with pressure).

☐ J.L. Anderson, "Non-Poisson Distributions Observed During Counting of Certain Carbon-14 Labeled (Sub) Monolayers," *Journal of Physical Chemistry*, Vol. 76, No. 4 (1972). (Shows that the decay rate of Carbon-14 is influenced by the local atomic environment.)

☐ G.T. Emery, "Perturbation of Nuclear Decay Rates," *Annual Review of Nuclear Science*, Vol. 22 (1972), pp. 165-202 (Shows that many radioactive elements, including Carbon-14 and Uranium-235, have had their decay rates altered in the laboratory.)

☐ J.L. Anderson, *Abstracts of Papers for the 161st National Meeting, Los Angeles* (American Chemical Society, 1971).

☐ SOME FEEL THIS PRECLUDES THE POSSIBILITY OF ACCURATE RADIOMETRIC DATING: See: A.F. Kovarik, "Calculating the Age of Minerals from Radioactivity Data and Principles," *Bulletin #80 of the National Research Council* (June 1931), p. 107.

☐ A unique study in regard to evidence of changing radioactive decay rates is being made by Robert Gentry (formerly associated with Oak Ridge National Laboratories, Atomic Energy Commission). Dr. Gentry believes the measurements of ancient radiohalos provide possible evidence of past rate variation. These halos are permanently etched into certain crystallized minerals and were caused by the energy released by the disintegration of the radioactive atom at their center. Dr. Gentry measured and compared the radiohalos in various rocks and discovered what appear to be significant variations in the measured ring diameters. This may indicate that radioactive decay rates have changed. *However, measurement uncertainty in the tiny radiohalo diameters may preclude any definitive statement on this matter.*

☐ **Robert V. Gentry**: Creationist / Physicist and chemist / D.Sc. (honorary) from Columbia Union College / M.S. in Physics from University of Florida / Graduate work at Georgia Institute of Technology / Often considered the world's foremost authority on radiohalos / Former Guest Scientist at Oak Ridge National Laboratories / Published scientific papers in *Nature, Science, Applied Physics Letters, Earth and Planetary Science Letters, Annual Review of Nuclear Science*, etc.

SOURCES FOR PROS AND CONS ON RADIOHALO EVIDENCE FOR CHANGES IN DECAY RATES

☐ Robert H. Brown, Harold G. Coffin, L. James Gibson, Ariel A. Roth, and Clyde L. Webster, "Examining Radiohalos," *Origins*, Vol. 15, No. 1 (Loma Linda, California: Geoscience Research Institute, Loma Linda University, 1988), pp. 32-38 (Creationists suggest problems with some aspects of Gentry's interpretations).

☐ Dennis Crews, "Mystery in the Rocks," *The Inside Report* (October/November 1987), pp. 3-6, (January 1988), pp. 3-6, (March/April 1988), pp. 3-10 (Provides a very interesting account of Gentry's research — described in layman's language).

☐ Robert V. Gentry, *Creation's Tiny Mystery*, 2nd edition (Knoxville, Tennessee, 37912-0067: Earth Science Associates, 1988), 347 pp.

☐ Paul D. Ackerman, *It's a Young World After All* (Grand Rapids, Michigan: Baker Book House, 1986), pp. 101-110 (easy layman-type explanation).

☐ Jim Melnick, "The Case of the Polonium Radiohalos," *Origins Research*, Vol. 5, No. 1 (1982), pp. 4-5.

66

☐ William D. Stansfield, *The Science of Evolution* (New York: Macmillan Publishing Co., 1977), p. 84.

☐ **William D. Stansfield**: Evolutionist / Ph.D. / Biology Department, California Polytechnic State University.

67

☐ Frederic B. Jueneman, "Secular Catastrophism," *Industrial Research and Development*, Vol. 24 (June 1982), p. 21.

LIST OF PROCESSES SUGGESTED BY SOME AS EVIDENCE FOR A MULTIPLE BILLIONS-OF-YEARS-OLD EARTH

68

☐ (listed in alphabetical order and not necessarily complete) (inclusion on this list is *NOT* an indication of the author's opinion of their relative validity.):

• **Coral "reefs" thickness.** [Dan Wonderly, *God's Time-Records in Ancient Sediments* (Flint, Michigan: Crystal Press Publishing, 1977). For rebuttals to this argument, see: Gerald Mallman, "Questions & Answers: Can the Rate of Coral Growth Be Used As Evidence for an Ancient Earth?", *Bible-Science Newsletter*, Vol. 27, No. 6 (P.O. Box 32457, Minneapolis, Minnesota 55432, Phone 612-635-0614: Bible-Science Association, June 1989), p. 16, and

"Questions & Answers on Creationism," *Bible-Science Newsletter*, Vol. 24, No. 3 (March 1986), p. 12.

- **"Expanding" universe** — Doppler effect interpretation of redshift of galaxies is said to indicate an expanding universe focused on an initial point. Extrapolation of "measured" velocities indicate the "Big Bang" at 2 to 20 billion years ago.
- **Lead** — ratio of accumulation of Lead-207 to Lead-206 (used with galena and pyrite) (accuracy is generally considered very doubtful for age estimation).
- **Lutetium** — rate of decay of Lutetium-176 into Hafnium-176 (rare earth minerals) (usefulness is generally considered very dubious).
- **Nuclides** — "Only 7" naturally occurring radioactive nuclides "are actually found." "If the earth were only 10,000 years old, there should be detectable amounts of all 47 in nature because 10,000 years is not enough time for them to decay totally... (yet) all 17 nuclides with half-lives longer than 50 million years are found in nature." [Stanley Freske, "Evidence for Supporting a Great Age for the Universe," *Creation/Evolution*, Vol. 1, No. 2 (1980), pp. 34-39.]
- **Potassium** — rate of decay of Potassium-40 into Argon-40 (used with muscovite, biotite, glauconite, potash feldspar.
- **Potassium** — rate of decay of Potassium-40 into Calcium-40 (used with sylvite) (usefulness for "dating" is generally considered very limited).
- **Rhenium** — rate of decay of Rhenium-187 into Osmium-187 (used with molybdenite) (usefulness for "dating" is generally considered very dubious).
- **Rubidium** — rate of decay of Rubidium-87 into Strontium-87 (used with muscovite, biotite, potash feldspar land epidolite).
- **Sedimentation** — estimates of rate of sedimentation of Earth's strata. (For rebuttal info see below *).
- **Sedimentation** — varve units in varved sediments. (For rebuttal info see below **.)
- **Stars** — speed of light and the distance of stars. (For rebuttal info see below ***.)
- **Thorium** — rate of decay of Thorium-232 into Lead-208 and Helium-4 (used with shale).
- **Uranium** — rate of decay of Uranium-237 into Lead-205 (used with monazite, rock containing uranium).
- **Uranium** — rate of decay of Uranium-235 into Lead-207 and Helium-4 (used with uraninite, zircon).
- **Uranium** — rate of decay of Uranium-238 into Lead-206 and Helium-4.
- **Uranium** — accumulation of helium in rocks due to the disintegration of uranium.

> *T*he timescale [the supposed 5-billion year old age of Earth] is grossly inadequate and the information content that is needed to produce life is so vast that it is impossible to actually arrive at that final step on Earth...
> *N. Chandra Wickramasinghe*

*It is highly questionable whether there is any reliable way to determine the speed at which sediments were deposited. And there is no way to measure the original thickness of rock laid down during the supposed geological periods. In regard to sedimentation rates, Evolutionist Adolph Knopf has stated:

"The great differences in the estimates of maximum thickness of many of the systems (geologic periods) manifestly indicate that thicknesses are unreliable measures of geologic time. As long ago as 1936 the conclusion had already been reached by Twenhofel that estimates of time based on thickness of strata 'are hardly worth the paper they are written on'... rocks generally give no internal evidence of the rate at which they were formed."

[J.F. White, *Study of the Earth* (Englewood Cliffs, New Jersey: Prentice-Hall, 1962), p. 46 (emphasis added).]

**There is increasing evidence that various varves and laminations in sediment were deposited far more quickly than had been thought. Examples of recent downscales:

John Horgan, "Blame It on the Moon: Australian 'Solar Varves' Turn Out to be Mostly Lunar," *Scientific American*, Vol. 260, No. 2 (February 1989), p. 18. / David I. Nutting, "Origin of Bedded Salt Deposits: A Critique of Evaporative Models and Defense of a Hydrothermal Model," Unpublished M.S. thesis (Santee, California: Institute for Creation Research, 1984), 107 p. / D.J.W. Piper, "Turbidite Origin of Some Laminated Mudstones," *Geology Magazine*, Vol. 109, pp. 115-126.

***For information in rebuttal to the starlight argument, see:**
- Richard Niessen, "Starlight and the Age of the Universe," ICR Impact Series, No. 121, *Acts & Facts* (July 1983).
- Harold S. Slusher, *Age of the Cosmos*, ICR Technical Monograph No. 9, (P.O. Box 2667, El Cajon, California 92021: Institute for Creation Research, 1980), pp. 25-37.
- Jerry Bergman, Ph.D. suggests that the starlight question is also a problem for Evolutionism: "The most distant galaxy ever observed is estimated to be 14.5 billion light years away. Thus, if this is true, the light we are now seeing is what the galaxy looked like 14.5 billion years ago. As this light shows it to be a mature galaxy, it is obviously likewise billions or even trillions of years old... As the sun and earth are believed to be only 4.6 billion years old, there are thus problems in explaining the newness of our solar system."

[Jerry Bergman, "The Problem of Time," in *Proceedings of the First Intl. Conference on Creationism*, Vol. 1 (362 Ashland, Pittsburgh, PA 15228: Creation Science Fellowship, 1986), p. 13.]

69

☐ **Harold S. Slusher**: Creationist / Geophysicist and astrophysicist / Ph.D. in Physics and Geophysics from Columbia Pacific University / D.Sc. (honorary) from Indiana Christian University / M.S. in Physics from University of Oklahoma / Director of Kidd Memorial Seismic Observatory at the University of Texas at El Paso / faculty member of Department of Physics at the University of Texas at El Paso / former Dean of the Graduate School and former Head of the Department of Planetary Sciences of the Institute for Creation Research / Current director of Geo/Space Research and Exploration Foundation, El Paso, Texas.

70

☐ Harold S. Slusher in Willem J.J. Glashouwer and Paul S. Taylor, writers, *The Earth, A Young Planet?* (Mesa, Arizona: Eden Films and Standard Media, 1983) (Creationist motion picture).

EARTH'S MAGNETIC FIELD

71

☐ Physicist and Creationist Thomas Barnes, Ph.D.:

"The best physical evidence that the earth is young is a dwindling resource that evolutionists refuse to admit is dwindling. To admit that it is dwindling is tantamount to admitting that the earth is young. To deny that it is a dwindling resource is phony physics. ... The dwindling resource is the magnetic energy in the field of the earth's dipole magnet." (p. 170) (emphasis is Barnes')

[Thomas G. Barnes, "Dwindling Resource Evidence of a Young Earth," *Creation Research Society Quarterly*, Vol. 25, No. 4 (P.O. Box 14016, Terre Haute, Indiana 47803: March 1989), pp. 170-171.]

☐ For a discussion of the 2nd Law of Thermodynamics, see this book's chapter, "The Origin of the Universe."

72

☐ Karl Gauss made the first evaluation of the strength of Earth's magnetic field in 1835.

☐ The U.S. Department of Commerce issued a publication which lists the evaluations starting with those by Gauss and states that the rate of decay is approximately 5% per 100 years. [See: Keith L. McDonald and Robert H. Gunst, *An Analysis of the Earth's Magnetic Field from 1835 to 1965*, Environmental Services Administration Technical Report IER 46-IES1 (Washington, D.C.: U.S. Government Printing Office, U.S. Dept. of Commerce, July 1967).]

A similar list can be found in:

☐ Ian T. Taylor, *In the Minds of Men* (Toronto, Canada: TFE Publishing, 1984), p. 439.

☐ D. Russell Humphreys, "The Creation of the Earth's Magnetic Field," *Creation Research Society Quarterly*, Vol. 20, No. 2 (P.O. Box 14016, Terre Haute, Indiana 47803: September 1983), p. 92.

73

☐ **Thomas G. Barnes**: Creationist / Physicist / D.Sc. from Hardin-Simmons University (1950) / Professor emeritus of Physics and Director Schellenger Research Laboratories of Texas Western College of the University of Texas at El Paso / Former consultant to Globe Universal Sciences, Inc. in El Paso / Former research physicist at Duke University (1942-45) / M.S. degree from Brown University (1936) while studying under the famous physicist R.B. Lindsay / Director of many important research projects on terrestrial magnetism and atmospheric physics / Published various scientific papers and textbooks / Member of the Editorial Board of the Creation Research Society Quarterly.

74

☐ According to Dr. Barnes, the equation for the half-life of Earth's magnetic field is:

Half-Life = 2.88×10^{-15} (Conductivity) (Radius^2)

Where the half-life is in years, the radius in meters, and the conductivity is in mhos/meter.

☐ The Magsat satellite launched by NASA in 1979 found a current half-life of 830 years for Earth's main magnetic field. ["Magsat Down, Magnetic Field Declining," *Science News*, Vol. 117, No. 26 (1980), p. 407.] Also, see: R.R. Langel, et al, "Initial Geomagnetic Field Model From Magsat Vector Data," *Geophysical Research Letters*, Vol. 7, No. 10 (1980), pp. 793-796.

☐ Dr. Barnes has published detailed rebuttals to claims that "the magnetic field has remained at essentially the same value during geologic time, except for intervals in which it went through a reversal, dying down to zero and rising up again with the reverse polarity." See the following by Dr. Barnes: "Depletion of the Earth's Magnetic Field", Impact No. 100, *Acts & Facts* (P.O. Box 2667, El Cajon, California 92021: Institute for Creation Research, October 1981).

☐ The primary evidence used against Dr. Barnes' findings are the paleomagnetic field present in many rocks. This is used to support the idea that Earth's magnetic field has reversed on numerous occasions. However, some researchers believe this evidence is questionable proof. Jacobs lists 4 processes having nothing to do with a reversal in Earth's magnetic field which can reverse magnetism in rocks. [Jacobs, *The Earth's Core and Geomagnetism*.]

☐ Lightning strikes are also said to regularly change the paleomagnetic field in rocks. Michael Aerate has published evidence that various possible mechanisms may cause reversals in rocks and sediments. It is shown that extreme bias in the astronomical theory has caused the manipulation of data by various means,

and the "reinforcement syndrome" acts like a traffic policeman to keep data and researchers in order.

[Michael J. Aerate, "Ice Ages: The Mystery Solved?, Part III: Paleomagnetic Stratigraphy and Data Manipulation," *Creation Research Society Quarterly*, Vol. 21, No. 4 (P.O. Box 14016, Terre Haute, Indiana 47803: March 1985), pp. 170-181.]

75

☐ Thomas Barnes in Willem J.J. Glashouwer and Paul S. Taylor, writers, *The Earth, A Young Planet?* (Mesa, Arizona: Eden Films and Standard Media, 1983) (Creationist motion picture).

☐ Concerning Earth's magnetic field, Henry M. Morris, Ph.D., comments:

"If any process is impervious to external influences which might change it, this one should be!"

[Henry Morris, *The Biblical Basis for Modern Science* (Grand Rapids, Michigan: Baker Book House, 1984), p. 263.]

☐ It is also interesting to note that if Earth's magnetic field was stronger in the ancient past, less cosmic radiation would have struck the planet's atmosphere. This would result in lower Carbon-14 production, which would mean the most ancient dates would need to be revised downward.

ADDITIONAL CREATIONIST INFORMATION ON EARTH'S MAGNETIC FIELD

☐ Thomas G. Barnes, "Dwindling Resource Evidence of a Young Earth," *Creation Research Society Quarterly*, Vol. 25, No. 4 (P.O. Box 14016, Terre Haute, Indiana 47803: March 1989), pp. 170-171.

☐ D. Russell Humphreys, "The Mystery of the Earth's Magnetic Field," *Impact*, No. 188 (P.O. Box 2667, El Cajon, California 92021: Institute for Creation Research, February 1989), 4 pp.

☐ D. Russell Humphreys, "Has the Earth's Magnetic Field Ever Flipped?", *Creation Research Society Quarterly*, Vol. 25, No. 3 (P.O. Box 14016, Terre Haute, Indiana 47803: December 1988), pp. 130-137 (suggests evidence for reversals in paleomagnetism in rocks and evidence for these reversals occurring rapidly during the Genesis Flood rather than slowly over millions of years).

☐ William M. Overn, "What Flips Earth's Field?", *Contrast: The Creation Evolution Controversy*, Vol. 7, No. 4 (P.O. Box 32457, Minneapolis, Minnesota 55432, Phone 612-635-0614: July/August 1988), p. 3 (suggests evidence that the Earth's dipole magnetic field probably does not reverse).

☐ D. Russell Humphreys, "Reversals of the Earth's Magnetic Field During the Genesis Flood," *Proceedings of the First International Conference on Creationism*, Vol. 2 (Pittsburgh: Creation Science Fellowship, 1986), pp. 113-126.

☐ Thomas G. Barnes, "Earth's Young Magnetic Age Confirmed," *Creation Research Society Quarterly*, Vol. 23, No. 1 (P.O. Box 14016, Terre Haute, Indiana 47803: June 1986), pp. 30-34.

☐ Thomas G. Barnes, "Earth's Young Magnetic Age: An Answer to Dalrymple," *Creation Research Society Quarterly*, Vol. 21, No. 3 (P.O. Box 14016, Terre Haute, Indiana 47803: December 1984), pp. 109-113.

☐ D. Russell Humphreys, "The Creation of Planetary Magnetic Fields," *Creation Research Society Quarterly*, Vol. 21, No. 3 (P.O. Box 14016, Terre Haute, Indiana 47803: December 1984), pp. 140-149.

☐ Thomas G. Barnes, *Origin and Destiny of the Earth's Magnetic Field*, Revised and expanded edition, Technical Monograph No.

4 (P.O. Box 2667, El Cajon, California 92021: Institute for Creation Research, 1983).

□ D. Russell Humphreys, "The Creation of the Earth's Magnetic Field," *Creation Research Society Quarterly*, Vol. 20, No. 2 (P.O. Box 14016, Terre Haute, Indiana 47803: September 1983), pp. 89-94.

HELIUM IN EARTH'S ATMOSPHERE

76

□ **Melvin Alonzo Cook**: Creationist / Physical Chemist / Ph.D. in physical chemistry from Yale University (1937) / M.A. University of Utah (1934) / Nobel Prize nominee (Nitro Nobel Gold Medalist, Swedish Academy, Stockholm (1969) / Professor of Metallurgy at the University of Utah (1947-70) / Explosives expert and Director of the Explosives Research Institute at the University of Utah / Founder (1958) and President (1962-72) and Chairman (1962-1974) of IRECO Chemicals in Salt Lake City / Chairman of Cook Slurry Company / Resident chemist at E.I. du Pont de Nemours & Co. (1937-47) / Chairman of Cook Associates, Inc. (1973-) / Chemistry Pioneer Award, American Institute of Chemists (1973) / E.V. Murphree Gold Medalist Award, American Chemical Society (1968) / Loomis Award from Yale University (1937).

77

□ Total quantity of Helium-4 in Earth's atmosphere = 3.9×10^{15} grams. Helium-3 in atmosphere = 5.3×10^9 grams. Ratio is 1.4×10^{-6}. [Larry Vardiman, "The Age of the Earth's Atmosphere Estimated by Its Helium Content," *Proceedings of the First International Conference on Creationism*, Vol. 1 (362 Ashland Ave., Pittsburgh, Pennsylvania 15228: Creation Science Fellowship, 1986), p. 188.]

78

□ Helium-4 and Helium-3.

79

□ Helium-3 and Helium-4 leaking through the crust is considered primordial helium by Evolutionists. Helium-4 outflow from this source is currently estimated at 2×10^6 atoms $cm^{-2} sec^{-1}$.

[W. Rison and H. Craig, "Helium Isotopes and Mantale Volatiles in Loihi Seamount and Hawaiian Island Basalts and Xenoliths," *Earth and Planetary Science Letters*, Vol. 66 (1983), pp. 407-426, and H. Craig and J.E. Lupton, "Primordial Neon, Helium, and Hydrogen in Oceanic Basalts," *Earth and Planetary Science Letters*, Vol. 31 (1976), pp. 369-385.]

□ Given 4.5 billion years, this source alone could produce 2 thousand times the amount of helium in Earth's current atmosphere. If primordial helium originally existed in Earth's atmosphere (which is a reasonable assumption), then the situation is even worse for those who assume an old Earth.

80

□ Despite the hopes and claims of Evolutionists that great amounts of helium can float out of Earth's atmosphere into space, it is apparently not possible in significant quantity. Dudley J. Benton, Ph.D., provides the following calculations indicating that under the most extreme upper atmospheric conditions

*I*s it really credible that random processes could have constructed a reality, the smallest element of which — a functional protein or gene — is complex beyond...anything produced by the intelligence of man?
Michael Denton, molecular biologist

only 1.4 helium atoms in 10 million helium atoms can escape from Earth's gravity via thermal effects.

"The CRC Handbook of Tables for Applied Engineering Science, second edition (p. 655) or CRC Handbook of Chemistry and Physics (pp. F160-F213) gives the following data:

extreme temperature at the upper limit of atmosphere (T) = 2100oK

escape velocity from the earth (vE) = 1.1E4 m/s

molecular weight of helium (w) = 4 (kg/kg-mole)

Avogadro's number (A) = 6.0E26 (atoms/kg-mole)

Boltzmann's constant (k) = 1.4E-23 J/oK/atom

The mass (m) of a single helium atom can be computed by:

m = w/A = (4 kg/kg-mole)/(6.0E26 atoms/kg-mole) = 6.6E-27 kg/atom

The fraction (F) of helium atoms having a speed greater than or equal to the escape velocity (vE) can be computed in integrating Maxwell's distribution from vE to infinity. The resulting formula is given by F.J. Pierce, Microscopic Thermodynamics (Scranton, Pennsylvania: International Textbook, 1968), pp. 38-45 in terms of the complimentary Gauss error function:

F = erfc{(mv2/(2kT))0.5} = erfc{((6.6E-27 kg/atom)(1.1E4 m/s)2)(2(1.4E-23 Joule/oK/atom)(2100oK))}0.5} = erfc(140.5) = erfc(3.7) = 1.4E-7."

"The theory that I used to obtain (the above)... indication of the helium escape from the Earth's atmosphere implicitly assumed continuous replenishment of those atoms which escape. Implied in the calculations was the assumption that this was an ongoing (not a one-time) process... Because helium is continuously produced and very little of this escapes... one may infer that for practical purposes the helium now present in the atmosphere is essentially the accumulation of that which has been produced plus whatever original helium there may have been. This inference may depend on the past temperature of the upper atmosphere; but it does not depend on the rate at which helium has been produced in the past. This is why I chose to compute the escaping population fraction rather than the escaping flux (which could also be computed by the same Maxwellian theory) as this would require some assumption about the rate of production."

[Dudley J. Benton, "Reply to Franklin," *Creation Research Society Quarterly*, Vol. 25 (P.O. Box 14016, Terre Haute, Indiana 47803: June 1988), p. 55.]

□ **Dudley J. Benton**: Creationist / Ph.D. in Mechanical Engineering from the University of Tennessee / Specialties: thermodynamics and numerical modeling / Published in various technical journals / Sole developer of over 50 large scale computer codes involving: thermodynamics, heat, mass, momentum transfer, chemical reactions, process plant equipment, numerical methods, and graphics.

□ Other suggested ways that significant quantities of helium might leak from Earth's atmosphere have been suggested by Evolutionists. These include: polar wind, solar wind sweeping, and hot ion exchange. According to expert Dr. Larry Vardiman:

"None of these have been accurately quantified nor have they been confirmed."

[Larry Vardiman in personal correspondence to the author (February 29, 1989) (emphasis added).]

□ *"Mechanisms other than thermal escape are considered even by the long-age scientific community to be speculative and of an undetermined significance."* (p. 192). *"Current diffusion models all indicate that helium escapes to space from the atmosphere at a rate much less than its production rate. The low concentration of helium actually measured would suggest that the earth's atmosphere must be quite young."* (p. 187)

[Larry Vardiman, "The Age of the Earth's Atmosphere Estimated by Its Helium Content," *Proceedings of the First International Conference on Creationism*, Vol. II (Pittsburgh: Creation Science Fellowship, 1986), pp. 187-194 (emphasis added).]

□ **Larry Vardiman:** Astrophysicist and geophysicist / Creationist / Ph.D. in Atmospheric Physics from Colorado State University (1974) / Former Academic Dean and Chairman of Physical Sciences and Mathematics at Christian Heritage College, Santee, CA / Chairman of Astro-Geophysics Department of the Institute for Creation Research Graduate School (beginning Summer 1989).

□ Evolutionist and atmospheric gases expert Chamberlain of Rice University (Department of Space Science and Astronomy) has stated that:

"The problem will not go away and it is unsolved." (p. 278 — emphasis added)

[Joseph W. Chamberlain, *Theory of Planetary Atmospheres: An Introduction to Their Physics and Chemistry* (New York: Academic Press, 1978), 330 pp.]

FURTHER CREATIONIST DOCUMENTATION ON HELIUM IN THE ATMOSPHERE, AS IT RELATES TO THE AGE OF THE EARTH

81

□ Larry Vardiman, "The Age of the Earth's Atmosphere Estimated by Its Helium Content," *Proceedings of the First International Conference on Creationism*, Vol. 1 (Pittsburgh: Creation Science Fellowship, 1986), pp. 187-194.

□ Larry Vardiman, "Up, Up and Away! The Helium Escape Problem," ICR Impact Series No. 143, *Acts & Facts* (P.O. Box 2667, El Cajon, California 92021: Institute for Creation Research, May 1985).

□ Henry M. Morris, editor, *Scientific Creationism*, general edition (San Diego: CLP Publishers, 1974), pp. 150-151.

□ Melvin A. Cook, *Prehistory and Earth Models* (London: Max Parrish, 1966), pp. 10-14.

□ Melvin A. Cook, "Where is the Earth's Radiogenic Helium?", *Nature*, Vol. 179, No. 213 (January 26, 1957), p. 213.

POPULATION GROWTH

82

□ Ian T. Taylor, *In the Minds of Men* (Toronto, Canada: TFE Publishing, 1984), pp. 337-339.

□ Henry M. Morris, *The Biblical Basis for Modern Science* (Grand Rapids, Michigan: Baker Book House, 1984), pp. 414-426.

□ Henry M. Morris, editor, *Scientific Creationism*, general edition (San Diego: CLP Publishers, 1974), pp. 167-169.

□ *"The actual data of population statistics, interpreted and applied in the most conservative and most probable manner, point to an origin of the human population only several thousand years ago. The present population could very easily have been attained in only about 6000 years or so, even if the average population growth rate throughout most of history*

were only one-sixth as much as it is at present." (Henry Morris, Ph.D.)

[Henry M. Morris, "Evolution and the Population Problem," *The Battle for Creation*, Acts/Facts/Impacts Volume 2 (San Diego: Creation-Life Publishers, 1976), pp. 259-269.]

□ Dr. John C. Whitcomb, Jr., believes Earth's present population could be reached in 3200 years since the Flood. Evolutionists suggest man has been here for over 100 times longer.

[John C. Whitcomb, Jr., *The World That Perished*, 2nd edition (Grand Rapids, Michigan: Baker Book House, 1988), p. 132.]

SHORT-PERIOD COMETS

83

□ The generally accepted theory (as proposed by astronomer Fred Whipple) is that comets are "dirty snowballs" consisting of frozen dust and various gases.

84

□ Most Evolutionary astronomers believe these comets were formed at the same time as the solar system. See: L. Wilkening, editor, *Comets* (Tucson, Arizona: University of Arizona Press, 1982), p. 219.

85

□ Harold S. Slusher in Willem J.J. Glashouwer and Paul S. Taylor, writers, *The Earth, A Young Planet?* (Mesa, Arizona: Eden Films and Standard Media, 1983) (creationist motion picture).

86

□ Named after Dutch astronomer Jan H. Oort who first proposed this theory in 1950. [Jan H. Oort, *Bulletin of the Astronomy Institute of the Netherlands*, Vol. 11, No. 408 (1950), p. 91; Jan H. Oort, editor, *The Solar System*, Vol. 4 (Chicago: University of Chicago, 1963).]

SOURCES CONCERNING COMETARY EVIDENCE FOR A YOUNG SOLAR SYSTEM AND/OR CONCERNING PROBLEMS WITH THE "OORT CLOUD" THEORY

87

□ Paul M. Steidl, "Comets and Creation," *Creation Research Society Quarterly*, Vol. 23, No. 4 (P.O. Box 14016, Terre Haute, Indiana 47803: March 1987), pp. 153-160 ("no way has been found either to create or maintain such a cloud" / Presents various evidences for a young age for comets.)

□ Paul D. Ackerman, *It's a Young World After All* (Grand Rapids, Michigan: Baker Book House, 1986), pp. 29-40 (Provides an easy-to-understand explanation of these theories for laypeople).

□ Harold S. Slusher, *Age of the Cosmos: ICR Technical Monograph #9* (P.O. Box 2667, El Cajon, California 92021: Institute for Creation Research, 1980), pp. 43-54.

□ Paul M. Steidl, *The Earth, the Stars, and the Bible* (Grand Rapids, Michigan: Baker Book House, 1979), pp. 58-59.

□ Harold Armstrong, "Comets and a Young Solar System," in George F. Howe, editor, *Speak to the Earth*, (New Jersey: Presbyterian and Reformed Publishing Company, 1975), pp. 327-330.

□ Raymond A. Lyttleton, "The Non-Existence of the Oort Cometary Shell," *Astrophysics and Space Science*, Vol. 31, No. 2 (December 1974), pp. 385-401.

☐ Harold S. Slusher, "Some Astronomical Evidences for a Youthful Solar System," *Creation Research Society Quarterly*, Vol. 8 (P.O. Box 14016, Terre Haute, Indiana 47803: June 1971), pp. 55-57.

☐ Thomas D. Nicholson, "Comets, Studied for Many Years, Remain an Enigma to Scientists," *Natural History* (March 1966), pp. 44-47.

THE ESCAPING MOON

88

☐ According to current Evolutionary theory, the Moon (and Earth) are supposed to be about 5 billion years old.

89

☐ Evolutionist Gordon Groves:

   "Thus the tidal friction tends to increase the length of day, to increase the distance between Earth and Moon, and to increase the lunar month."

   [Gordon W. Groves, "Tidal Friction," in *McGraw-Hill Encyclopedia of Science and Technology*, Vol. 18 (New York: McGraw-Hill, 1987), p. 361.]

90

☐ Currently a rate equal to losing 0.00002 seconds per year (approximately). [Figure supplied in personal correspondence June 1, 1983 from Creationist physicist Dr. Donald DeYoung.]

☐ The current measured rate is approximately 4 centimeters per year. ["Moon Slipping Away from Earth," *Geo*, Vol. 3 (July 1981), p. 137 (*"Signals from a laser reflector placed on the moon by Apollo 11 astronauts 12 years ago this month have confirmed what scientists have long theorized: the Moon is pulling away from the earth. The rate at which it is receding has been calculated at 4 centimeters per year. Tidal friction — caused by a bulge, or pileup, of water in the middle of the earth's oceans — is partly responsible for this phenomenon and for... the slowing down of the earth in its own daily revolution. What all this means, according to British physicist David W. Hughes, is that the length of the day will increase by one second every 50,000-years..."*). Also see: John Wahr, "The Earth's Rotation Rate," *American Scientist*, Vol. 73, No. 1 (January-February 1985), pp. 41-46.]

☐ *"One cannot linearly extrapolate the present 4 cm/year separation rate back into history. It has that value today, but was more rapid in the past because of tidal effects. In fact, the separation rate depends on the distance to the 6th power, a very strong dependence. ...the rate is now 4 cm/year, was perhaps 20 m/year 'long' ago, and the average is 1.2 m/year."*

   [Physicist Donald B. DeYoung, Ph.D., in personal correspondence to Paul S. Taylor (January 6, 1989).]

91

☐ Dr. Dudley J. Benton supplies the following calculations for an *approximate* time for the separation between the Moon and Earth (an unknown amount of the involved energy is dissipated in tidal friction on Earth and the Moon instead of going into orbital motion):

   The *CRC Handbook of Chemistry and Physics* (pp. F160-F216):

Earth's rotational speed (ω) = 7.3E-5 radians/second

Rotational moment of inertia (I) = 8.1E37 kg-m^2

Relative change in rotational speed of Earth = -2.8E-8 per 100 years

Mass of Earth (M_E) = 6.0E24 kg

Mass of Moon (M_M) = 7.3E22 kg

Mean orbital radius of Moon (R) = 3.8E8 meters

Gravitational constant (G) = 6.7E-11 N-m^2/kg^2

The corresponding rate of change in rotational kinetic energy of the Earth can be computed by taking the time derivative of the rotational kinetic energy as given by S. Borowitz and A. Beiser in Essentials of Physics (Reading, Massachusetts: Addison-Wesley, 1971), pp. 164-172.

$E_E = 0.5\, I\, \omega^2$ which becomes:

$dE_E/dt = I\omega\, d\omega/dt =$

$$\frac{(8.1E37\ kg{-}m^2)(7.3E{-}5\ radians\ per\ second)^2(-2.8E{-}8\ per\ 100\ years)}{(3600\ seconds\ per\ hour)(24\ hours\ per\ day)(365\ days\ per\ year)}$$

$= -3.8E12$ Joules per second

The total energy of the Moon (potential + kinetic) is given by Borowitz and Beiser: $E_M = -\dfrac{GM_E M_M}{2R}$

Taking the derivative with respect to time of the above equation:

$$dE_M/dt = \frac{GM_E M_M}{2R^2}\, dR/dt \quad or \quad dR/dt = \frac{2R^2 E_M/dt}{GM_E M_M}$$

If this energy from Earth were transferred to the Moon as suggested, the rate of change of the Moon's orbital radius would be:

$$dR/dt = \frac{2(3.8E8\ m)^2(3.8E12\ Joules\ per\ second)}{(6.7E{-}11\ N{-}m^2/kg^2)(6.0E24\ kg)(7.3E22\ kg)}$$

$= 3.8E{-}8$ meters per second = 1.2 meters per year

This separation rate value is an overall average. Using this overall theoretical average for the separation rate value, it can be divided into the orbit radius, yielding the following time.

$$\frac{(3.8E8\ meters)}{(3.8E{-}8\ meters\ per\ sec.)(3600\ seconds\ per\ hour)(24\ hours\ per\ day)}$$

$= 320$ million years

Further reference: Stuart R. Taylor, *Lunar Science: A Post-Apollo View* (New York: Pergamon Press, 1975), p. 3.

92

☐ Thomas G. Barnes, "Young Age for the Moon and Earth," ICR Impact Series, No. 110, *Acts & Facts* (P.O. Box 2667, El Cajon, California 92021: Institute for Creation Research, August 1982).

☐ Louis B. Slichter, "Secular Effects of Tidal Friction Upon the Earth's Rotation," *Journal Geoph. Res.*, Vol. 8, No. 14 (1964), pp. 4281-4288.

*A*n intelligible communication via radio signal from some distant galaxy would be widely hailed as evidence of an intelligent source. Why then doesn't the message sequence on the DNA molecule also constitute prima facie evidence for an intelligent source?

Chemists Thaxton, Bradley, and Olsen

OTHER EVIDENCE FOR A YOUNG MOON

93

☐ Paul D. Ackerman, *It's a Young World After All* (Grand Rapids, Michigan: Baker Book House, 1986), pp. 41-47, 49-53 (Lunar rock viscosity).

☐ Glenn R. Morton, Harold S. Slusher, and Richard E. Mandock, "The Age of Lunar Craters," *Creation Research Society Quarterly*, Vol. 20, No. 2 (P.O. Box 14016, Terre Haute, Indiana 47803: September 1983), pp. 105-108.

☐ John C. Whitcomb and Donald B. DeYoung, *The Moon: Its Creation, Form and Significance* (Winona Lake, Indiana 46590: BMH Books, 1978), pp. 105-127. (The authors have gathered evidence that *"...the moon is still active geologically. It is not the cold, dead body that the pre-space-age theories had depicted. Yet, it should be cold and dead if it is indeed billions of years old."* — p. 126).

☐ Randy L. Wysong, *The Creation-Evolution Controversy* (Midland, Michigan: Inquiry Press, 1976), p. 177-178 (points out that short-lived Uranium-236 and Thorium-230 have been found in lunar materials).

☐ One recent example concerns the "surprising" youthful appearance of the rings of Saturn:

"...new observations have uncovered a stunning number of variations on the few, broad rings expected by researchers and have even suggested that the rings formed only recently, a most unpalatable prospect to astronomers...

...there is no easy way of explaining away the youthful appearance of the rings. Planetary dynamics abhor youthfulness in the solar system; everything is much tidier if the general arrangements of the planets, satellites, and rings was determined early on as formation processes petered out and violent collisions became rare. Theorists would have no problem with a broad, featureless disk surviving 4.5 billion years since the early days of the solar system, but features such as spiral density waves are clear evidence that satellites, including the profusion of small ones found near the rings, are draining angular momentum from the rings."

[Richard Kerr, "Making Better Planetary Rings," *Science*, Vol. 229 (September 1985), pp. 1376-1377 (emphasis added).]

IS THE SUN SHRINKING?

94

☐ Dozens of different observers at the Royal Greenwich Observatory and independently at the U.S. Naval Observatory have participated in direct visual measurements of the Sun since 1836. These measurements indicate a continuing decrease in the Sun's diameter. Based on these findings, it was suggested the Sun is shrinking at a rate of almost 6 feet per hour — suggesting a very young Sun.

☐ John A. Eddy (astrophysicist with the Harvard-Smithsonian Center for Astrophysics and High Altitude Observatory in Boulder) and Aram A. Boornazian (mathematician with S. Ross and company in Boston) reported that the sun is "shrinking" at a rate of almost 10 miles per year (16 kilometers) or 0.1% per century (more than 2 seconds of arc per 100 years).

☐ John A. Eddy and Aram A. Boornazian, "Secular Decrease in the Solar Diameter, 1836-1953," *Bulletin of the American Astronomical Society*, Vol. 11 (1979), p. 437.

☐ Gloria B. Lubkin, "Analysis of Historical Data Suggest Sun Is Shrinking," *Physics Today*, Vol. 32, No. 9 (September 1979), pp. 17-19.

HOWEVER, OTHER MEASUREMENTS HAVE BEEN INTERPRETED AS EVIDENCE THE SHRINKAGE IS SLOWER OR MUCH SLOWER

☐ Approximately **0.6 foot per hour** (1 mile per year) — estimate from geologist Andrew Snelling, Ph.D.:

"...the best analyses of the solar diameter data now suggest a 76 to 80 year cycle of variation superimposed upon a secular decrease in the solar diameter of about 1/10th the figure suggested originally by Eddy and Boornazian, a shrinkage rate of about 0.2 seconds of arc per century or 1 mile per year. This I would regard as the most conservative position on this issue and fits quite well with many of the other figures..."

[Andrew A. Snelling, personal correspondence to Paul S. Taylor (January 25, 1989).]

Also see Snelling and Gilliland articles mentioned in endnote (see index entries on "Snelling, A." and "Gilliland, R.").

☐ Approximately **2 feet per hour** (60 centimeters) — Eddy's later recalculation using the figures from the *vertical* diameter Greenwich readings, rather than the horizontal. For an easy-to-understand explanation of Eddy's alternate figure, see: Snelling article Part 1.

☐ Approximately **5 to 6 feet per hour** (1.5 to 1.8 meters) — measurements made with photoelectric scanner by astronomer Howard at Mt. Wilson Observatory. [K. Frazier, *Our Turbulent Sun* (Englewood Cliffs, New Jersey: Prentice-Hall, 1982), pp. 74-83.]

☐ Approximately **1 to 2 feet** (30 to 60 centimeters) (0.5 seconds of arc per century) — based on 50 years of solar photos, 1930 to 1980. [K. Frazier, *Our Turbulent Sun* (Englewood Cliffs, New Jersey: Prentice-Hall, 1982), pp. 74-83.]

☐ Less than **1 foot per hour** (30 centimeters) (approximately 0.2 seconds of arc per year). [D.W. Dunham, S. Sophia, A.D. Fiala, et al., "Observations of a Probable Change in the Solar Radius Between 1715 and 1979," *Science*, Vol. 210 (1980), pp. 1243-1245 (compares special eclipse measurement done by Dunham in 1979 with that of Halley in 1715).]

☐ Less than **1 foot per hour** (30 centimeters). This is still a significant decrease rate. [S. Sophia, J. O'Keefe, J.R. Lesh, and A.S. Endal, "Solar Constant: Constraints on Possible Variations Derived from Solar Diameter Measurements," *Science*, Vol. 204 (1979), pp. 1306-1308.]

☐ Some even claim there is no shrinkage. See Snelling article on problems with claims the Sun is not shrinking. The best analyses seem to indicate the sun is shrinking, although not as fast as the first summary report concluded.

95

☐ Currently, Earth is said to be 5 billion years old.

$$\frac{5,000,000,000}{10,000,000} = \frac{100}{0.2}$$

96

☐ Using the original figures of Eddy and Boornazian, the time required for the Sun to double in size (backward in time) would have been:

$$\frac{1}{1,000,000 \text{ years}} = (100,000 \text{ years})(10 \text{ the suggested adjustment}) =$$

$$(0.001/100 \text{ years})$$

97

☐ The *CRC Handbook of Chemistry and Physics*, 54th edition (pp. F160-F216), lists the diameter of the sun as 1.4E9 meters and gives the mean radius of Earth's orbit as 1.5E11 meters.

Assuming a constant rate of expansion in the past, this would indicate contact with the Earth in:

$$\frac{(1.5E11 \; meters)}{0.5(1.4E9 \; meters)(0.001/100 \; years)} = 210 \; million \; years$$

It should be noted that Evolutionists extrapolating back to the "Big Bang" are extending 95 times further than this extrapolation!

$$\frac{20,000,000,000}{210,000,000} - 95$$

SOURCES FOR FURTHER INFORMATION ON THE SHRINKAGE OF THE SUN, AND ON THE RELATED AND ADDED PROBLEM OF MISSING SOLAR NEUTRINOS

98

☐ Andrew A. Snelling, "Is the Sun Shrinking?", Parts 1-3, *Creation: Ex Nihilo*, Vol. 11, No. 1 (December 1988 - February 1989), pp. 14-19, No. 2 (March/May 1989), No. 3 (June/August 1989).

☐ Dudley J. Benton, "The Effect of Non-Uniform Density on Solar Contraction Energy," *Creation Research Society Quarterly*, Vol. 24, No. 3 (P.O. Box 14016, Terre Haute, Indiana 47803: December 1987), pp. 145-147.

☐ Thomas G. Barnes, "The Dilemma of a Theistic Evolutionist: An Answer to Howard Van Till," *Creation Research Society Quarterly*, Vol. 23 (P.O. Box 14016, Terre Haute, Indiana 47803: 1987), pp. 167-171.

☐ Paul D. Ackerman, *It's a Young World After All* (Grand Rapids, Michigan: Baker Book House, 1986), pp.55-64 (includes a good layman's explanation).

☐ Harold L. Armstrong, "Questions Remain About the Sun's Operation," *Creation Research Society Quarterly*, Vol 22, No. 3 (P.O. Box 14016, Terre Haute, Indiana 47803: December 1985), p. 123.

☐ Paul M. Steidl, "Recent Developments About Solar Neutrinos," letter, *Creation Research Society Quarterly*, Vol. 17, No. 4 (P.O. Box 14016, Terre Haute, Indiana 47803: March 1981), p. 233.

☐ Ronald L. Gilliland, "Solar Radius Variations Over the Past 265 Years," *The Astrophysical Journal*, Vol. 248, No. 3 (September 15, 1981), pp. 1144-1155 (there is a steady, long-term shrinkage of almost 0.2 seconds of arc per year or 150 kilometers/93 miles per century or less than 1 foot per hour (approximately 30 centimeters — superimposed on a 76 to 80 year cycle of increase and decrease over a range of 0.8 seconds of arc / based on thorough analysis of 5 different data sets, including the meridian circle of Greenwich and Washington observations, the Mercury solar transit timings, and the durations of total solar eclipses / says the strongest evidence supporting a cyclic solar radius change with overall shrinkage is the remarkable agreement between independent data sets in predicting the maximum 20th century radius near 1910-1911 with a cycle time of about 76 years / the Mercury transits figures support a long-term solar shrinkage of over 0.1 seconds of arc per century and basically agree with the Dunham et al. polar radius decrease / says that the preponderance of evidence indicates the Sun is shrinking — even with allowance for possible systematic errors

in both the meridian circle and Mercury transit timing observations).

☐ David W. Dunham, et al., "Observations of a Probable Change in the Solar Radius Between 1715 and 1979," *Science*, Vol. 210, (December 12, 1980), pp. 1243-1245.

☐ Hilton Hinderliter, "The Inconsistent Sun: How Has It Been Behaving, and What Might It Do Next?," *Creation Research Society Quarterly*, Vol. 17, No. 3 (P.O. Box 14016, Terre Haute, Indiana 47803: December 1980), pp. 143-145.

☐ Hilton Hinderliter, "The Shrinking Sun: A Creationist's Predictions, Its Verification, and the Resulting Implications for Theories of Origins," *Creation Research Society Quarterly*, Vol. 17, No. 1 (P.O. Box 14016, Terre Haute, Indiana 47803: June 1980), pp. 57-59.

☐ Paul M. Steidl, "Solar Neutrinos and a Young Sun," *Creation Research Society Quarterly*, Vol. 17, No. 1 (P.O. Box 14016, Terre Haute, Indiana 47803: June 1980), pp. 60-64.

☐ G. Russell Akridge, "The Sun is Shrinking," Impact No. 82, *Acts & Facts* (P.O. Box 2667, El Cajon, California 92021: Institute for Creation Research, April 1980).

99

☐ John Eddy in R.G. Kazmann, "It's About Time: 4.5 Billion Years," (report on Symposium at Louisiana State University), *Geotimes*, Vol. 23 (September 1978), p. 18.

METEORITES

100

☐ Paul D. Ackerman, *It's a Young World After All* (Grand Rapids, Michigan: Baker Book House, 1986), pp. 25-28.

☐ Randy L. Wysong, *The Creation-Evolution Controversy* (Midland, Michigan: Inquiry Press, 1976), p. 171.

☐ Peter A. Steveson, "Meteoric Evidence for a Young Earth," *Creation Research Society Quarterly*, Vol. 12, No. 1 (P.O. Box 14016, Terre Haute, Indiana 47803: June 1975), pp. 23-25.

☐ Barbara M. Middlehurst and Gerard P. Kuiper, editors, *The Moon, Meteorites and Comets* (Chicago: University of Chicago, 1963), pp. 219, 406.

☐ Brian H. Mason, *Meteorites* (New York: John Wiley, 1962), p. 4.

SPACE DUST

SOURCES FOR FURTHER INFORMATION ON EVOLUTIONISTS' EXPECTED THICKNESS OF MOON DUST PRIOR TO ACTUAL MOON EXPLORATION

101

☐ Paul Bartz, *Contrast: The Creation-Evolution Controversy*, Vol. 7, No. 5 (September/October 1988), p. 4.

☐ Harold S. Slusher in Willem J.J. Glashouwer and Paul S. Taylor, writers, *The Earth, A Young Planet?* (Mesa, Arizona: Eden Films and Standard Media, 1983) (Creationist motion picture) (Slusher refers to earlier Evolutionist calculations that the in-

> *When I make an incision with my scalpel, I see organs of such intricacy that there simply hasn't been enough time for natural evolutionary processes to have developed them.*
>
> C. Everett Koop, former U.S. Surgeon General

coming dust on the Moon could yield 440 to 990 feet of compacted dust in 4.5 to 5 billion years).

☐ Harold S. Slusher, *Age of the Cosmos*, ICR Technical Monograph No. 9 (P.O. Box 2667, El Cajon, California 92021: Institute for Creation Research, 1980), p. 41 (discusses rate of 14.3 million tons per year) (see Petterson and Asimov references, below).

☐ N.H. Apfel and Joseph A. Hynek, *Architecture of the Universe* (Menlo Park: Benjamin/Cummings Publishing, 1979), p. 349.

☐ Jay M. Pasachoff, *Contemporary Astronomy* (Philadelphia: W.B. Saunders Company, 1977), pp. 294-295.

☐ Randy L. Wysong, *The Creation-Evolution Controversy* (Midland, Michigan: Inquiry Press, 1976), pp. 175-177.

☐ Robert T. Dixon, *Dynamic Astronomy* (Englewood Cliffs, New Jersey: Prentice Hall, Inc. 1971) (p. 149 — "*The moon was for many years characterized as having a thick layer of dust covering its surface, into which an object would sink if it landed on the moon.*").

☐ Harold S. Slusher, "Some Astronomical Evidences for a Youthful Solar System," *Creation Research Society Quarterly*, Vol. 8, No. 1 (P.O. Box 14016, Terre Haute, IN 47803: June 1971), pp. 55-57.

☐ John W. Salisbury and Peter Glaser, editors, *The Lunar Surface Layer* (New York: Academic Press, 1964) (discusses erosive factors on Moon and suggests "*an equivalent dust layer of at least 300 feet in thickness, and probably more*...").

☐ Hans Petterson, "Cosmic Spherules and Meteoritic Dust," *Scientific American*, Vol. 202 (February 1960), pp. 123-132 (estimated 14.3 million tons per year deposited on Earth).

☐ Isaac Asimov, "14 Million Tons of Dust Per Year," *Science Digest*, Vol. 45, No. 1 (January/February 1959), pp. 33-36.

☐ Fred W. Whipple, "On the Lunar Dust Layer," in *Vistas in Astronautics*, Vol. 2 (New York: Pergamon Press, 1959) (estimated 700 thousand tons per year deposited on Earth).

☐ Fletcher G. Watson, *Between the Planets* (Cambridge, Massachusetts: Harvard University Press, 1956) (estimates accumulation of 300 thousand to 3 million tons per year deposited on Earth).

☐ Raymond A. Lyttleton, *The Modern Universe* (New York: Harper and Brothers, 1956) (predicted layer "*several miles in thickness*" — p. 72 / Also suggests that ultraviolet light and X-rays striking the Moon's rocks would produce additional dust — p. 72).

☐ Thomas Gold, "The Lunar Surface...," *Royal Astronomical Society of London: Monthly Notices*, Vol. 115 (1955), pp. 598-599 (speculates that the Moon "*is acquiring a layer one centimeter in thickness every 10^7 years*" for a total of about 18 inches — and speculates the maria could be filled to 1 thousand feet deep and that there would be a hazard to landing spacecraft).

102

☐ Astronaut Neil Armstrong reportedly said his greatest fear in landing on the Moon was the expected thick layer of dust. [Nancy Pearcey, "The Age of the Earth: Does Mother Nature Tell?", *Bible-Science Newsletter*, Vol. 25, No. 2 (P.O. Box 32457, Minneapolis, Minnesota 55432, Phone 612-635-0614: Bible-Science Association, February 1987), p. 9.]

☐ Franklyn M. Branley, *Apollo and the Moon* (Garden City, New Jersey: Natural History Press, 1964) (published for American Museum / Hayden Planetarium) ("*Some astronomers think that, in places,* lunar *meteoritic dust may be a hundred feet or more deep. Also, it may be so loosely packed that a spaceship would sink into it, never to be seen again.*")

☐ *The Rand McNally New Concise Atlas of the Universe* (London: Mitchell Beazley Publishers, 1978) (p. 41 — "*The theory that the Maria were covered with deep layers of soft dust was current until well into the 1960s.*").

103

☐ Hans Petterson gave the deposition of meteoritic dust on Earth as 5 to 14 million metric tons per year. This is the amount that survives entry through Earth's atmosphere! Certainly most of the incident dust is burned up in the atmosphere and does not make it to the surface as such. [Hans Petterson, "Cosmic Spherules and Meteoritic Dust," *Scientific American*, Vol. 202, No. 2 (1960), pp. 123-132.]

☐ The deposition rate on the Moon has not been measured over a period of millions of years, but considering the fact that Earth has a substantial atmosphere and the Moon does not, this may outweigh the difference in the surface area of the Moon and its lesser gravitational attraction.

The *CRC Handbook of Chemistry and Physics* (p. F160) lists the diameter of the Moon as (D) = 3.5E6 meters. The surface area of a sphere (S) can be computed from the diameter (D): S = π D^2. The density of dry earth (dirt) is 1400 kg/m^3 (*CRC Handbook of Tables for Applied Engineering Science*, 2nd edition, p. 177). Using the high value for deposition rate and the density of "dry earth," the approximate thickness (t) over 4.5 billion year period can be computed.

The following calculation is supplied by Dudley J. Benton, Ph.D., Knoxville, Tennessee. If the deposition rate were as much as 14 million metric tons per year, then over a 4.5 billion year period the thickness would be:

$$t = \frac{(1.4E7 \text{ tons per yr.})(1000 \text{ kg per ton})(3.28 \text{ ft per meter})}{(1400 \text{ kg/}m^3)\pi(3.5E6 \text{ m})^2} =$$

3800 *feet in 4.5 billion years*

104

☐ Paul D. Ackerman, *It's a Young World After All* (Grand Rapids, Michigan: Baker Book House, 1986), pp. 15-23.

☐ Harold S. Slusher, *Age of the Cosmos* (P.O. Box 2667, El Cajon, CA 92021: Institute for Creation Research, 1980), pp. 39-42.

☐ Peter A. Steveson, "Meteoric Evidence for a Young Earth," *Creation Research Society Quarterly*, Vol. 12, No. 1 (P.O. Box 14016, Terre Haute, Indiana 47803: June 1975), pp. 23-25.

☐ Henry M. Morris, *Scientific Creationism* (San Diego: Creation-Life Publishers, 1974, pp. 151-153.

105

☐ G.S. Hawkins, "Meteor Orbits and Dust," *Smithsonian Contributions to Astrophysics*, Vol. 2 (Washington, D.C.: Smithsonian Institution, 1967).

ESTIMATES OF RATE OF COSMIC DUST FALLING ON EARTH:

106

☐ Petterson's estimate of 14 million tons per year falling on Earth is in the range of 1 thousand times higher than later reports of 10 to 20 thousand tons per year.

☐ Also see index entries on "dust," "Moon dust," "dating methods, space dust."

(the following estimates are listed in descending order of year of publication)

☐ 16,000 tons per year [David W. Hughes, "Meteors," in James A.M. McDonnell, editor, *Cosmic Dust* (New York: John Wiley and Sons, 1978), pp. 123-185, especially pp. 154-155.]

☐ 365,000 tons per year ["Space Dust Falls to Earth Every Day," Associated Press dispatch from Washington, D.C., *Peoria Journal Star* (March 6, 1978), p. A-10 ("*A little bit of space falls to earth every day, says* National Geographic. *About a thousand tons of space dust, space particles and micrometeoroids reach the earth's surface daily, they report.").]*

☐ 10,950 tons per year [Peter M. Millman, "Dust in the Solar System," in George B. Field and Alstair G.W. Cameron, editors, *The Dusty Universe* (New York: Published for the Smithsonian Astrophysical Observatory by Neale Watson Academic Publications, Inc., 1975), pp. 185-209, especially p. 191 (Note: p. 190-191 — *"On the other side of the picture, fluxes calculated from most of the near-earth microphone recordings on satellites and rockets are several orders of magnitude higher than the fluxes found from penetration data (McDonnel, 1971). The discrepancy is particularly marked for particle masses below 10^{-10}g. ...when we see the spread of flux values for small particles exhibited in Figure 3 and we remember that this still does not include the controversial microphone results, we cannot expect to define the overall average flux near the earth-moon system to much better than an order of magnitude. If some of the fine material does not register by penetrating or cratering, it could well be that we should allow for this by raising the flux estimate. It should also be noted that the Prairie Network fireballs (McCrosky, 1968), which are outside the above integration, could add appreciably to the flux estimate if the preliminary mass distribution found by McCrosky is verified by more extensive observation.).]*

☐ 20,000 tons per year [Donald E. Gault, et al., "Effects of Microcratering on the Lunar Surface," *Proceedings of the Third Lunar Science Conference* (Cambridge, Massachusetts: MIT Press, 1972), pp. 2713-2734.]

☐ 5,000,000 to 14,000,000 tons per year. [Hans Petterson, "Cosmic Spherules and Meteoritic Dust," *Scientific American*, Vol. 202, No. 2 (1960), pp. 123-132.]

☐ 70,000 tons per year. [Fred W. Whipple, "On the Lunar Dust Layer," in *Vistas in Astronautics*, Vol. 2 (New York: Pergamon Press, 1959).]

☐ 14,000,000 tons per year. [Isaac Asimov, "14 Million Tons of Dust Per Year," *Science Digest*, Vol. 45, No. 1 (Jan.-Feb. 1959), pp. 33-36.]

☐ 30,000 to 3,000,000 tons per year. [Fletcher G. Watson, *Between the Planets* (Cambridge, Massachusetts: Harvard University Press, 1956).]

107

☐ 294 centimeter core drilled by Apollo 17 team using electric drill (approximately 9 feet 8 inches).

108

☐ Warning: The composition of all (or even most) meteors is, of course, not actually known. Only a relatively small number of samples have been made in comparison to the great numbers of meteors probably in existence. Therefore, determination of what is or is not meteoritic dust (as opposed to Moon dust) is somewhat conjectural depending as it does upon various assumptions concerning the supposed composition of meteoroids.

109

☐ Stuart R. Taylor, *Lunar Science: A Post-Apollo View* (New York: Pergamon Press, 1975).

110

☐ Donald B. DeYoung, *Questions and Answers on Astronomy and the Bible* (Grand Rapids, Michigan: Baker Books, 1989), p. 34.

W̶e ourselves would be less concerned about falsifiability if neo-Darwinism were a powerful theory with major successes to its credit. But this is simply not the case.
Mathematician P. Saunders and biologist M. Ho

CONCERNING: LIST OF YOUNG-AGE ESTIMATION PROCESSES

111

☐ SOURCES FOR FURTHER INFORMATION ON AGE ESTIMATION METHODS WHICH SOME SUGGEST AS EVIDENCE OF A RELATIVELY YOUNG EARTH OR AS EVIDENCE TO DISPUTE THE OLD-AGE ESTIMATES OF EVOLUTIONISTS

A. A.W. Mehlert, "Another Look at the Age and History of the Mississippi River," *Creation Research Society Quarterly*, Vol. 25, No. 3 (P.O. Box 14016, Terre Haute, Indiana 47803: December 1988), pp. 121-123.

B1. Jerry Bergman and Robert Doolan, "The Oldest Living Things," *Creation: Ex Nihilo*, Vol. 10, No. 1 (P.O. Box 302, Sunnybank, Queensland 4109, Australia: Creation Science Foundation, February 1988), p. 10.

B2. Eugene F. Chaffin, "A Young Earth? — A Survey of Dating Methods," *Creation Research Society Quarterly*, Vol. 24, No. 3 (P.O. Box 14016, Terre Haute, Indiana 47803: December 1987), pp. 109-117 (includes a large list of important references).

C1. Henry M. Morris and Gary E. Parker, *What is Creation Science?*, revised and expanded edition (San Diego: Master Books, 1987), pp. 273-293 (Lists 68 ways to determine the age of the Earth).

C2. Paul D. Ackerman, *It's a Young World After All* (Grand Rapids, Michigan: Baker Book House, 1986), p. 30.

D1. Robert V. Gentry, *Creation's Tiny Mystery* (Knoxville, Tennessee, 37912-0067: Earth Science Associates, 1986), 315 pp.

D2. Ariel A. Roth, "Some Questions About Geochronology," *Origins*, Vol. 13, No. 2 (Loma Linda, California: Geoscience Research Institute, Loma Linda University, 1986), pp. 80-81.

E1. Stephen R. Schrader, "Was the Earth Created a Few Thousand Years Ago? Yes.", in Ronald Youngblood, editor, *The Genesis Debate* (Nashville: Thomas Nelson Publishers, 1986), pp. 56-83.

E2. Frederic R. Howe, "The Age of the Earth: An Appraisal of Some Current Evangelical Positions," Part II, *Bibliotheca Sacra*, Vol. 143 (March/June 1985), pp. 114-129.

F1. Michael J. Oard, "Ice Ages: The Mystery Solved?, Part II: The Manipulation of Deep-Sea Cores," *Creation Research Society Quarterly*, Vol. 21, No. 3 (P.O. Box 14016, Terre Haute, Indiana 47803: December 1984), pp. 125-137.

F2. Henry M. Morris, *The Biblical Basis for Modern Science* (Grand Rapids, Michigan: Baker Book House, 1984), pp. 477-480 (68 "global processes indicating recent Creation").

G1. Ian T. Taylor, *In the Minds of Men* (Toronto, Canada: TFE Publishing, 1984), pp. 282-339.

G2. Glenn R. Morton, Harold S. Slusher, and Richard E. Mandock, "The Age of Lunar Craters," *Creation Research Society Quar-*

terly, Vol. 20 (P.O. Box 14016, Terre Haute, Indiana 47803: September 1983), pp. 105-108.

H1. Robert V. Gentry, "Letters," *Physics Today*, Vol. 36, No. 4 (April 1983), p. 13.

H2. Russell Arndts and William Overn, *Isochron Dating and the Mixing Model* (P.O. Box 32457, Minneapolis, Minnesota 55432, Phone 612-635-0614: Bible-Science Association, 1983), 36 pp.

I1. Harold S. Slusher and Stephen J. Robertson, *The Age of the Solar System: A Study of the Poynting-Robertson Effect and Extinction of Interplanetary Dust*, revised edition (P.O. 2667, El Cajon, California 92021: Institute for Creation Research, 1982), 131 pp.

I2. G. Russell Akridge, "Radiometric Dating Using Isochrons," *Impact* series No. 113, *Acts & Facts* (P.O. 2667, El Cajon, California 92021: Institute for Creation Research, November 1982).

J1. Robert V. Gentry, "Creationism Discussion Continued," *Physics Today*, Vol. 35, No. 13 (October 1982).

J2. Randal L.N. Mandock, *Scale Time Versus Geologic Time in Radioisotope Age Determination*, Master of Science Thesis (P.O. Box 2667, El Cajon, California 92021: Institute for Creation Research, 1982).

K1. Robert V. Gentry, T.J. Sworski, H.S. McKown, et al., "Differential Lead Retention in Zircons: Implications for Nuclear Waste Containment," *Science*, Vol. 296, No. 216 (1982).

K2. Robert V. Gentry, G.L. Glis and E.H. McBay, "Differential Helium Retention in Zircons: Implications for Nuclear Waste Containment," *Geophysical Research Letters 9*, Vol. 1129 (1982).

L1. Harold S. Slusher, *Critique of Radiometric Dating* (P.O. Box 2667, El Cajon, California 92021: Institute for Creation Research, 1981), pp. 58.

L2. Harold S. Slusher, *Age of the Cosmos*, ICR Technical Monograph #9 (P.O. Box 2667, El Cajon, California 92021: Institute for Creation Research, 1980), 76 pp.

M1. Robert H. Brown, "The Interpretation of C-14 Dates," *Origins*, Vol. 6, No. 1 (Loma Linda, California: Geoscience Research Institute, Loma Linda University, 1979), pp. 30-44.

M2. Robert H. Brown, *Interpretation of C-14 Dates* (Berrien Springs, Michigan: Geoscience Research Institute, Loma Linda University, 1979).

N1. John Woodmorappe, "Radiometric Geochronology Reappraised," *Creation Research Society Quarterly*, Vol. 16, No. 2 (P.O. 14016, Terre Haute, Indiana 47803: September 1979), pp. 102+.

N2. Robert V. Gentry, "Time: In Full Measure," *EOS Transactions, Am. Geophysical Union*, Vol. 60 (January 9, 1979), pp. 21-22.

O1. Paul M. Steidl, The Earth, the Stars, and the Bible (Grand Rapids, Michigan: Baker Book House, 1979), pp. 51-52, 55.

O2. Robert H. Brown, *How Old Is the World?* (Berrien Springs, Michigan: Geoscience Research Institute, Loma Linda University, 1978).

P1. Harold S. Slusher and Thomas P. Gamwell, *The Age of the Earth: A Study of the Cooling of the Earth Under the Influence of Radioactive Heat Sources*, ICR Monograph No. 7 (P.O. 2667, El Cajon, California 92021: Institute for Creation Research, 1978).

P2. Randy L. Wysong, *The Creation-Evolution Controversy* (Midland, Michigan: Inquiry Press, 1976), pp. 145-179.

Q1. R. Samec, "Effect of Radiation on Micrometeoroids, and Existence of Micrometeoroids as Evidence of a Young Solar System," *Creation Research Society Quarterly*, Vol. 12, No. 1 (P.O. Box 14016, Terre Haute, Indiana 47803: June 1975), p. 7.

Q2. Henry M. Morris, "The Young Earth," *Creation Research Society Quarterly* (P.O. Box 14016, Terre Haute, Indiana 47803: Vol. 12, No. 1, June 1975), p. 21.

R1. Harold L. Armstrong, "Misleading Concentrations of Isotopes," *Creation Research Society Quarterly*, Vol. 11, No. 3 (P.O. 14016, Terre Haute, Indiana 47803: Dec, 1974), p. 163.

R2. Harold S. Slusher, "A Young Universe," *Bible-Science Newsletter*, Vol. 13 (P.O. Box 32457, Minneapolis, Minnesota 55432, Phone 612-635-0614: Bible-Science Assn., January 1975).

S1. Thomas G. Barnes, "Physics, A Challenge to Geologic Time," ICR Impact Series, *Acts & Facts*, No. 16 (July 1974).

S2. Harold Camping, "Let the Oceans Speak," *Creation Research Society Quarterly*, Vol. 11 (P.O. Box 14016, Terre Haute, Indiana 47803: June 1974), pp. 39-45.

T1. Harold L. Armstrong, "Bacteria May Alter Element Concentrations," *Creation Research Society Quarterly*, Vol. 11, No. 1 (P.O. Box 14016, Terre Haute, Indiana 47803: June 1974), pp. 75-76.

T2. R.D. Wilson, et al., "Natural Marine Oil Seepage," *Science*, Vol. 184 (May 24, 1974), pp. 857-865.

U1. Henry M. Morris, editor, *Scientific Creationism*, general edition (San Diego: CLP Publishers, 1974), pp. 131-169.

U2. Stuart E. Nevin, "Evolution: The Ocean Says No," ICR Impact Series, *Acts & Facts*, Vol. 2, No. 8 (November 1973).

V1. Harold L. Armstrong, "C-14 and Hard Water," *Creation Research Society Quarterly*, Vol. 9, No. 3 (P.O. Box 14016, Terre Haute, Indiana 47803: March 1973), p. 241.

V2. Benjamin F. Allen, "The Geologic Age of the Mississippi River," *Creation Research Society Quarterly*, Vol. 9 (P.O. Box 14016, Terre Haute, Indiana 47803: September 1972), pp. 96-114.

W1. V.A. Hughes and D. Routledge, "An Expanding Ring of Interstellar Gas with Center Close to the Sun," *Astronomical Journal*, Vol. 77, No. 3 (1972), pp. 210-214.

W2. Halton Arp, "Observational Paradoxes in Extragalactic Astronomy," *Science*, Vol. 174 (December 17, 1971), pp. 1189-1200.

X1. John Whitcomb, Jr. and Henry M. Morris, *The Genesis Flood* (Philadelphia: Presbyterian and Reformed, 1970), pp. 387-391.

X2. Melvin A. Cook, "Do Radiological Clocks Need Repair?", *Creation Research Society Quarterly*, Vol. 5 (P.O. Box 14016, Terre Haute, Indiana 47803: October 1968), p. 70.

X3. Melvin A. Cook, *Prehistory and Earth Models* (London: Max Parrish, 1966), 354 pp.

Y1. J.P. Riley and G. Skirrow, editors, *Chemical Geography*, Vol. 1 (London: Academic Press, 1965), p. 164.

Y2. Maurice Ewing, J.I. Ewing, and M. Talwan, "Sediment Distribution in the Oceans — Mid-Atlantic Ridge," *Bulletin of the Geophysical Society of America*, Vol. 75 (January 1964), pp. 17-36.

Y3. Dudley J. Whitney, *The Face of the Deep* (New York: Vantage Press, 1955).

Z1. Lord Kelvin, "On the Age of Sun's Heat," in *Popular Lectures and Addresses* (London: MacMillan, 1889), p. 415.

Z2. Lord Kelvin, *Mathematical and Physical Papers* (Cambridge, England: Cambridge University, 1882)

112

☐ Henry M. Morris, *The Biblical Basis for Modern Science* (Grand Rapids, Michigan: Baker Book House, 1984), p. 478.

☐ Thomas G. Barnes, "Physics, A Challenge to Geologic Time," ICR Impact Series, *Acts & Facts*, No. 16 (July 1974).

113

☐ Harold S. Slusher, *The Origin of the Universe*, revised edition (P.O. Box 2667, El Cajon, California 92021: Institute for Creation Research, 1980), p. 52.

114

☐ Dr. Harold S. Slusher:

"...*Must be of recent origin or they would have long ago disintegrated the groupings by their tremendous velocities exceeding the escape speeds of the clusters.*" (p. 52)

[Harold S. Slusher, *The Origin of the Universe*, revised edition (P.O. Box 2667, El Cajon, California 92021: Institute for Creation Research, 1980), pp. 52, 59-66.]

115

☐ Harold S. Slusher, *The Origin of the Universe*, revised edition (P.O. Box 2667, El Cajon, California 92021: Institute for Creation Research, 1980), pp. 53-57.

☐ "*We know of no process that can maintain a spiral arm for more than two galactic revolutions.*"

[Hadley Wood, *Unveiling the Universe* (New York: American Elsevier Publishing Company, 1968), p. 188.]

☐ "*If this theory is true, the universe is young, since it has so many rapidly revolving spirals.*"

[C.B. Clason, *Exploring the Distant Stars* (New York: G.P. Putnam's Sons, 1958), p. 326.]

116

☐ 100 cm per 1,000 years figure is from: John C. Whitcomb, Jr., *The World That Perished*, 2nd edition (Grand Rapids, Michigan: Baker Book House, December 1988), pp. 132. (55,000,000 years/1,000 years = 55,000. 55,000 x 100 centimeters = 5,500,000 centimeters = 55 kilometers. 55 km x 0.62 miles per km = 34.1 miles. Mt. Everest = 29,028 feet = 5.5 miles. 34.1 miles less 5.5 miles = 28.6 miles. 28.6 miles/5.5 miles = 5.2.)

117

☐ Henry M. Morris, *The Biblical Basis for Modern Science* (Grand Rapids, Michigan: Baker Book House, 1984), p. 478.

☐ "Natural Plutonium," *Chemical and Engineering News*, Vol. 49 (September 20, 1971), p. 29.

118

☐ Paul D. Ackerman, *It's a Young World After All* (Grand Rapids, Michigan: Baker Book House, 1986), pp. 81-85.

☐ Also see references in index to this subject.

119

☐ Harold S. Slusher, *The Origin of the Universe*, revised edition (P.O. Box 2667, El Cajon, California 92021: Institute for Creation Research, 1980), p. 59 (Time for Breakup of Star Clusters).

☐ Harold S. Slusher, *Age of the Cosmos*, ICR Technical Monograph No. 9 (P.O. Box 2667, El Cajon, California 92021: Institute for Creation Research, 1980), p. 16.

120

☐ Paul D. Ackerman, *It's a Young World After All* (Grand Rapids, Michigan: Baker Book House, 1986), pp. 55-61.

☐ Harold S. Slusher, "A Young Universe," *Bible-Science Newsletter*, Vol. 13 (P.O. Box 32457, Minneapolis, Minnesota 55432, Phone 612-635-0614: Bible-Science Association, January 1975).

121

☐ Henry M. Morris, *The Biblical Basis of Modern Science* (Grand Rapids, Michigan: Baker Book House, 1984), p. 477.

☐ Salman Bloch, "Some Factors Controlling the Concentration of Uranium in the World Ocean," *Geochimica et Cosmochimica Acta*, Vol 44 (1980), pp. 373-377.

EARTH'S AGE — SOME CREATIONISTS SUGGEST ANOTHER POSSIBILITY

Some Creationists suggest there is a historic record of value in estimating Earth's approximate age, if one is willing to consider an alternative source. Their point of view may be of particular interest to those readers who are Christians or Jews.

*T*he mass of evidence shows that all, or almost all, known mutations are unmistakably pathological and the few remaining ones are highly suspect.
C. Martin in American Scientist

☐ Most people realize the book of Genesis, honored by both Christians and Jews, implies that this planet is not extremely old. Although the biblical books do not give an exact age, they do provide indications that Earth's age should be measured in thousands rather than millions — or billions — of years. For thousands of years, a literal, straightforward, common-sense reading of Genesis and the related biblical books have led millions of intelligent people to believe these records are saying:

- Adam was the first human being.
- Earth existence began only 5 days prior to Adam. (This seems to be clearly claiming that these days were literal days, including daylight and night during each. If the biblical writers had meant to indicate an indefinite time, they could have used the Hebrew word "olam". The use of connective "ands" throughout Genesis 1, plus the repetitious use of "the evening and the morning were the first day" [etc.], and the use of the Hebrew "yom" for "day" connected with these numbers leaves no gaps and speaks clearly of normal days.
- Furthermore, Exodus 20:11 and 31:17,18 claim that the biblical Creator wrote on tablet of stone that he had created all things in 6 days. These verses state that he rested on the 7th day as a pattern for man to follow — working 6 literal days and resting on the 7th. Thus, records accepted by both Christians and Jews imply that the Creator in whom they believe purposely chose to perform the entire act of Creation in one literal week as an example to humankind to a literal six days and rest every 7th – for necessary refreshment of body and soul.

Exodus 20:9-11 – "*Six days you shall labor and do all your work... For in six days the Lord made the heavens and the earth, the sea, and all that is in them, but he rested on the seventh day...*"

Exodus 23:12 – *"Six days do your work, but on the seventh day do not work, so that your ox and your donkey may rest and the slave born in your household, and the alien as well, may be refreshed."*

Exodus 31:17, 34:21 – *"It will be a sign between me and the Israelites forever, for in six days the Lord made the heavens and the earth, and on the seventh day he abstained from work and rested. ...Six days you shall labor, but on the seventh day you shall rest; even during the plowing season and harvest you must rest."*] [New International Version]

The most reasonable conclusion is that Genesis and Exodus are saying that the Creation week was 7 literal days.

- In the Christian New Testament, genealogies are provided apparently listing every important patriarch descended from the first man (Adam) till the time of Abraham and on to Jesus Christ. Hebrew records provide considerable detail on most of the patriarchs prior to Christ, including many ages, life spans, and relationships. Thus, the time span between Creation and the birth of Jesus Christ of Nazareth is represented as being only thousands of years (not millions or billions). This surely gives at least a general idea of the amount of time these records say has elapsed. Certainly there is no reasonable way for one to insert periods of millions of years between each described generation.
- The genealogies of Genesis 5 and 11 give every indication of intending to convey a continuous backward record from Abraham to the Creation (130 years before Adam was said to have fathered Seth). The genealogies provide the ages of each father at the birth of each mentioned son. The Christian New Testament reiterates the Hebrew genealogies. It also agrees that Enoch was the 7th patriarch since Adam (Jude 14).
- Jewish scholar Leo Levi: *"Science does not claim a 10 billion year history of the world. Such a claim is beyond its scope. It only claims that, if we assume that the present laws of nature were always in force, then the world is that old. But, according to the simple meaning of the Torah's narrative, the world – and the laws of nature with it – were created 5,740 years ago. This denies the non-scientific assumption of the scientists and does not quarrel with their scientific reasoning. In other words, the Torah does not at all contradict the claims of science, but only the hypothesis of scientists, which is not science at all."* [Leo Levi, *Torah and Science* (New York: Feldheim Publish., 1983.]
- The biblical records thereby claim only about 6 thousand to 8 thousand years have passed since the creation of the first human being. And, as has been shown, there is no scientific proof that such an age is radically in error.
- Note: The question of the veracity of Genesis and the veracity of Jesus Christ seem to be linked, since Christ quoted from Genesis on various occasions. There is also good indication that he accepted Genesis as historical truth. He built doctrines, such as those involving marriage, on events in Genesis which he evidently accepted as literal history.
- In the final analysis, whatever age one accepts for Earth is, of course, a *belief* — a position based on one's presuppositions about origins and history. There is no scientific way to *prove* an age of billions (or thousands) of years.

SOURCES FOR EVIDENCES THAT THE "DAYS" OF GENESIS 1 AND 2 ARE LITERAL DAYS, NOT "INDEFINITE AGES"

- Kenneth A. Ham and Paul S. Taylor, *The Genesis Solution* (Grand Rapids, Michigan: Baker Book House, 1988).
- James Stambaugh, "The Meaning of 'Day' in Genesis," ICR Impact Series, No. 184, *Acts & Facts* (P.O. Box 2667, El Cajon, California 92021: Institute for Creation Research, October 1988).
- David Malcolm, "The Seven-Day-Cycle," *Creation: Ex Nihilo*, Vol. 9, No. 2 (P.O. Box 302, Sunnybank, Queensland 4109, Australia: Creation Science Foundation, 1987), pp. 32-35.
- John C. Whitcomb, Jr., *The Early Earth*, revised edition (Grand Rapids, Michigan: Baker Book House, 1986), pp. 28-49.
- John Rendle-Short, *Man: Ape or Image* (San Diego: Master Books, 1984).
- Henry M. Morris, *The Biblical Basis for Modern Science* (Grand Rapids, Michigan: Baker Book House, 1984), pp. 117-132.
- Paul A. Bartz, "Questions & Answers on Creationism," *Bible-Science Newsletter*, Vol. 22, No. 5 (P.O. Box 32457, Minneapolis, Minnesota 55432, Phone 612-635-0614: Bible-Science Association, May 1984), p. 12.
- John C. Whitcomb, Jr. and Donald B. DeYoung, *The Moon: Its Creation, Form and Significance* (Winona Lake, Indiana: BMH Books, 1978), pp. 76-83.
- Arthur F. Williams, "The Genesis Account of Creation," in Walter E. Lammerts, editor, *Why Not Creation?* (Grand Rapids, Michigan: Baker Book House, 1970), pp. 24-38, esp. 24-33 (p. 27 —*"Those who hold to the day-age theory ask us to give the word "day" a meaning which it has nowhere else in the five books of Moses."*).

OTHER SOURCES WHICH CLAIM THE GENEALOGIES ARE ACCURATE

- Robert H. Brown, "Chronologic Constraints of the Patriarchal Period," Unpublished manuscript available from the Geoscience Research Institute, Loma Linda University, Loma Linda, California 92350 (1987).
- Thomas M. Strouse, "The Biblical Date for Creation," *Bible-Science Newsletter*, Vol. 22, No. 10 (P.O. Box 32457, Minneapolis, Minnesota 55432, Phone 612-635-0614: Bible-Science Association, October 1984), p. 12.
- Richard Niessen, "A Biblical Approach to Dating the Earth: A Case for the Use of Genesis 5 and 11 as an Exact Chronology," *Creation Research Society Quarterly*, Vol. 19, No. 1 (P.O. Box 14016, Terre Haute, Indiana 47803: June 1982), pp. 60-66.
- Gerhard F. Hasel, "Genesis 5 and 11: Chronogenealogies in the Biblical History of Beginnings," *Origins*, Vol. 7, No. 1 (Loma Linda, California: Geoscience Research Institute, Loma Linda University, 1980), pp. 23-37.
- Gerhard F. Hasel, "The Meaning of the Chronogenealogies of Genesis 5 and 11," *Origins*, Vol. 7, No. 2 (Loma Linda, California: Geoscience Research Institute, Loma Linda University, 1980), pp. 53-70.
- Fred Kramer, "A Critical Evaluation of the Chronology of Ussher," in Paul Zimmerman, editor, *Rock Strata and the Bible Record* (St. Louis: Concordia Publishing House, 1970), pp. 57-67 (Reveals problems with Bishop Ussher chronology, but provides evidence that the Bible cannot accommodate billions of years).
- Arthur C. Custance, *The Genealogies of the Bible: A Neglected Subject*, Doorway Paper No. 24 (P.O. Box 291, Brockville, Ontario, Canada K6V 5V5: Doorway Publications, 1988 reprint — first published in 1967), 53 pp.

SOURCES FOR CHRISTIAN ARGUMENTS AGAINST THEISTIC EVOLUTIONISM

- Kenneth A. Ham and Paul S. Taylor, *The Genesis Solution* (Grand Rapids, Michigan: Baker Book House, 1988), 126 pp.
- Kenneth A. Ham, *The Lie: Evolution* (El Cajon, California: Master Books, 1987), 186 pp.

The Origin of Life

122

- Arthur E. Wilder-Smith in Willem J.J. Glashouwer and Paul S. Taylor, writers, *The Origin of Life* (Mesa, Arizona: Eden Films and Standard Media, 1983) (a Creationist motion picture).

SPONTANEOUS GENERATION

123

☐ Pasteur's experiments disproved the form of spontaneous generation called heterogenesis, but did not yet conclusively disprove the concept of abiogenesis

☐ Peter Mora in the scientific journal *Nature*:

"*...how life originated, I am afraid that, since Pasteur, this question is not within the scientific domain.*"

[Peter T. Mora, "Urge and Molecular Biology," *Nature*, Vol. 199, No. 4890 (July 20, 1963), p. 212 (emphasis added).]

124

☐ There are two forms of spontaneous generation theories:

(a) Heterogenesis — life coming from dead organic matter

(b) Abiogenesis — life coming from inorganic matter.

Of the two, abiogenesis would actually be the more difficult, in the final analysis.

125

☐ Technically, it is not humanly possible to totally disprove atheistic abiogenesis, since it is not falsifiable. Thaxton, Bradley, and Olsen:

"*Why will many predictably persist in their acceptance of some version of chemical evolution? Quite simply, because chemical evolution has not been falsified. One would be irrational to adhere to a falsified hypothesis. We have only presented a case that chemical evolution is highly implausible. By the nature of the case that is all one can do. In a strict, technical sense, chemical evolution cannot be falsified because it is not falsifiable. Chemical evolution is a speculative reconstruction of a unique past event, and cannot therefore be tested against recurring nature.*"

[Charles B. Thaxton, Walter L. Bradley, and Roger L. Olsen, *The Mystery of Life's Origin: Reassessing Current Theories* (New York: Philosophical Library, 1984), p. 186 (emphasis added).]

126

☐ The existence of a creator god is the only alternative to belief in life being created by matter and physical laws alone.

☐ Evolutionist Michael Denton, Ph.D.:

"*Considering the way the prebiotic soup is referred to in so many discussions of the origin of life as an already established reality, it comes as something of a shock to realize that there is absolutely no positive evidence for its existence.*"

[Michael Denton, *Evolution: A Theory in Crisis* (Bethesda, Maryland: Adler and Adler Publishers, 1985) p. 261 (emphasis added).]

127

☐ A.I. Oparin, *The Origin of Life* (New York: Academic Press, 1957).

128

☐ Various energy sources have been tried in the attempt to create life from many different chemical mixtures. These include electric currents, electric sparks, ultraviolet radiation, shock waves and chemical compounds which give off high energy. None has produced results necessary to create life.

SCIENCE TRIES TO CREATE LIFE
(Miller/Urey/Fox and other abiogenesis experiments)

129

☐ Sidney W. Fox, editor, *The Origin of Prebiological Systems and of Their Molecular Matrices* (New York: Academic Press, 1965).

☐ Stanley L. Miller and H.C. Urey, "Organic Compound Synthesis On the Primitive Earth," *Science*, Vol. 130 (1959).

☐ Stanley L. Miller, "A Production of Amino Acids Under Possible Primitive Earth Conditions," *Science*, Vol. 117, No. 3046 (1953), pp. 528-529.

☐ Sidney W. Fox and K. Baal, *Molecular Evolution and the Origin of Life* (New York: Dover Publishing, 1953).

130

☐ A protein is a molecule constructed of linked amino acids.

131

☐ Charles B. Thaxton, Walter L. Bradley, and Roger L. Olsen, *The Mystery Of Life's Origin: Reassessing Current Theories* (New York: Philosophical Library, 1984).

☐ Rene Evard and David Schrodetzki, "Chemical Evolution," *Origins*, Vol. 3, No. 1 (Loma Linda, California: Geoscience Research Institute, Loma Linda University, 1976), pp. 9-37.

☐ Arthur E. Wilder-Smith, *The Natural Sciences Know Nothing of Evolution* (San Diego: CLP Publishers, 1981).

☐ Richard B. Bliss and Gary E. Parker, *Origin of Life* (San Diego: CLP Publishers, 1979).

☐ Duane T. Gish, "A Consistent Christian-Scientific View of the Origin of Life," *Creation Research Society Quarterly*, Vol. 15, No. 4 (P.O. Box 14016, Terre Haute, Indiana 47803: March 1979), pp. 185-203.

☐ Duane T. Gish, *Speculations and Experiments Related to the Origin of Life*, Technical Monograph No. 1 (P.O. Box 2667, El Cajon, California 92021: Institute for Creation Research, 1972).

☐ A.J. White, "Uniformitarianism, Probability and Evolution," *Creation Research Society Quarterly*, Vol. 9, No. 1 (P.O. Box 14016, Terre Haute, Indiana 47803: June 1972), pp. 32-37.

132

☐ **stereochemistry:** study which deals with the spatial arrangements of atoms and molecules. The amino acids which the Miller/Fox experiments produced are racemates — an even mixture of both left- and right-handed amino acid molecules.

133

☐ Arthur E. Wilder-Smith, *The Natural Sciences Know Nothing of Evolution* (San Diego: Master Books, 1981), p. 18.

☐ Duane T. Gish, "A Consistent Christian-Scientific View of the Origin of Life," *Creation Research Society Quarterly*, Vol. 15, No. 4 (P.O. Box 14016, Terre Haute, Indiana 47803: March 1979), p. 193.

134

☐ Thaxton, Bradley, and Olsen:

"*...in the atmosphere and in the various water basins of the primitive earth, many destructive interactions would have so vastly diminished, if not altogether consumed, essential precursor chemicals, that chemical evolution rates would have*"

*N*o *matter how numerous they may be, mutations do not produce any kind of Evolution.*
Pierre-Paul Grosse, Evolutionist

been negligible. The soup would have been too dilute for direct polymerization to occur. Even local ponds for concentrating soup ingredients would have met with the same problem. Furthermore, no geological evidence indicates an organic soup, even a small organic pond, ever existed on this planet. It is becoming clear that however life began on earth, the usually conceived notion that life emerged from an oceanic soup of organic chemicals is a most implausible hypothesis. We may therefore with fairness call this scenario 'the myth of the prebiotic soup.'"

[Charles B. Thaxton, et al, *The Mystery of Life's Origin: Reassessing Current Theories* (New York: Philosophical Library, 1984), p.66 (emphasis added).]

☐ **Charles B. Thaxton:** Creationist / Chemist / Ph.D. in Chemistry from Iowa State University / Postdoctoral Fellow at Harvard University (2 years), history and philosophy of science / Postdoctoral appointment in molecular biology laboratory at Brandeis University (3 years) / Director of Curriculum Research of the Foundation for Thought and Ethics in Dallas / Staff member of the Julian Center in Julian, California.

☐ **Walter L. Bradley:** Ph.D. in materials science from University of Texas / Professor of Mechanical Engineering at Texas A&M University / Principal or co-principal investigator on over a million dollars' worth of contract research / Consultant to many major corporations / Texas Engineering Experimental Station Research Fellowship / Published over 30 research papers in refereed journals.

☐ **Roger L. Olsen:** Geochemist / Ph.D. in geochemistry from Colorado School of Mines / Former Senior Research Chemist with Rockwell International / Project Geochemist for D'Appolonia Waste Management Services of Englewood, Colorado / Published several technical papers and has written over 40 confidential engineering-scientific reports / Member Sigma Xi.

135

☐ 10^{67} = 10,000,000,000,000,000,000,000,000,000,000,000,000,-000,000,000,000,000,000,000,000,000.

☐ A.J. White, "Uniformitarianism, Probability and Evolution," *Creation Research Society Quarterly* (P.O. Box 14016, Terre Haute, Indiana 47803: Vol. 9, No. 1, June 1972), pp. 32-37.

☐ **A.J. ("Monty") White:** Creationist / Chemist / Ph.D. in chemistry from University of Wales / Research fellow at the Edward Davies Chemical Laboratories, Aberystwyth, United Kingdom.

136

☐ I.L. Cohen, *Darwin Was Wrong — A Study in Probabilities* (P.O. Box 231, Greenvale, New York 11548: New Research Publications, Inc., 1984), p. 205.

☐ Mathematician Emil Borel agrees that the laws of probability demonstrate that *"events whose probabilities are extremely small never occur."*

[Emil Borel, *Elements of the Theory of Probability* (New Jersey: Prentice-Hall, 1965), p. 57 (emphasis added).]

137

☐ Evolutionist Paul Erbrich:

"The probability... of the convergent evolution of two proteins with approximately the same structure and function is too low to be plausible, even when all possible circumstances are present which seem to heighten the likelihood of such convergence. If this is so, then the plausibility of a random evolution of two or more different but functionally related proteins seems hardly greater."

[Paul Erbrich, "On the Probability of the Emergence of a Protein with a Particular Function," *Acta Biotheoretica*, Vol. 34 (1985), pp. 53-80 (quote is from the abstract — emphasis added).]

138

☐ Arthur E. Wilder-Smith in Willem J.J. Glashouwer and Paul S. Taylor, writers, *The Origin of Life* (Mesa, Arizona: Eden Films and Standard Media, 1983) (Creationist motion picture).

☐ Also, see: Arthur E. Wilder-Smith, *The Natural Sciences Know Nothing of Evolution* (San Diego: Master Books, 1981), pp. 9-89.

IS THERE EVIDENCE THAT LIFE COULD EVOLVE FROM MINERALS AND WATER?

☐ Evolutionist and biochemist Klause Dose, Ph.D., a leading origin-of-life researcher:

"(A) mineral origin of life? This thesis is beyond the comprehension of all biochemists or molecular biologists who are daily confronted with the experimental facts of life. The poor response of life scientists to (A.G.) Cairns-Smith's thesis is therefore no surprise."

[Klause Dose, "Book Review of *Clay Minerals and the Origin of Life* by A.G. Cairns-Smith and H. Hartman," *Biosystems*, Vol. 22, No. 1 (1988), p. 89 (emphasis added).]

THE DNA MOLECULE: THE ODDS AGAINST EVOLUTION

139

☐ Chromosomes are thread-like structures made of DNA and protein. There are 46 chromosomes in man.

140

☐ DNA is Deoxyribonucleic Acid.

141

☐ Robert F. Weaver, "ATGC: A Simple Code of Four Parts Spells Out Life," *National Geographic*, Vol. 166, No. 6 (December 1984), p. 822.

142

☐ This analogy, which points out the great complexity of DNA, was suggested by Francis C. Crick, the co-discoverer of DNA and a 1962 Nobel Prizewinner.

☐ *"The set of genetic instructions for humans is roughly three billion letters long."* (genetics experts Radman and Wagner, p. 40)

[Miroslav Radman and Robert Wagner, "The High Fidelity of DNA Duplication," *Scientific American*, Vol. 259, No. 2 (August 1988), pp. 40-46 (emphasis added).]

143

☐ Nucleotides.

144

☐ Researcher and author Luther Sunderland:

"When Watson and Crick discovered the helical structure of the DNA molecule and the general way that it coded the formation and replication of proteins in cells, there were great expectations that a plausible scientific explanation for the origin of life was just over the horizon. The laboratory synthesis of amino acids from basic chemicals further heightened the expectations that man, with all his intelligence and resources, could synthesize a living cell. These hopes have also been dashed with the failure to generate life in the laboratory, and researchers are stating that new natural laws will need to be discovered to explain how the high degree of order and

specificity of even a single cell could be generated by random, natural processes."

[Luther D. Sunderland, *Darwin's Enigma: Fossils and Other Problems*, 4th edition (Santee, California: Master Book Publishers, 1988), p. 8.]

☐ *"The chance that useful DNA molecules would develop without a Designer are approximately zero. Then let me conclude by asking which came first — the DNA (which is essential for the synthesis of proteins) or the protein enzyme (DNA-polymerase) without which DNA synthesis is nil? ...there is virtually no chance that chemical 'letters' would spontaneously produce coherent DNA and protein 'words'."* (George I lowe, expert in biological sciences and Creation/Evolution issues)

[George Howe, "Addendum to As a Watch Needs a Watchmaker," *Creation Research Society Quarterly*, Vol. 23, No. 2 (P.O. Box 14016, Terre Haute, Indiana 47803: September 1986), p. 65.]

☐ **George F. Howe:** Botanist and Biologist / Creationist / Ph.D. and M.Sc. in Botany from Ohio State University (1959, 1956) / Postdoctoral studies in radiation biology, Cornell University (1965-66) / Postdoctoral studies in botany, Washington State University (1961) / Postdoctoral studies in desert biology, Arizona State University (1963) / Former Assistant Professor of biology and botany at Westmont College, Santa Barbara, California / Charter member and former President of the Creation Research Society / Director of CRS Grand Canyon Experimental Station / Professor and Chairman of the Division of Natural Sciences, The Master's College, Newhall, California / Published papers in scientific journals including: *Bulletin of the Southern California Academy of Sciences, Ohio Journal of Science,* and *Creation Research Society Quarterly* / Twice voted Teacher of the Year by students at The Master's College.

☐ *"Evolution lacks a scientifically acceptable explanation of the source of the precisely planned codes within cells without which there can be no specific proteins and hence, no life."* (Creationist David A. Kaufmann, Ph.D., University of Florida, Gainesville)

[David A. Kaufmann, "Human Growth and Development, and Thermo II," *Creation Research Society Quarterly*, Vol. 20, No. 1 (P.O. Box 14016, Terre Haute, Indiana 47803: June 1983), p. 28.]

☐ *"The immensity of the problem is rarely appreciated by laymen, and is generally ignored by Evolutionary scientists, themselves... The process by which life originated was thus a supernatural process and cannot be accounted for by natural processes and natural laws now operating on planet Earth."* (Creationist Duane T. Gish, Ph.D. in Biochemistry from University of California at Berkeley, former research biochemist at Cornell University and Upjohn Company)

[Duane Gish, "A Consistent Christian-Scientific View of the Origin of Life," *Creation Research Society Quarterly*, Vol. 15, No. 4 (P.O. Box 14016, Terre Haute, Indiana 47803: March 1979), p. 185.]

VARIOUS EVOLUTIONISTS HAVE WRITTEN BOOKS AND ARTICLES WHICH SHOW THE MATHEMATICAL IMPOSSIBILITY OF LIFE BY PURELY NATURAL MEANS

☐ Harold F. Blum, *Time's Arrow and Evolution* (Princeton, New Jersey: Princeton University Press, 1968).

☐ P.S. Moorhead and M.M. Kaplan, editors, *Mathematical Challenges to the Neo-Darwinian Interpretation of Evolution* (Philadelphia: Wistar Institute, 1967).

☐ D.E. Hull, "Thermodynamics and Genetics of Spontaneous Generation," *Nature*, Vol. 186 (1955), pp. 693-694.

145

☐ **Dr. John Grebe:** Chemist / Creationist / D.Sc. from Case Institute of Technology (1935) (Case is now part of Western Reserve University) / Honorary Doctor of Laws degree from Hillsdale College (1967) / M.S. also from Case / Former researcher at Oak Ridge National Laboratory Reactor School and Engineering Team (1946-1947) / Former Director of the Dow Chemical Company Physical Chemistry Research Laboratories in Midland, Michigan / Served as Chief Scientist to the Army Chemical Corps at Edgewood Arsenal New Baltimore (1948-1949) / In 1943 became the youngest recipient ever to receive the Chemical Industry Medal / Certificate of Merit from The Franklin Institute (1942) / A founder of the Creation Research Society / Deceased.

146

☐ Honored chemist John Grebe, D.Sc.:

"The DNA assembly uses only 20 out of 64 possible sub-assemblies. The basic units are called nucleotides. They are arranged in a spiral rope ladder-like structure, made of a purine, pyrimidine, sugar, and phosphate unit, each group of four forming one of many rung sections. The 15,000 or more atoms of the individual sub-assemblies, if left to chance as required by the evolutionary theory, would go together in any of 10^{87} different ways. (This is ten billion with 77 more ciphers behind it.) It is like throwing 15,000 dice at one time to determine what specific molecule to make; and then to test each one for the survival of the fittest until the one out of 10^{87} different possibilities is proven by the survival of the fittest to be the right one.

Just think, only 20 of these possible amino acids are actually used in nature to form, describe and prescribe all the kinds of life known. And only a small amount of each individual cell of each living organism is made up of the DNA molecule... Now, let us try to locate, and hold for assembly, the sub-assemblies of 20 kinds out of the 10^{87} kinds that should form at random, if any did form. Lo and behold! The dice are loaded.

Not all the types of sub-assemblies expected at random are available in the same numbers. One of them is more than 10^{61} (100 billion plus 50 zeroes behind it) times as predominant as the average because of its greater thermodynamic stability – as determined by well-established laws of equilibrium concentrations.

I **n the meantime, the educated public continues to believe that Darwin has provided all the relevant answers by the magic formula of random mutations plus natural selection — quite unaware of the fact that random mutations turned out to be irrelevant and natural selection a tautology.**

Arthur Koestler, author

This is governed by the same kind of scientific facts as those used in the oil industry to get the best kind of much smaller petroleum molecules out of a refinery process. Even this pre-dominant one is available only one in more than a thousand billion billion. But while you may want two of that predominant one, for finding each of the other units you have to wade through more than 10^{51} (more than 10 billion multiplied by itself 6 times).

Fortunately, one can find five more kinds of molecules that are used in the DNA for every 100,000 or so of the first. But then, the picking gets that much leaner for the other 14 kinds out of the 10^{87} possible ones, diluted by the predominant ones, which are there and reform in the equilibrium that must be maintained, if any of them are in position to form. Obviously, the creation of order out of random positions and rotations in each of the six degrees of freedom calls for the reversal of the laws of thermodynamics on a fantastic scale, in addition to the required activation energies...

Let us now assume we have overcome the laws of chance generation which would call for the production of more than 10^{87} kinds of amino acids to pick and test from the survival of the fittest and to be put together in one specific way out of $4^{10,000}$ alternate ways (yes, that is four multiplied by itself ten thousand times), for each and every one species. We find that this is for asexual reproduction.

Sexual reproduction requires that the same unique macro-molecular composition would appear (a) at the same place, (b) at the very same instant, (c) twice, (d) with exactly the correct temperature, (e) velocity, (f) direction to meet and to stay together, (g) without interference from others for a long enough time to entwine together to make the first DNA pair in (h) a specific nutrient medium that is then protected somehow by, (i) a membrane, which permits (j) the RNA-smaller than DNA and (k) the hundreds of enzymes to (l) function together simultaneously (m) in a complex pattern of action, (n) somehow pre-trained or by 'inherited' self-control.

Now, if the exact kind and number of amino acid molecules were counted out and confined and somehow, <u>against the laws of nature</u>, also protected against 'the survival of the fittest' in a thermodynamic equilibrium, one would still have only one chance out of 10^{91} (10 billion with 21 ciphers added) to obtain the one combination for any one species as a dead agglomerate.

[John J. Grebe, "DNA Studies in Relation to Creation Concepts," in Walter E. Lammerts, editor, *Why Not Creation?* (Grand Rapids, Michigan: Baker Book House, 1970), pp. 316-317.]

Also, see: John J. Grebe, "Youth's Dilemma with Answers from Modern Biology," *Creation Research Society Quarterly*, Vol. 8, No. 1 (P.O. Box 14016, Terre Haute, Indiana 47803: June 1971), pp. 60-62.

147

☐ Universe sheds 10 billion years?

"Brent Jully of the University of Hawaii now claims that astronomers who believe in a larger and older universe, have been misled ... His analysis gives the universe an age of 10 billion years instead of 20 billion years."

[Nigel Henbest, "Universe Sheds 10 Billion Years," *New Scientist*, Vol. 119, No. 1624 (August 4, 1988), p. 34.]

148

☐ Illustration adapted from a presentation made by Dr. Grebe before the State Board of Education in Austin, Texas, as reported by Mel Gabler, Longview, Texas.

149

☐ John J. Grebe, "DNA Complexity Points to Divine Design," *Science & Scripture*, Vol. 3, No. 3 (San Diego: Creation-Science Research Center, 1973), p. 20 (p. 20 — "No scientific evidence has shown the slightest chance of one code mutating to another.").

150

☐ I.L. Cohen, *Darwin Was Wrong — A Study in Probabilities* (P.O. Box 231, Greenvale, New York 11548: New Research Publications, Inc., 1984), pp. 4,5,8.

☐ **I.L. Cohen:** Engineer / Mathematician / Researcher / Author / Member of the New York Academy of Sciences / Officer of the Archaeological Institute of America (N. Shore Society).

151

☐ Michael Denton, *Evolution: A Theory in Crisis* (Bethesda, Maryland: Adler and Adler Publishers, 1985), p. 264.

152

☐ Sir Fred Hoyle is a well-known British mathematician, astronomer, and cosmologist. He originated the steady state theory of nucleogenesis, and he is Professor of Astronomy at Cambridge University. Hoyle is also the co-author of the book, *Evolution from Space*, which states:

"Once we see, however, that the probability of life originating at random is so utterly minuscule as to make it absurd, it becomes sensible to think that the favorable properties of physics, on which life depends, are in every respect deliberate... It is, therefore, almost inevitable that our own measure of intelligence must reflect higher intelligence — even to the limit of God."

[Fred Hoyle and N. Chandra Wickramasinghe, *Evolution from Space* (London: J.M. Dent and Company, 1981), pp. 141, 144.]

CONCERNING THE HIGH IMPROBABILITY OF LIFE EVOLVING

153

☐ An article in the journal *Nature* reported Hoyle's statements at the Kellogg Laboratory Symposium explaining why he does not believe conventional views about Evolution. He says that the calculated time since the origin of the universe is not enough time to account for the emergence of life. He states that the information content of simplest life is about $10^{40,000}$ and there is simply not enough time for the degree of specificity to occur by random processes:

"The likelihood of the formation of life from inanimate matter is one to a number with 40,000 noughts after it... <u>It is big enough to bury Darwin and the whole theory of (E)volution</u>. There was no primeval soup, neither on this planet nor on any other, and if the beginnings of life were not random, they must therefore have been the product of purposeful intelligence."

["Hoyle on Evolution," *Nature*, Vol. 294, No. 5837 (November 12, 1981), p. 148 (emphasis added).]

☐ DNA expert Francis Crick (the co-discoverer of the DNA double helix and a Nobel Prize winner) agrees there is virtually no chance that the first life could have spontaneously generated from Earth's chemistry. For this reason, he wrote a book which suggests the first living cell must have been brought to Earth by a spaceship from outside this solar system. See: Francis Crick, *Life Itself* (New York: Simon and Schuster, 1981), pp. 117-141; Francis Crick, "Francis Crick: The Seeds of Life," *Discover* (October 1981), pp. 256, especially pp. 62-67.

☐ Sir Fred Hoyle has taken a similar tack. [See: Fred Hoyle and N. Chandra Wickramasinghe, *Evolution from Space* (New York: Simon and Schuster, 1981), and "Where Microbes Boldly Went," *New Scientist*, Vol. 91, No. 1266 (August 13, 1981), pp. 412-415.]

☐ *"However, the macromolecule-to-cell transition is a <u>jump of fantastic dimensions</u>, which lies <u>beyond the range of testable hypothesis</u>. In this area, <u>all is conjecture</u>. <u>The available facts do not provide a basis for postulating that cells arose on this planet</u>... We simply wish to point out the fact that there is <u>no scientific evidence</u>."*

(Biochemists and Evolutionists David Green, University of Wisconsin, and Robert Goldberger, National Institutes of Health, Bethesda, Maryland)

[David E. Green and Robert F. Goldberger, *Molecular Insights Into the Living Process* (New York: Academic Press, 1967), pp. 406-407 (emphasis added).]

☐ "*By adding up the energy content of all the chemical bonds in a 'simple' bacterium and comparing this to the energy content at equilibrium of the constituent atoms from which it was formed, Morowitz calculated the probability of this cell to be* $10^{10 \text{ to the } 11\text{th}}$, *that is, one chance out of a number formed by writing the number one followed by 100 billion zeroes! That number is so large that it would require 100 thousand volumes of 500 pages each just to print! Yet, the improbability of the existence of a single-celled organism, in comparison to inanimate matter, is of that order of magnitude. Are there natural processes at work that could enable this monstrous improbability to be overcome? Of course not. In fact, increase the probability a quadrillion times (one followed by 15 zeroes) and the probability would still be only one out of one followed by 99 billion, 999 million, 999 thousand, 985 zeroes!*" (Biochemist and Creationist Dr. Gish)

[Duane T. Gish, "A Consistent Christian-Scientific View of the Origin of Life," *Creation Research Society Quarterly*, Vol. 15, No. 4 (P.O. Box 14016, Terre Haute, Indiana 47803: March 1979), pp. 201-202 (emphasis added).]

☐ Some Evolutionists have suggested that chance would not be involved in the original evolution of DNA; it would be the inevitable outcome of nature's laws. But this is wishful thinking. Biochemistry/Geochemistry experts Thaxton, Bradley and Olsen state:

"*No one to date has published data indicating that bonding preferences could have had any role in coding the DNA molecules.*"

[Charles B. Thaxton, Walter L. Bradley, and Roger L. Olsen, *The Mystery of Life's Origin: Reassessing Current Theories* (New York: Philosophical Library, 1984), p. 148.]

☐ Arthur E. Wilder-Smith, *The Creation of Life: A Cybernetic Approach to Evolution* (Wheaton, Illinois: Harold Shaw Publishers, 1970), pp. 66-69 (discusses the Fox experiment with hot lava which produced proteinoids with amino acid sequences that were not totally random (p. 66+), but why this still does no good / etc.).

☐ Expert Michael Polanyi further points out that if a DNA molecule could be put together by such means:

"*...such a DNA molecule would have no information content. Its codelike character would be effaced by an overwhelming redundancy.*"

[Michael Polanyi, "Life's Irreducible Structure," *Science*, Vol. 160, No. 3834 (June 21, 1968), p. 1309 (emphasis added).]

154

☐ Gregg Easterbrook observes that no Evolutionary scientist has:

"*any idea what makes chemicals start living. The origin of life is perhaps the leading unknown of contemporary science.*"

[Gregg Easterbrook, "Are We Alone?", *Atlantic* (August 1988), pp. 25-38 (quote is from p. 32).]

☐ Evolutionist N. Chandra Wickramasinghe:

"*...there are very few empirical facts of direct relevance and perhaps no facts relating to the actual transition from organic material to material that can even remotely be described as*

living. ... *The timescale (the supposed 5 billion year old age of Earth) is grossly inadequate and the information content that is needed to produce life is so vast that it is impossible to actually arrive at that final step on Earth...*"

[N. Chandra Wickramasinghe in Vol. 325 of *Philosophical Transcripts of the Royal Society of London* (1988), pp. 611-618 (quote is from p. 611) (emphasis added).]

☐ "*One must conclude that, contrary to the established and current wisdom, a scenario describing the genesis of life on earth by chance and natural causes which can be accepted on the basis of fact and not faith has not yet been written.*"

[Hubert P. Yockey, "A Calculation of the Probability of Spontaneous Biogenesis by Information Theory," *Journal of Theoretical Biology*, Vol. 67 (1977), p. 398 (emphasis added).]

SUGGESTED SOURCES FOR A LAYMAN-LEVEL EXPLANATION OF PROBABILITY AS IT RELATES TO THE ORIGIN OF LIFE (including more evidence of the extreme odds against the Evolution of proteins, DNA molecules, cells, etc.)

☐ I.L. Cohen, *Darwin Was Wrong — A Study in Probabilities* (P.O. Box 231, Greenvale, New York 11548: New Research Publications, Inc., 1984).

☐ Henry M. Morris, "Probability and Order Versus Evolution," Impact series no. 73, *Acts & Facts* (P.O. Box 2667, El Cajon, California 92021: Institute for Creation Research, July 1979).

☐ Randy L. Wysong, *The Creation-Evolution Controversy* (Midland, Michigan: Inquiry Press, 1976), pp. 69-144.

155

☐ Hubert P. Yockey, "Self Organization Origin of Life Scenarios and Information Theory," *Journal of Theoretical Biology*, Vol. 91, No. 1 (July 7, 1981), p. 13.

☐ Experts Thaxton, Bradley, and Olsen therefore rightly wonder:

"*...an intelligible communication via radio signal from some distant galaxy would be widely hailed as evidence of an intelligent source. Why then doesn't the message sequence on the DNA molecule also constitute prima facie evidence for an intelligent source? After all, DNA information is not just analogous to a message sequence such as Morse code, it is such a message sequence.*"

[Charles B. Thaxton, Walter L. Bradley, and Roger L. Olsen, *The Mystery of Life's Origin: Reassessing Current Theories* (New York: Philosophical Library, 1984), pp. 211-212.]

☐ Also see Ernst Mayr quote in endnotes (see index).

156

☐ Arthur E. Wilder-Smith, *The Natural Sciences Know Nothing of Evolution* (San Diego: Master Books, 1981), p. 4.

☐ Also see: Arthur E. Wilder-Smith, *The Scientific Alternative to Neo-Darwinian Evolutionary Theory: Information Sources & Structures* (P.O. Box 8000, Costa Mesa, California 92683: TWFT Publishers, 1987).

157

☐ Arthur E. Wilder-Smith in Willem J.J. Glashouwer and Paul S. Taylor, writers, *The Origin of Life* (Mesa, Arizona: Eden Films and Standard Media, 1983) (Creationist motion picture).

D*arwinism has failed in practice.*
Norman Macbeth

THE INCREDIBLE COMPLEXITY OF MAN

158

☐ Concerning the great complexity of one-celled creatures, Dr. Ilya Prigogine, Professor and Director of the Physics Department of the Universite Libre de Bruxelles, confirms:

"But let us have no illusions — our research would still leave us quite unable to grasp the extreme complexity of the simplest of organisms."

[Ilya Prigogine, "Can Thermodynamics Explain Biological Order?," *Impact of Science on Society*, Vol. 23, No. 3 (1973), p. 178.]

☐ A one-celled animal may be made up of millions of molecular parts.

☐ It is also interesting to note that there is a large gap between the many single-celled animals and the multi-celled animals. There is no known animal with 2 cells, for instance — or with 3, 4.... even 20 cells.

[Lynn Margulis and Karlene V. Schwartz, *Five Kingdoms: An Illustrated Guide to the Phyla of Life on Earth* (San Francisco: W.H. Freeman and Company, 1982), pp. 178-179; E. Lendell Cockrum and William J. McCauley, *Zoology* (Philadelphia: W.B. Saunders Company, 1965), p. 163.]

☐ The least complex multicellular animals are the sponges (which Evolutionists don't think evolved into any other type of animal) and the mesozoa (a parasite to a more complex creature).

☐ Some scientists now view bacteria as highly complex multicellular organisms:

"Although bacteria are tiny, they display biochemical, structural and behavioral complexities that outstrip scientific description. In keeping with the current microelectronics revolution, it may make more sense to equate their size with sophistication rather than with simplicity... Without bacteria, life on earth could not exist in its present form."

[James A. Shapiro, "Bacteria as Multicellular Organisms," *Scientific American*, Vol. 258, No. 6 (June 1988), p. 82.]

INTERESTING COMMENTS ON THE COMPLEXITY OF THE HUMAN BRAIN

159

☐ Concerning the human brains' complexity Judson Herrick, Professor of Neurology at the University of Chicago, states that:

"If a million cortical nerve cells were connected one with another in groups of only two neurons each in all possible combinations, the number of different patterns of interneuronic connection thus provided would be expressed by $10^{2,783,000}$. This, of course, is not the actual structure, as we shall see; but the illustration may serve to impress upon us the inconceivable complexity of the interconnections of the ninety-two hundred million (9,200,000,000) nerve cells known to exist in the cerebral cortex." (p. 5)

"On the basis of the known structure of the cortex, the following computation may be regarded as a <u>conservative</u> statement of the number of intercellular connections that are anatomically present and available for use in a short series of cortical associational processes. Starting again with a million (10^6) cortical neurons of the visual area simultaneously excited by some retinal image, each of these certainly activates at least ten others (10^7), and each of these in turn ten others (10^8)... If for simplicity of computation we limit ourselves to one million of the 10^8 neurons already activated in the process, and if we assume that these may be recombined among themselves in all theoretically possible patterns, the total number of such connections would <u>far exceed</u> the $10^{2,783,000}$ already mentioned as the theoretically possible combinations in groups of two only." (pp. 7-8).

[C. Judson Herrick, *Brains of Rats and Man: A Survey of the Origin and Biological Significance of the Cerebral Cortex* (New York: Hafner Publishing Co., 1963), 382 pp. (emphasis added), and see Paul G. Roofe, p. "x" of the introduction to the same edition.]

☐ Thus, there is an astonishingly large number of interconnections possible within the brain, *far* exceeding the estimate of the total number of atoms in the whole visible universe —

"Probably the whole visible sidereal universe does not contain more than 10^{66} atoms!"

[Korzybski, *Psychophysiology*, Chapter XII.]

☐ *"In crude terms, the human brain is a natural computer composed of 10 to 100 billion neurons, each of which connects to about 10,000 others, and all of which function in parallel. ... Neuronal systems take about 100 processing steps <u>to perform a complex task of vision or speech which would take an electronic computer billions of processing steps</u>."*

[Michael Recce and Philip Treleavan, "Computing from the Brain," *New Scientist*, Vol. 118, No. 1614 (May 26, 1988), p. 61 (emphasis added).]

☐ Neurologist, brain surgeon, and Evolutionist Dr. Wilder Penfield concluded there must be more to man's brain than just the physical, there must be another element — what some people call a mind or a soul. He believes this 2nd element is what programs *and* reads the cerebral computer:

"...<u>after years of striving</u> to explain the mind on the basis of <u>brain-action alone</u>, I have come to the conclusion that it is <u>simpler (and far easier to be logical)</u> if one adopts the hypothesis that our being <u>does consist of two fundamental elements</u>." (brain and mind (or soul)) (p. 80 — emphasis added)

"Because it seems to be <u>certain</u> that it will <u>always be quite impossible to explain the mind on the basis of neuronal action within the brain</u>, and because it seems to me that the mind develops and matures independently throughout an individual's life as though it were a continuing element, and because a computer (which the brain is) must be programmed and operated by an agency capable of <u>independent understanding</u>, I am <u>forced</u> to choose the proposition that our being is to be explained on the basis of two fundamental elements." (brain and mind, or body and soul) (p. 80 — emphasis added)

"I conclude that there is <u>no good evidence... that the brain alone can carry out the work that the mind does</u>..." (p. xxi)

"...to expect the highest brain-mechanism or any set of reflexes, however <u>complicated,</u> to carry out what the mind does, and thus perform all the functions of the mind, is quite <u>absurd</u>." (p. 79, emphasis added)

"...the mind seems to act <u>independently</u> of the brain in the same sense that a programmer acts independently of his computer, however he may depend upon the action of that computer for certain purposes." (pp. 79-80)

"...in order to survive after death, the mind <u>must</u> establish a connection with a source of energy other than that of the brain (p. 88 — emphasis is Penfield's)

[Wilder Penfield, *The Mystery of the Mind: A Critical Study of Consciousness and the Human Brain* (Princeton, New Jersey: Princeton University Press, 1975), 123 pp.]

☐ Concerning the human brain, Arthur E. Wilder-Smith, Ph.D., D.Sc., Dr.es.Sc., states:

"Any scientist who holds the view that the teleonomy and information required to build an organ such as the <u>human cortex</u> developed by chance with the aid of the laws of nature is either not familiar with the second law of thermodynamics or he is superstitious, for as a scientist he should know that teleonomy and intelligence are required to build an intelligent electronic computer, because the computer matter does not possess the required teleonomy, and neither do the laws of nature governing the behavior of atoms and

inorganic molecules when a biological organism is synthesized."

[Arthur E. Wilder-Smith, *The Natural Sciences Know Nothing of Evolution* (San Diego: Master Books, 1981), p. 154 (emphasis added).]

160

☐ Quote from biochemist and atheistic author Dr. Isaac Asimov:

"In man is a three-pound brain which, as far as we know, is the most complex and orderly arrangement of matter in the universe."

[Isaac Asimov, "In the Game of Energy and Thermodynamics You Can't Even Break Even," *Smithsonian* (June 1970), p. 10.]

☐ Evolutionist Michael Denton has made a similar comment regarding the marvelous protein synthesis apparatus found within every living thing:

"It is <u>astonishing</u> to think that this remarkable piece of machinery, which possesses the ultimate capacity to construct every living thing that ever existed on Earth, from a giant redwood to the human brain, can construct all of its own components in a <u>matter of minutes</u> and weigh less than 10⁻¹⁶ grams. It is the order of <u>several thousand million million times smaller than the smallest piece of functional machinery constructed by man</u>."

[Michael Denton, *Evolution: A Theory in Crisis* (Bethesda, Maryland: Adler and Adler Publishers, 1985), p. 338 (emphasis added).]

161

☐ Evolutionist Michael Denton:

"The almost irresistible force of the analogy has completely undermined the complacent assumption, prevalent in biological circles over most of the past century, that the <u>design hypothesis</u> can be excluded on the grounds that the notion is fundamentally a metaphysical a priori concept and therefore scientifically unsound. On the contrary, <u>the inference to design is a purely posteriori induction based on a ruthlessly consistent application of the logic of analogy. The conclusion may have religious implications, but it does not depend on religious presuppositions</u>."

[Michael Denton, *Evolution: A Theory in Crisis* (Bethesda, Maryland: Adler and Adler Publishers, 1985), p. 341 (emphasis added).]

☐ *"I never operate without having a subconscious feeling that there's no way this extraordinarily complicated mechanism known as the human body just happened to come up from slime and ooze someplace. When I make an incision with my scalpel, I see <u>organs of such</u> intricacy that there simply hasn't been enough time for natural evolutionary processes to have developed them."*

(Surgeon Dr. C. Everett Koop, former Surgeon General of the United States of America, former editor of *The Journal of Pediatric Surgery*, recipient of at least 8 honorary degrees stemming from his surgical expertise, member of more than a dozen medical societies worldwide, former president of the Surgical section of the American Academy of Pediatric Surgery, and former Professor at the University of Pennsylvania School of Medicine)

[C. Everett Koop, in Eric C. Barrett and David Fisher, editors, *Scientists Who Believe* (Chicago: Moody Press, 1984), p. 163 (emphasis added).]

SUGGESTED SOURCES FOR FURTHER EVIDENCE OF MAJOR PROBLEMS FOR THE EVOLUTION OF DNA AND LIFE

☐ Charles B. Thaxton, Walter L. Bradley, and Roger L. Olsen, *The Mystery of Life's Origin: Reassessing Current Theories* (New York: Philosophical Library, 1984) (Very complete and detailed / quantifies the information content in DNA and protein / includes the important work of Ilya Prigogine).

☐ Magnus Verbrugge, *Alive: An Inquiry Into the Origin and Meaning of Life* (Vallecito, California: Ross House Books, 1984).

☐ Luther D. Sunderland, *Darwin's Enigma: Fossils and Other Problems* (San Diego: Master Books, 1984), pp. 127-140.

☐ S.E. Aw, *Chemical Evolution: An Examination of Current Ideas* (San Diego: CLP Publishers, 1982), 206 pp.

☐ Henry M. Morris and Gary E. Parker, *What Is Creation Science?*, revised and expanded edition (San Diego: Master Books, 1982), pp. 31-52, 269-273.

☐ Arthur E. Wilder-Smith, *The Natural Sciences Know Nothing of Evolution* (San Diego: Master Books, 1981).

☐ Duane T. Gish, "The Origin of Biological Order and the Second Law" in Emmett L. Williams, editor, *Thermodynamics and the Development of Order* (Norcross, Georgia: Creation Research Society Books, 1981), pp. 77-86.

☐ Duane T. Gish, "A Consistent Christian-Scientific View of the Origin of Life," *Creation Research Society Quarterly*, Vol. 15, No. 4 (P.O. Box 14016, Terre Haute, Indiana 47803: March 1979), pp. 185-203.

☐ M. Trop, "Polyamino Acid — The Missing Link," *Creation Research Society Quarterly*, Vol. 15, No. 4 (P.O. Box 14016, Terre Haute, Indiana 47803: March 1979), pp. 205-209.

☐ Duane T. Gish, *Speculations and Experiments Related to Theories on the Origin of Life* (P.O. Box 2667, El Cajon, California 92021: Institute for Creation Research, 1972).

☐ Duane T. Gish, "Critique of Biochemical Evolution," in Walter E. Lammerts, *Why Not Creation?* (Grand Rapids, Michigan: Baker Book House, 1970), pp. 283-289.

☐ Arthur E. Wilder-Smith, *The Creation of Life* (Wheaton, Illinois: Harold Shaw Publishers, 1970).

☐ Murray Eden, "Inadequacies of Neo-Darwinian Evolution as a Scientific Theory," in P.S. Moorehead and M.M. Kaplan, *Mathematical Challenges to the Neo-Darwinian Interpretation of Evolution*, The Wistar Symposium Monograph No. 5 (Philadelphia: Wistar Institute Press, 1967) (Shows the impossibility of producing even a very simple single pair of ordered genes in 5 billion years).

---

*M*odern apes... seem to have sprung out of nowhere. They have no yesterday, no fossil record. And the true origin of modern humans... is, if we are to be honest with ourselves, an equally mysterious matter.

Lyall Watson, Ph.D., Evolutionist

162

☐ Michael Denton:

"It is the sheer universality of perfection, the fact that every-where we look, to whatever depth we look, we find an elegance and ingenuity of an absolute transcending quality, which so mitigates against the idea of chance."

[Michael Denton, *Evolution: A Theory in Crisis* (Bethesda, Maryland: Adler and Adler Publishers, 1985), p. 342 (emphasis added).]

163

☐ Dr. Wilder-Smith's personal conclusion:

"I, as a scientist, must postulate a source of information to supply the teleonomy or know-how. I don't find it in this universe, and, therefore, I assume that it is transcendent to this universe. I believe, myself, in a living God who did it. I believe that this God, who supplied the information, revealed Himself in the form of a man — so that man could understand Him. We are made to understand. If God made us to understand, I want to understand. I want to understand God. But I can only do it if He comes down to my wavelength, the wavelength of man. I believe that God revealed Himself in the form of Christ, and that we can serve Him and know Him in our hearts as the source of the Logos — all information necessary to make the universe and to make life itself."

[Arthur E. Wilder-Smith in Willem J.J. Glashouwer and Paul S. Taylor, writers, *The Origin of the Universe* (Mesa, Arizona: Eden Films and Standard Media, 1983) (Creationist motion picture).]

"Look at the beauty of nature around us. When you consider that it all grew out of matter injected with information of the type I have been describing, you can only be filled with wonder at the wisdom of a Creator, who, first of all, had the sense of beauty to do it, and then the technical ability. I am filled with wonder as I look at nature, to see how God technically did it and realized the beauty of His own soul in doing it.

The Scripture teaches perfectly plainly, and it fits in with my science perfectly well, that the one who did that called Himself THE LOGOS. That Logos was Jesus. Jesus called Himself the Creator who made everything — 'for Him and by Him'. Now, if that is the case, then I am very happy and filled with joy that He made the Creation so beautiful and that He also valued me enough to die for me, to become my redeemer, as well."

[Arthur E. Wilder-Smith in Willem J.J. Glashouwer and Paul S. Taylor, writers, *The Origin of Life* (Mesa, Arizona: Eden Films and Standard Media, 1983) (Creationist motion picture).]

☐ Similar expressions of acceptance of the Genesis origins account have been made by thousands of scientists.

☐ **logos**: the ultimate source of all teleonomy in the cosmos; mind; creative, revelatory thought; alogos (non-logos) = chance, randomness, non-thought, no concept; the Word (Logos) — a term often used to refer to the second person of the Trinity. Christians believe that Christ is the source of all teleonomy — The Logos.

☐ The Bible claims that when one looks upon nature, one's mind — by that simple act alone — can come to the conclusion that there is a Creator. Since life can only come from pre-existing life. "In the beginning God created..." may be the most tenable statement that can be made concerning the origin of life.

FOR FURTHER INFORMATION ON WILDER-SMITH'S VIEWS ON TELEONOMY AND LOGOS

☐ Arthur E. Wilder-Smith, *God: To Be or Not to Be: A Critical Analysis of Monod's Scientific Materialism* (Neuhausen-Stuttgart, West Germany: Telos International, 1975), 117 pp.

THE ORIGIN OF SPECIES

164

☐ Henry M. Morris, *The Genesis Record* (Grand Rapids, Michigan: Baker Book House, 1976), pp. 85-86, 96-98.

☐ Book of Genesis 2:19.

SAMPLE, PRELIMINARY CREATIONIST GROUPINGS OF ANIMALS ACCORDING TO POSSIBLE BARAMINS (ILLUSTRATING GREAT DIVERSITY WITHIN ORIGINAL CREATED KINDS OF ANIMALS)

165

☐ **The original BEARS.** Descendants: Possibly all living and extinct members of the Family: *Ursidae*, including black bears, grizzly bears (and giant "cave bear" — practically the same, except in size), and brown bears.

☐ **The original BEAVERS.** Descendants: Probably all living and extinct members of the Family: *Castoridae*, including the North American and European beavers and the fossil giant beaver.

☐ **The original CAMELS.** Descendants: Possibly all living and extinct members of the Family: *Camelidae*.

☐ **The original CATS.** Descendants: Probably all 30+ breeds of living domestic cats (species: *Felis catus*); probably all extinct domestic cats; Possibly the wildcats (living species: *Felis sylvestris*); Possibly the pumas (living species: *Felis concolor*); Possibly the lynxes (genus: *Lynx*). The great cats would be a separate baramin or else early offshoots of this baramin (genus: *Panthera*, includes lions, tigers, and leopards).

☐ **The original CATTLE.** Descendants: Possibly all living and extinct members of the genus *Bos*, including all varieties of dairy and beef cattle, the oxen (species: *Bos taurus*), the Brahman (species: *Bos indicus*), the yak (species: *Bos mutus*), the gaur, the gayal, the banteng and the kouprey; possibly all of the bison (species: *Bison bison* — American, and *Bison bonasus* — European).

☐ **The original CERATOPIAN DINOSAURS.** Descendants: Possibly all members of the Family: *Ceratopids*, including Triceratops. Since these animals are extinct and only known from fossils, relatively little is known about them. It is certainly possible that they involve more than one baramin.

☐ **The original "CHICKENS" (DOMESTIC FOWL).** Descendants: Possibly all living and extinct members of the Family: *Phasianidae*, including the domestic hen and the Indian Jungle Fowl); Also, possibly all living and extinct members of the Family: *Meleagrididae*, including the turkeys; Also, possibly the members of the Family: *Numididae*, the guinea fowl.

☐ **The original COCKROACHES.** Descendants: Possibly all living and extinct members of the Family: *Blattidae* (supposedly includes 4 thousand or more species today).

☐ **The original DOGS.** Descendants: Probably all living and extinct members of the genus *Canis*, including all 200+ breeds of living and extinct domestic dogs (species: *Canis familiaris*), the dingos (species: *canis dingo* or *canis familiaris dingo*), the wolves (species: *Canis lupus*), the coyotes (species: *Canis latrans*), and possibly the jackals and foxes; Possibly all of the Family: *Canidae*. The hyenas and aardwolves would be either a separate baramin or an early offshoot of this baramin.

☐ **The original ELEPHANTS.** Descendants: Possibly all living and extinct members of the Family: *Elephantidae*, including the African elephant (species: *Loxodonta africana*), the Indian elephant (species: *Elephas indicus*), the mammoths and the mastodons.

☐ **The original FLAMINGOS.** Descendants: Probably all living and extinct members of the Family: *Phoenicopteridae*.

☐ **The original HORSES.** Descendants: Probably all living and extinct members of the genus *Equus*, including the many modern horse breeds (species: *Equus caballus*), the zebras (species: *Equus zebra*), and the mules. The donkeys and asses (species: *Equus asinus*) are possibly part of this baramin or else are a separate baramin of their own.

☐ **The original PIGS.** Descendants: Possibly all living and extinct members of the Family: *Suidae*, including the many modern breeds of pigs, the wild boars (species: *Sus scrofa*), and possibly the warthogs (species: *Phacochoerus aethiopicus*).

☐ **The original SERPENTS.** Descendants: Possibly all living and extinct members of the Order: *Squamata* (snakes), including the supposed 2300+ modern species.

☐ **The original SHEEP.** Descendants: Possibly all living and extinct members of the genus *Ovis*, including the 400+ modern breeds of domestic sheep, the bighorn sheep, and the mouflon (species: *Ovis musimon*). The goats (genus: *Capra*) might possibly be an early offshoot of this baramin, since there is some cross fertilization possible. Otherwise the goats are in their own baramin(s).

166

☐ The term "baramin" was first coined by Frank L. Marsh, *Life, Man, and Time* (Mountain View, California: Pacific Press Publishing Association, 1957), p. 118, and Frank L. Marsh *Variation and Fixity in Nature* (Mountain View, California: Pacific Press Publishing Association, 1976), pp. 36-37.

☐ Plural = baramins.

167

☐ Creationists Lane Lester (Ph.D. in genetics) and Raymond Bohlin:

"We would predict that speciation events would not affect the basic design of the organism. This would simply be a splitting up of the gene pool of one species to create two. With the constraining factors of the regulatory mechanisms still operating and the inability of mutations of any type to produce new genetic information, the maintenance of the basic plan is to be expected." (p. 168)

"There are limits to biological change and... these limits are set by the structure and function of the genetic machinery." (p. 153)

[Lane P. Lester and Raymond G. Bohlin, *The Natural Limits of Biological Change* (Grand Rapids, Michigan: Zondervan/Probe, 1984), 207 pp. (emphasis added).]

168

☐ Book of Genesis, chapter 1.

☐ Henry M. Morris, *The Genesis Record* (Grand Rapids, Michigan: Baker Book House, 1976), pp. 62-64.

THE THEORIES OF CHARLES DARWIN

169

☐ *Angels, Apes and Men* (LaSalle: Sugden, 1983).

170

☐ Full title of Darwin's book: *The Origin of Species by Means of Natural Selection or The Preservation of Favored Races in the Struggle for Life.*

171

☐ Patricia G. Horan in Foreword of Charles R. Darwin, *The Origin of Species...*, (New York: Avenel Books, 1979), p. v.

172

☐ Many have noted that Darwin's belief system sounds curiously religious in concept.

173

☐ Darwin admitted that one difficulty with his theory could be seen throughout the animal kingdom. This problem remains till this day. Charles Darwin:

"Firstly, why, if species have descended from other species by insensibly fine gradations, do we not everywhere see innumerable transitional forms? Why is not all nature in confusion instead of the species being, as we see them, well defined?"

[Charles R. Darwin, *The Origin of Species...*, first edition reprint (New York: Avenel Books, 1979), p. 205 (in 2nd paragraph of Chapter 6 on "Difficulties on Theory").]

174

☐ Concerning Darwinism and neo-Darwinism:

"We ourselves would be less concerned about falsifiability *if neo-Darwinism were a powerful theory with major successes to its credit. But this is simply not the case.*

Neo-Darwinist textbooks on evolution keep citing the same comparatively few examples: industrial melanism, sickle cell anemia, DDT resistance. All are comparatively minor evolutionary changes; all involve variations in which a large and obvious selective advantage can be obtained by a single allele substitution.

The real question, however, and this is what the claim to sufficiency is all about, is whether all of evolution can be explained as an extrapolation from these examples, i.e., as arising from the natural selection of many random variations. Is evolution nothing more than industrial melanism writ large? On this — the crucial issue — there is no evidence in favor of the synthetic theory. *From the claims that are made for neo-Darwinism one could easily get the impression that it has made great progress towards explaining evolution, mostly leaving the details to be cleared up. In fact, quite the reverse is true.* Neo-Darwinism can account for some of the details, but the *major* problems remain unsolved. Samuel Butler's (1911) complaint that *Darwin had given us 'an Origin of the Species with the 'Origin' cut out'* is true today as when he wrote it." (P. Saunders, mathematician, Queen Elizabeth College of the University of London, and M. Ho, biologist, Open University)

[Peter T. Saunders and Mae-Wan Ho, "Is Neo-Darwinism Falsifiable? And Does It Matter?," *Nature and System*, Vol. 4, No. 4 (Tucson, Arizona 85722-3368: Nature and System, December 1982), pp. 179-196 (quote is from p. 191 — emphasis added).]

175

☐ Some Creationists call these changes within a baramin "microevolution," a term evidently coined by Evolutionist Theodosius Dobzhansky.

[Theodosius Dobzhansky, "Further Data on the Variation of the Y Chromosome in *Drosophila pseudoobscura*," *Gen.*, Vol. 22 (1937), pp. 340-346.]

*T*he Evolutionist thesis has become more stringently unthinkable than ever before...
Wolfgang Smith, Ph.D.

☐ Microevolution (small changes or variations) involves small-scale biological changes only (e.g., color, size). Microevolution does not produce new genetic information; it only reshuffles existing genes. The gene pool remains constant.

☐ Macroevolution has never been observed, but Evolutionists suppose it is possible and commonplace. Macroevolution would involve the production of new genetic information enabling large-scale biological changes (e.g., amphibian to reptile).

☐ Creationists have no problem with the idea of microevolution. They believe God designed the genetic code with this ability to produce interesting variety within each baramin. Also, they believe this allows various baramins to survive despite changing environments (which have occurred since man's fall into sin and the worldwide Flood of Noah's day).

☐ The author prefers to avoid use of the term "microevolution" since some laypeople confuse it with true Evolution (macroevolution).

SUGGESTED SOURCES FOR INFORMATION ON PROBLEMS WITH DARWIN'S INTERPRETATION OF THE GALAPAGOS FINCHES

176

☐ "The Galapagos Islands — A World All Its Own," *Bible-Science Newsletter*, Vol. 22, No. 2 (P.O. Box 32457, Minneapolis, Minnesota 55432, Phone 612-635-0614: Bible-Science Association, February 1984), pp. 7-10.

☐ Walter E. Lammerts, "Effect of Drought on the Finches of a Galapagos Island," *Creation Research Society Quarterly*, Vol. 19, No. 1 (P.O. Box 14016, Terre Haute, Indiana 47803: June 1982), pp. 70-71.

☐ G.H. Harper, "Speciation or Irruption: The Significance of the Darwin Finches," *Journal of Biological Education*, Vol. 14, No. 2 (1980), pp. 99-106 (provides data to show that the 13 finch "species" on the Galapagos did not evolve there, but rather, all flew there / provides scientific reasons to believe the 13 "species" did not originate from a single species).

☐ Frank L. Marsh, *Variation and Fixity in Nature* (Mountain View, California: Pacific Press Publishing, 1976).

☐ Norman Macbeth, *Darwin Retried* (New York: Dell Publishing Co., Delta Books, 1971), p. 154 — Macbeth says there is nothing revolutionary about what Darwin found on Galapagos: "This was all old stuff.") (Macbeth is an Evolutionist with a doctorate (J.D.) from Harvard Law School. He has made the study of Darwinian theory his avocation.).

☐ Walter E. Lammerts, "The Galapagos Island Finches," in Walter E. Lammerts, editor, *Why Not Creation?* (Grand Rapids, Michigan: Baker Book House, 1970), pp. 354-366.

LAMARCK AND DARWIN

177

☐ Darwin initially rejected Lamarck's hypothesis of acquired traits in favor of natural selection. But, further research and debate caused him to return to Lamarck's theory (unpopular as it was). In the sixth edition of his book *The Origin of Species*, Charles Darwin abandoned natural selection as the force behind Evolution due to the continuing lack of evidence and theoretical problems.

[Charles Darwin, *The Origin of Species*, 6th edition (New York: The Modern Library, 1872) (p. 66 — Darwin: "*natural selection is incompetent to account for the incipient stages of useful structures...*").]

☐ Randall Hedtke, "The Divine Essence in Evolutionary Theorizing - An Analysis of the Rise and Fall of Evolutionary Natural Selection, Mutation, and Punctuated Equilibria as Mechanisms of Megaevolution," *Creation Research Society Quarterly*, Vol. 21, No. 1 (Terre Haute, Indiana 47803: June 1984), pp. 40-46.

☐ Randall Hedtke, *The Secret of the Sixth Edition* (New York: Vantage Press, 1983), pp. 1-48.

☐ Francis Hitching, *The Neck of the Giraffe: Where Darwin Went Wrong (New Haven, Connecticut: Ticknor and Fields, 1982), 258 pp.*

GENETICS

178

☐ Botanist and geneticist Gregor J. Mendel's scientific theory of genes was first submitted in 1865, just 6 years after the first publication of Darwin's *Origin of Species*. The results of Mendel's important research were neglected until 1900, when they were made public by DeVries (Holland), Correns (Germany), and Tschermak (Austria).

179

☐ Biologist Frank Marsh, Ph.D., Emeritus Professor of Biology of Andrews University:

"*Microevolution, yes. Macroevolution, no!* This is a natural fact (i.e., it can be demonstrated) of tremendous importance, one which merits deep and thoughtful study."

[Frank L. Marsh, "Genetic Variation, Limitless or Limited?," *Creation Research Society Quarterly*, Vol. 19, No. 4 (P.O. Box 14016, Terre Haute, Indiana 47803: 1983), pp. 204-206 (quote from p. 206 — emphasis added) (A biological principle of limited variation pervades: genetic variability in organisms can go no farther than to produce new variants within already existing basic types. No exception has been demonstrated.)]

☐ "*People are misled into believing that since microevolution is a reality, that therefore macroevolution is such a reality also. Evolutionists maintain that over long periods of time small-scale changes accumulate in such a way as to generate new and more complex organisms... This is sheer illusion, for there is no scientific evidence whatever to support the occurrence of biological change on such a grand scale. In spite of all the artificial breeding which has been done, and all the controlled efforts to modify fruit flies, the bacillus escherichia (E-coli), and other organisms, fruit flies remain fruit flies, E-coli bacteria remain E-coli bacteria, roses remain roses, corn remains corn, and human beings remain human beings.*" (Creationist researcher Darrel Kautz)

[Darrel Kautz, *The Origin of Living Things* (10025 W. Nash St., Milwaukee, Wisconsin 53222: Darrel Kautz, 1988), p. 6 (emphasis added).]

☐ A meeting of the world's leading Evolutionists discussed "*whether the mechanisms underlying microevolution can be extrapolated to explain the phenomena of macroevolution.*" The answer was "*a clear No.*").

[Roger Lewin, "Evolutionary Theory Under Fire," *Science*, Vol. 210, No. 4472 (November 21, 1980), pp. 883 (emphasis added).]

180

☐ "The High Fidelity of DNA Duplication":

"*Generation after generation, through countless cell divisions, the genetic heritage of living things is scrupulously preserved in DNA. ... All of life depends on the accurate transmission of information. As genetic messages are passed along through generations of dividing cells, even small mistakes can be life-threatening. ...If mistakes were as rare as one* in a million, 3,000 mistakes would be made during each duplication of the human genome. Since the genome replicates about a million billion times In the course of building a human being from a single fertilized egg, it is unlikely that the human organism could tolerate such a high rate of error. In fact, the actual rate of mistakes is more like one in 10 billion."

[Miroslav Radman and Robert Wagner, "The High Fidelity of DNA Duplication," *Scientific American*, Vol. 259, No. 2 (August 1988), pp. 40-46 (quote is from p. 24).]

MUTATIONS

181

☐ Ernst Mayr, *Populations, Species and Evolution* (Cambridge, Massachusetts: Harvard University Press, 1970) [p. 98 - Evolutionist Mayr says mutations are the "*ultimate* source of genetic novelties." (emphasis added)].

182

☐ Dr. Colin Patterson, British Museum of Natural History:

"The main reason for *inventing* these macromutations is that there are some features of plants and animals which *can hardly be imagined* as arising by gradual steps; the adaptive value of the perfected structure is easily seen, but intermediate steps seem to be useless, or even harmful. For example, what use is a lens in the eye unless it works? A distorting lens might be worse than no lens at all... How can the segments of an animal like the earthworm or centipede arise bit by bit? An animal is either segmented or it is not. The usual answer to such questions is that they are due only to the failure of the imagination."

[Colin Patterson, *Evolution* (London: British Museum of Natural History, 1978), p. 142 (emphasis added).]

☐ Evolutionary paleontologist Stephen J. Gould:

"But how do you get from nothing to such an elaborate something if Evolution must proceed through a long sequence of intermediate stages, each favored by natural selection? You can't fly with 2% of a wing or gain much protection from an iota's similarity with a potentially concealing piece of vegetation. How, in other words, can natural selection explain these incipient stages of structures that can only be used (as we now observe them) in much more elaborated forms?... one point stands high above the rest: the dilemma of incipient stages. Mivart identified this problem as primary and *it remains so today*."

[Stephen Jay Gould, "Not Necessarily a Wing," *Natural History*, Vol. 94, No. 10 (October 1985), pp. 12-13.]

ON THE HARMFULNESS OF MUTATIONS

183

☐ Scientists M. Radman, Ph.D from the Free University of Brussels and a research director at the National Center for Scientific Research in Paris, and R. Wagner, Ph.D. from Harvard University:

Eighty to eighty-five percent of Earth's land surface does not have even 3 geologic periods appearing in 'correct' consecutive order. ...it becomes an overall exercise of gargantuan special pleading and imagination for the evolutionary-uniformitarian paradigm to maintain that there ever were geologic periods.

John Woodmorappe, geologist

"In human beings the substitute of a *single* 'letter' in the genetic message is responsible for such *lethal* hereditary diseases as sickle-cell anemia and thalassemia. *Several* common cancers are also associated with a *single-letter change*." (p. 40)

[Miroslav Radman and Robert Wagner, "The High Fidelity of DNA Duplication," *Scientific American*, Vol. 259, No. 2 (August 1988), pp. 40-46 (emphasis added).]

☐ "If the genetic blueprint for an organism is initially optimal — like, say, the design for a new TV set — then *mutations appear as damage* incurred by wear and tear or misuse. Kicking a damaged TV set might improve its performance but the treatment is not generally recommended. In no way could random — or even well-directed — kicking have been responsible for the origin of the TV set in the first place. But the neo-Darwinian, who asserts that mutations are the raw material of evolution, and the only source of novelty for natural selection to work on, is both denying the existence of an optimal genetic blueprint (or archetype) for a life-form, and accepting 'kicking' as a rational means of improving it out of recognition." (M. Pitman, Cambridge University)

[Michael Pitman, *Adam and Evolution* (London: Rider, 1984), pp. 66-67 (emphasis added).]

☐ "Viewing mutations as degradations is in line with the Second Law of Thermodynamics which states that matter goes from order to disorder." (Creationist R. Hedtke)

[Randall Hedtke, "The Divine Essence in Evolutionary Theorizing — An Analysis of the Rise and Fall of Evolutionary Natural Selection, Mutation, and Punctuated Equilibria as Mechanisms of Megaevolution," *Creation Research Society Quarterly*, Vol. 21, No. 1 (P.O. Box 14016, Terre Haute, Indiana 47803: June 1984), p. 44.]

☐ "For a mutation is a random change of a highly organized, reasonably smoothly functioning human body. A random change in the highly integrated system of chemical processes which constitute life is certain to impair — just as a random interchange of connections in a television set is not likely to improve the picture." (Radiation and mutation specialist James Crow)

[James F. Crow, "Genetic Effects of Radiation," *Bulletin of the Atomic Scientists*, Vol. 14 (1958), pp. 19-20.]

☐ "It is entirely in line with the accidental nature of mutations that extensive tests have agreed in showing the vast majority of them detrimental to the organism in its job of surviving and reproducing, just as changes accidentally introduced into any artificial mechanism are predominantly harmful to its useful operation... *good ones are so rare that we can consider them all bad*." (Radiation and mutation expert H. Muller)

[H.J. Muller, "How Radiation Changes the Genetic Constitution," *Bulletin of the Atomic Scientists*, Vol. 11, No. 9 (November 1955), p. 331 (emphasis added).]

☐ "There is no single instance where it can be maintained that any of the mutants studied has a higher viability than the mother species." (p. 1212)

"A review of known facts about their ability to survive has led to no other conclusion than that they are always constitutionally weaker than their parent form or species, and in a popu-

lation with free competition they are eliminated... Therefore they are never found in nature (e.g., not a single one of the several hundreds of Drosophila mutations), and therefore, they are able to appear only in the favorable environment of the experimental field or laboratory..." (famous Swedish Evolutionist Heribert Nilsson of Lund University, p. 1186)

[N. Heribert Nilsson, *Synthetische Artbildung* (Lund, Sweden: Verlag CWK Gleerup, 1953), p. 1212.]

☐ *"...all mutations seem to be in the nature of injuries that, to some extent, impair the fertility and viability of the affected organisms. I doubt if among the many thousands of known mutant types one can be found which is superior to the wild type in its normal environment; only very few can be named which are superior to the wild type in a strange environment... the mass of evidence shows that all, or almost all, known mutations are unmistakably pathological and the few remaining ones are highly suspect."* (Expert C. Martin of McGill University)

[C.P. Martin, "A Non-Geneticist Looks at Evolution," *American Scientist*, Vol. 41, No. 1 (January 1953), pp. 100, 103 (emphasis added).]

ALSO SEE:

☐ John W. Klotz, "The Philosophy of Science in Relation to Concepts of Creation Vs. the Evolution Theory," in Walter E. Lammerts, editor, *Why Not Creation?* (Grand Rapids, Michigan: Baker Book House, 1970), pp. 17-18.

☐ Duane T. Gish, "Critique of Biochemical Evolution," in Walter E. Lammerts, *Why Not Creation?* (Grand Rapids, Michigan: Baker Book House, 1970), pp. 288-289.

☐ Gary E. Parker, "Darwin and the Nature of Biologic Change," in Henry M. Morris and Gary E. Parker, *What Is Creation Science?*, Revised and Expanded edition (San Diego: CLP Publishers, 1987), pp. 100-108.

☐ Randy L. Wysong, *The Creation-Evolution Controversy* (Midland, Michigan: Inquiry Press, 1976), pp. 266-278.

NATURAL SELECTION

184

☐ Charles Darwin later became uncertain about natural selection as a cause of Evolution, eventually bowing to the weight of scientific evidence and abandoning it in the 6th edition of his book, *The Origin of Species*. See: Randall Hedtke, *The Secret of the Sixth Edition* (New York: Vantage Press, 1983).

185

☐ Concerning the importance of natural selection to Darwinism, Evolutionist Stephen Jay Gould states:

"The essence of Darwinism lies in a single phrase: natural selection is the creative force of evolutionary change. No one denies that selection will play a negative role in eliminating the unfit. Darwinian theories require that it create the fit as well."

[Stephen Gould, "The Return of Hopeful Monsters," *Natural History*, Vol. 86 (June/July 1977), p. 28.]

☐ Norman Macbeth on Darwin's stress on the analogy between natural selection and the work of the plant and animal breeders:

"This stimulated Darwin's thinking, but clouded his judgment as to the serious dissimilarities. Several eminent evolutionists have followed Darwin in this error, creating great confusion in biology."

[Norman Macbeth, "Danger: Analogies Ahead," *Rivista di Biologia (Biology Forum)*, Vol. 79, No. 2 (1986), pp. 191-202 (quote is from his abstract).]

186

☐ I.L. Cohen:

"'Survival of the fittest' and 'natural selection.' No matter what phraseology one generates, the basic fact remains the same: any physical change of any size, shape or form is strictly the result of purposeful alignment of billions of nucleotides (in the DNA). Nature or species do not have the capacity or rearranging them nor to add to them. Consequently no leap (saltation) can occur from one species to another. The only way we know for a DNA to be altered is through a meaningful intervention from an outside source of intelligence — one who knows what it is doing, such as our genetic engineers are now performing in their laboratories."

[I.L. Cohen, *Darwin Was Wrong — A Study in Probabilities* (P.O. Box 231, Greenvale, New York 11548: New Research Publications, Inc., 1984), p. 209 (emphasis added).]

☐ *"No one has ever produced a species by mechanisms of natural selection. No one has ever gotten near it..."* (Evolutionist Dr. Colin Patterson)

[Colin Patterson, interview on the subject of Cladistics, British Broadcasting Corporation television (March 4, 1982).]

☐ *"But natural selection per se does not work to create new species."* (Well-known Evolutionist Niles Eldredge, a curator of the American Museum of Natural History in New York City)

[Niles Eldredge, "An Extravagance of Species (The Diversity of Fossil Trilobites Poses a Challenge to Traditional Evolutionary Theory)," *Natural History*, Vol. 89, No. 7 (July 1980), p. 46 (emphasis added).]

☐ *"The role assigned to natural selection in establishing adaptation, while speciously probable, is based on not one single sure datum."* (Evolutionist P. Grosse)

[Pierre-Paul Grosse, *Evolution of Living Organisms* (New York: Academic Press, 1977), p. 170.]

187

☐ Michael Pitman, Cambridge University:

"...natural selection can only reduce rather than increase genetic variability... It is indeed a force counteracting the tendency for mutation to cause a degeneration in the quality of living organisms — but it cannot be creative."

[Michael Pitman, *Adam and Evolution* (London: Rider, 1984), p. 76.]

MUTATIONS + NATURAL SELECTION

188

☐ Evolutionist S. Lovtrup:

"Micromutations do occur, but the theory that these alone can account for evolutionary change is either falsified, or else it is an unfalsifiable, hence metaphysical theory. I suppose that nobody will deny that it is a great misfortune if an entire branch of science becomes addicted to a false theory. But this is what has happened in biology: ...I believe that one day the Darwinian myth will be ranked the greatest deceit in the history of science. When this happens many people will pose the question: How did this ever happen?..."

[S. Lovtrup, *Darwinism: The Refutation of a Myth* (London: Croom Helm, 1987), p. 422 (emphasis added).

☐ Jeffrey Wicken:

"As a generative principle, providing the raw material for natural selection, random mutation is inadequate both in scope and theoretical grounding."

[Jeffrey S. Wicken, "The Generation of Complexity in Evolution...", *Journal of Theoretical Biology*, Vol. 77, No. 3 (April 7, 1979), p. 349.]

□ Evolutionist Dr. Pierre-Paul Grosse, former President of the French Academie des Sciences and the scientist who held the Chair of Evolution at the Sorbonne in Paris for twenty years, confirms:

"No matter how numerous they may be, *mutations do not produce any kind of (E)volution.*" (p. 88 — emphasis added)

"The opportune appearance of mutations permitting animals and plants to meet their needs *seems hard to believe*. Yet the Darwinian theory is even more demanding: a single plant, a single animal would require thousands and thousands of lucky, appropriate events. *Thus, miracles would become the rule:* events with an infinitesimal probability could not fail to occur... *There is no law against day dreaming, but science must not indulge in it.*" (p. 103 — emphasis added)

[Pierre-Paul Grosse, *Evolution of Living Organisms* (New York: Academic Press, 1977), pp. 88, 103.]

COULD NATURAL SELECTION CAUSE MACROEVOLUTION BY MAINTAINING THEORETICALLY GOOD MUTATIONS IN THE POPULATION?

189

□ I.L. Cohen:

"To propose and argue that mutations even in tandem with 'natural selection' are the root-causes for 6,000,000 viable, enormously complex species, is to mock logic, deny the weight of evidence, and reject the fundamentals of mathematical probability."

[I.L. Cohen, *Darwin Was Wrong — A Study in Probabilities* (P.O. Box 231, Greenvale, New York 11548: New Research Publications, Inc., 1984), p. 81.]

□ Paleontologist and Evolutionist Dr. Stephen Jay Gould:

"A mutation doesn't produce major new raw material. *You don't make a new species by mutating the species.*"

[Stephen Gould, "Is a New and General Theory of Evolution Emerging?," lecture at Hobart and William Smith College (February 4, 1980) (emphasis added).]

□ "The central question of the Chicago Conference was whether the mechanisms of microevolution (mutations and natural selection) could be extrapolated to explain the phenomenon of macroevolution. At the risk of doing violence to the positions of some people at the meeting, the answer can be given as a clear 'NO'!"

[Roger Lewin, "Evolutionary Theory Under Fire," *Science*, Vol. 210, No. 4472 (November 21, 1980), pp. 883-887.]

□ "In the meantime, the educated public continues to believe that Darwin has provided all the relevant answers by the magic formula of random mutations plus natural selection — quite unaware of the fact that *random mutations turned out to be irrelevant* and natural selection a tautology."

[Arthur Koestler, *Janus: A Summing Up* (New York: Vintage Books, 1978), p. 185 (emphasis added).]

□ Evolutionist Richard Goldschmidt, Ph.D., M.D., D.Sc., outstanding geneticist and Professor of Zoology at the University of California, frequently pointed out that no one has ever succeeded in producing even one new species by the accumulation of micromutations.

[Richard B. Goldschmidt, *The Material Basis of Evolution* (New Haven, Connecticut: Yale University Press, 1940) (p. 8 — "*the facts of microevolution do not suffice for an understanding of macroevolution*."); Richard B. Goldschmidt, "Evolution, as Viewed by One Geneticist," *American Scientist*, Vol. 40 (January 1952).]

□ "If one allows the unquestionably largest experimenter to speak, namely nature, one gets a clear and incontrovertible answer to the question about the significance of mutations for the formation of species and Evolution. They disappear under the competitive conditions of natural selection, as soap bubbles burst in a breeze." (Swedish Evolutionist Heribert Nilsson)

[N. Heribert Nilsson, *Synthetische Artbildung* (Lund, Sweden: Verlag CWK Gleerup Press, 1953), p. 174.]

190

□ Dr. Richard Lewontin, Professor of Zoology, University of Chicago, Co-editor of *American Naturalist*:

"...natural selection over the long run *does not seem to improve a species' chance of survival* but simply enables it to 'track', or keep up with, the constantly changing environment."

[Richard C. Lewontin, "Adaptation," *Scientific American*, Vol. 239, No. 3 (September 1978), pp. 212-230 (quote from p. 215) (emphasis added).]

191

□ Arthur E. Wilder-Smith in Willem J.J. Glashouwer and Paul S. Taylor, writers, *The Origin of Species* (Mesa, Arizona: Films for Christ, 1983) (Creationist motion picture).

□ Also, see: Arthur E. Wilder-Smith, *The Natural Sciences Know Nothing of Evolution* (San Diego: Master Books, 1981), pp. 123-146.

CONCERNING THE EXTREME IMPROBABILITY OF EVOLVING EYES

192

□ Charles Darwin:

"To suppose that the eye, with all its inimitable contrivances for adjusting the focus to different distances, for admitting different amounts of light, and for the correction of spherical and chromatic aberration, could have been formed by natural selection, seems, I freely confess, absurd in the highest possible degree."

[Charles R. Darwin, *The Origin of Species...*, first edition reprint (New York: Avenel Books, 1979), p. 217 (Chapter 6, "Difficulties on Theory"). First edition: 1859.]

□ "That a mindless, purposeless, chance process such as natural selection, acting on the sequelae of recombinant DNA or random mutations, most of which are injurious or fatal, could fabricate such complexity and organization as in the vertebrate eye, where each component part must carry out its own distinctive task in an harmoniously functioning optical unit, is

*R*adiometric dating "is an exceedingly crude instrument with which to measure our strata and I can think of no occasion where it has been put to an immediate practical use. Apart from very 'modern' examples, which are really archaeology..."
Derek Ager, geologist and Evolutionist

inconceivable. *The absence of transitional forms between the invertebrate retina and that of the vertebrates poses another difficulty. Here there is a great gulf fixed which remains inviolate with no seeming likelihood of ever being bridged. The total picture speaks of intelligent creative design of an infinitely high order."*

[H.S. Hamilton (M.D.), "The Retina of the Eye — An Evolutionary Road Block," *Creation Research Society Quarterly*, Vol. 22, No. 2 (P.O. Box 14016, Terre Haute, Indiana 47803: September 1985), pp. 59-64.]

☐ *"The curious thing, however, is that in their distribution the eyes of the invertebrates form no series of continuity and succession. Without obvious phylogenic sequence, their occurrence seems haphazard; analogous photoreceptors appear in unrelated species, an elaborate organ in a primitive species, or an elementary structure high in the Evolutionary scale, and the same animal may be provided with two different mechanisms with different spectral sensitivities subserving different types of behavior."*

[Sir Stewart Duke-Elder, *The Eye in Evolution* (St. Louis: C.V. Mosby, 1973), p. 178.]

SUGGESTED SOURCES FOR A MORE IN-DEPTH DISCUSSION OF PROBLEMS THE EYE POSES FOR EVOLUTIONISTS

☐ Joseph L. Calkins, "Design in the Human Eye," *Bible-Science Newsletter*, Vol. 24, No. 3 (P.O. Box 32457, Minneapolis, Minnesota 55432, Phone 612-635-0614: Bible-Science Association, March 1986), pp. 1-2, 5.

☐ "Darwin on the Evolution of the Eye: The Full Context," *Origins Research*, Vol. 8, No. 2 (Colorado Springs, Colorado 80937-8069: Students for Origins Research, 1985), pp. 12-13.

☐ I.L. Cohen, "The Eyes," in *Darwin Was Wrong — A Study in Probabilities* (P.O. Box 231, Greenvale, New York 11548: New Research Publications, Inc., 1984), pp. 112-130.

☐ Michael Pitman, *Adam and Evolution* (London: Rider & Company, 1984), pp. 215-218.

193

☐ Evolutionist R. Dawkins

*"...species-level selection *can't explain* the evolution of adaptations: eyes, ears, knee joints, spider webs, behavior patterns, everything, in short, that many of us want a theory of evolution to explain. Species selection may happen, but it doesn't seem to *do* anything much."*

[Richard Dawkins, "What Was All the Fuss About?," *Nature*, Vol. 316 (August 22, 1985), pp. 683-684 (emphasis added).]

194

☐ Randall Hedtke:

*"Darwin finally did deal honestly and objectively with the data; he *abandoned Evolutionary natural selection*. Then, in order to avoid conceding to special Creation and continue to meet the scientific requirement of postulating an ongoing mechanism, he *switched to Jean Lamarck's theory of acquired characters, which never had credibility."*

[Randall Hedtke, "The Divine Essence in Evolutionary Theorizing...," *Creation Research Society Quarterly*, Vol. 21, No. 1 (P.O. Box 14016, Terre Haute, Indiana 47803: June 1984), p. 40 (emphasis added).]

☐ *"*Darwinism has failed in practice*. The whole aim and purpose of Darwinism is to show how modern forms descended from ancient forms, that is, to construct reliable phylogenies (genealogies or family trees). In this *it has utterly failed."* (Retired attorney and Evolutionism researcher Norman Macbeth, author of *Darwin Retried* / J.D. degree from Harvard Law School, B.A. from Stanford University)

[Norman MacBeth, "A Third Position in the Textbook Controversy," *American Biology Teacher*, Vol. 38, No. 8 (November 1976), pp. 495-496 (quote is from p. 495 — emphasis added).]

SUGGESTED SOURCES CONCERNING CREATIONISTS' BELIEF THAT THE GENETIC LAWS STABILIZE THE BASIC KINDS OF ANIMALS (WHAT THEY CALL BARAMINS) WITHIN THEIR OWN BOUNDARIES

☐ Lane Lester and Ray Bohlin, *The Natural Limits of Biological Change* (Grand Rapids, Michigan: Zondervan/Probe, 1984), 207 pp. (careful and refreshing evaluation of Darwinism, neo-Darwinism, and punctuated equilibrium — shows there are limits to biological change).

☐ Michael Denton, *Evolution: A Theory in Crisis* (Bethesda, Maryland: Adler & Adler, 1985, and London: Burnett Books, 1985).

☐ A.J. Jones, "The Genetic Integrity of the 'Kinds' (Baramins): A Working Hypothesis," *Creation Research Society Quarterly*, Vol. 19, No. 1 (P.O. Box 14016, Terre Haute, Indiana 47803: June 1982), pp. 13-18.

☐ Lawrence R. Davie, "A Re-examination of the Role of Mutations and Natural Selection in the Evolution Model of Origins," *Origins Research*, Vol. 3, No. 1 (Colorado Springs, Colorado 80937-8069: Students for Origins Research, 1980), pp. 6-8 (discusses failure of both gene mutations and chromosomal aberrations to account for Evolution).

☐ Frank L. Marsh, *Variation and Fixity in Nature* (Omaha, Nebraska: Pacific Press, 1976).

195

☐ Gordon Taylor:

*"In all the thousands of fly-breeding experiments carried out all over the world for more than fifty years, a distinct new species has *never* been seen to emerge... or even a new enzyme."*

[Gordon R. Taylor, *The Great Evolution Mystery* (New York: Harper and Row, 1983), pp. 34, 38 (emphasis added).]

196

☐ Evolutionist and paleontologist David Kitts of the School of Geology and Geophysics of the University of Oklahoma:

*"Evolution, at least in the sense that Darwin speaks of it, *cannot be detected within the lifetime of a single observer*."*

[David Kitts, "Paleontology and Evolutionary Theory," *Evolution*, Vol. 28 (September 1974), p. 466 (emphasis added).]

☐ *"No one has *ever* produced a species by mechanisms of natural selection. No one has gotten *near* it..."* (C. Patterson, Senior Principal Scientific Officer in the Paleontology Department of the British Museum of Natural History)

[Colin Patterson, "Cladistics," Interview by British Broadcasting Corporation (March 4, 1982) (emphasis added).]

☐ *"Evolution by natural selection would be established today beyond any reasonable doubt, *even without* empirical evidence of intermediates, *if* it had been shown that all the great divisions of nature could *at least theoretically* have been crossed by *inventing* a really convincing series of hypothetical and fully functional transitional forms. However, as we shall see this has never been achieved."* (non-Creationist Dr. Denton)

[Michael Denton, *Evolution: A Theory in Crisis* (Bethesda, Maryland: Adler and Adler Publishers, 1985, and London: Burnett Books, 1985), pp. 200-201 (emphasis added).]

OTHER USEFUL SOURCES OF INFORMATION ON THE ORIGIN OF SPECIES

197

☐ Nancy Pearcey, "World View: What Species of Species? — or, Darwin and the Origin of What?", *Bible-Science Newsletter*, Vol. 27, No. 6 (P.O. Box 32457, Minneapolis, Minnesota 55432, Phone 612-635-0614: Bible-Science Association, June 1989), pp. 7-9 (layman-level article).

☐ Walter E. Lammerts, "Does Chromosomal Reorganization Really Lead to the Origin of New Species?," *Creation Research Society Quarterly*, Vol. 19, No. 1 (P.O. Box 14016, Terre Haute, Indiana 47803: June 1982), pp. 10-13.

☐ Frank L. Marsh, *Variation and Fixity in Nature: The Meaning of Diversity and Discontinuity in the World of Living Things, and Their Bearing on Creation and Evolution* (Mountain View, California: Pacific Press Publishing Association, 1976).

☐ Arthur LaGrange Battson III, "The Paradox of Natural Selection," *Origins Research*, Vol. 9, No. 2 (1986), pp. 1, 3, 6.

☐ Francis Hitching, *The Neck of the Giraffe: Darwin, Evolution and the New Biology* (1982), 258 pp. (written by a non-Creationist / shows the demise of Darwinism / treats the fossil evidence, the insufficiency of mutation and chance, punctuated equilibrium, cladism, etc. / well-documented).

☐ Tom Bethell, "Agnostic Evolutionists: The Taxonomic Case," *Harpers* (February 1985), pp. 49-61 (an article that has had Evolutionists up in arms / includes interviews with Colin Patterson, Gareth Nelson, Norman Platnick, and Richard Lewontin).

THE ORIGIN OF MANKIND

198

☐ Robert Eckhardt:

"*Amid the bewildering array of early fossil hominoids, is there one whose morphology marks it as man's hominid ancestor? If the factor of genetic variability (naturally occurring differences between individuals within a species) is considered, the answer appears to be no.*"

[Robert B. Eckhardt, "Population Genetics and Human Origins," *Scientific American*, Vol. 226, No. 1 (January 1972), p. 94 (emphasis added).]

☐ "*So one is forced to conclude that there is no clearcut scientific picture of human evolution.*" (Dr. R. Martin, Senior Research Fellow at the Zoological Society of London)

[Robert Martin, "Man Is Not an Onion," *New Scientist*, Vol. 75, No. 1063 (August 4, 1977), p. 285.]

RAMAPITHECUS

199

☐ *Ramapithecus* had teeth and dental characteristics very similar to the Gelada baboon (*Theropithecus gelada*). See:

---

*T*he intelligent layman has long suspected circular reasoning in the use of rocks to date fossils and fossils to date rocks. The geologist has never bothered to think of a good reply...

J. O'Rourke in the American Journal of Science

- Richard E. Leakey and Roger Lewin, *Origins* (London: Macdonald and Janes, 1977), p. 68+.
- W.C.O. Hill, *Primates: Comparative Anatomy and Taxonomy*, Vol. VIII—Cynopithecinae (Edinburgh: Edinburgh University Press, 1970), pp. 536-538.

☐ David Pilbeam and Peter Andrews proved that *Ramapithecus* was not in the lineage of man, but rather "part of the orangutan lineage." See:

J. Greenburg, "Fossils Trigger Questions of Human Origins," *Science News*, Vol. 121, No. 5 (January 30, 1982), p. 84.

Peter Andrews, "Hominoid Evolution," *Nature*, Vol. 295, No. 5846 (1982), pp. 185-186.

☐ David Pilbeam, "New Hominoid Skull Material From the Miocene of Pakistan," *Nature*, Vol. 295, No. 5846 (1982), pp. 232-234.

☐ Allen L. Hammond, "Tales of an Elusive Ancestor," *Science 83*, Vol. 4, No. 9 (November 1983), pp. 36-43.

☐ Adrienne L. Zihlman and Jerold M. Lowenstein, "False Start of the Human Parade," *Natural History*, Vol. 88, No. 7 (1979), pp. 86-91 (p. 91 — "The case for Ramapithecus as an ancestral human has been weak from the start and has not strengthened with the passage of time." / also discusses the fact that Louis Leakey incorrectly pieced the skull fragments together to resemble a human jaw).

☐ Leonard O. Greenfield, "A Comment on Relative Molar Breadth in *Ramapithecus*," *Journal of Human Evolution*, Vol. 4, No. 3 (May 1975), pp. 267-273 (*Ramapithecus* molars indicate it was an ape / Greenfield is an Evolutionist and was a faculty member of the Department of Anthropology of the University of Michigan. He measured and examined all the *Ramapithecus* specimens at Yale Peabody Museum, The Geological Survey of India in Calcutta, and the National Museums of Kenya in Nairobi. / p. 268 — Greenfield says, concerning the evidence of the broad molars, "These comparisons suggest that *Ramapithecus* is like its closely related Indian relatives, D. [Dryopithecus] indicus and D. [Dryopithecus] sivalensis.") / p. 272 — *Ramapithecus* broad molars are not relatively broader than those of most pongids.) (The Family. *Pongidae* includes such apes as the orangutan.)

AUSTRALOPITHECUS

200

☐ Evolutionist and paleoanthropologist Professor Joseph Weiner, although claiming *Australopithecus* as an ancestor of man, has conceded:

"*The first impression given by all the skulls from the different populations of Australopithecus is of a distinctly ape-like creature... The ape-like profile of Australopithecus is so pronounced that its outline can be superimposed on that of a female chimpanzee with a remarkable closeness of fit. In this respect, and also in the lack of chin and in the possession of strong supra-orbital ridges, Australopithecus stands in strong contrast to modern (man) Homo sapiens.*"

[Joseph S. Weiner, *The Natural History of Man* (New York: Universe Books, 1971), 255 pp. (quote from pp. 45-46 — emphasis added).]

201

☐ John W. Cuozzo's testimony can be viewed in the Creationist motion picture, *The Origin of Mankind* (Mesa, Arizona: Eden Films and Standard Media, 1983).

☐ Dr. Cuozzo has found examples of modern human jaws which are extremely similar to those of modern apes in the degree of angulation in the jaw and demonstrated a large range of variability in the degree of jaw angulation within both humans and apes. For example, he says there are modern human jaws which are extremely similar to those of known apes in this particular feature. He found a little girl that had a 10- to 12-degree angulation between the two rows of her lower teeth. This happens to be very similar to that of a young chimpanzee.

☐ SUGGESTED SOURCE FOR RELATED EVIDENCE:

Gerald Duffett, "Some Implications of Variant Cranial Capacities for the Best-Preserved Australopithecine Skull Specimens," *Creation Research Society Quarterly*, Vol. 20, No. 2 (P.O. Box 14016, Terre Haute, Indiana 47803: September 1980), pp. 96-104.

202

☐ See: Malcolm Bowden, *Ape-Men: Fact or Fallacy*, second edition (Bromley, Kent, England: Sovereign Publications, 1981).

☐ **Malcolm Bowden**: Civil Engineer / Author / Creationist / An independent Christian researcher, specializing in Creation-Evolution topics, especially the origin of man / Member of the Institute of Civil Engineering.

203

☐ In fact, *Australopithecus* literally means "southern ape."

204

☐ Malcolm Bowden in Willem J.J. Glashouwer and Paul S. Taylor, writers, *The Origin of Mankind* (Mesa, Arizona: Eden Films and Standard Media, 1983) (a Creationist motion picture).

AUSTRALOPITHECUS AND MULTIVARIATE ANALYSIS EXPERT DR. OXNARD

☐ Evolutionist Dr. Charles Oxnard of the University of Chicago:

"These fossils clearly differ more from both humans and African apes, than these two living groups from each other. The australopithecines are unique."

[Charles E. Oxnard, *Fossils, Teeth and Sex: New Perspectives on Human Evolution* (Seattle: University of Washington Press, 1987), p. 227.]

☐ Oxnard conducted multivariate computer analysis on all the fossil parts in 1974 and subsequently strongly rejected australopithecines as being hominids or having anything to do with the ancestry of man. They were simply an extinct form of ape.

[See: Charles E. Oxnard, *University of Chicago Magazine* (Winter 1974), p. 11.]

☐ Paul DuBois, "Lucy Out of Context: A Reply," *Creation Research Society Quarterly*, Vol. 24, No. 3 (P.O. Box 14016, Terre Haute, Indiana 47803: December 1987), pp. 117-119 (discusses Oxnard's views).

☐ Charles E. Oxnard, *The Order of Man: A Biomathematical Anatomy of the Primates* (New Haven, Conn.: Yale University Press, 1983).

☐ Charles E. Oxnard, "Relationship of *Australopithecus* and *Homo*: Another View," *Journal of Human Evolution*, Vol. 8, No. 4 (May 1979), pp. 427-432.

☐ Charles E. Oxnard, "Human Fossils: New Views of Old Bones," *American Biology Teacher*, Vol. 41, No. 5 (May 1979), pp. 264-276.

☐ Charles E. Oxnard, "The Place of *Australopithecus* in Human Evolution: Grounds for Doubt," *Nature*, Vol. 258, No. 5534 (December 4, 1975), pp. 389-395.

205

☐ Sir Solly Zuckerman:

"The australopithecine skull is in fact so <u>overwhelmingly simian, (ape) as opposed to human that the contrary proposition could be equated to an assertion that black is white.</u>" (Zuckerman has been Professor of Anatomy at the University of Birmingham, Secretary of the Zoological Society of London, and chief scientific advisor to the British government.)

[Solly Zuckerman, *Beyond the Ivory Tower* (London: Taplinger Publishing Company, 1970), p. 78 (emphasis added).]

206

☐ Donald C. Johanson, D.Johanson and Maitland A. Edey, *Lucy: The Beginnings of Mankind* (New York: Simon and Schuster, 1981).

207

☐ Richard Leakey is the Director of National Museums of Kenya, Africa. He is the son of Louis Leakey, whose "missing link" research was often reported in *National Geographic*.

☐ *"Echoing the criticism made of his father's Homo habilis skulls, he (Richard Leakey) added that Lucy's skull was so incomplete that most of it was 'imagination, made of plaster of paris,' thus making it impossible to draw any firm conclusion about what species she belonged to."*

[*The Weekend Australian* (May 7-8, 1983), p. 3.]

208

☐ Henry M. McHenry, "The Capitate of *Australopithecus Afarensis* and *A. Africanus*," *American Journal of Physical Anthropology*, Vol. 62, No. 2 (1983), pp. 187-198 (p. 187 — Compares the post-cranium of both *Australopithecus afarensis* and *Australopithecus africanus*, and shows they are "strikingly similar" / p. 196 — Says "Lucy's" pelvis is "astoundingly similar" to some specimens of *africanus*).

☐ Ivan M. Suzman, "A Comparative Study of the Hadar and Sterkfontein Australopithecine Innominates," *American Journal of Physical Anthropology*, Vol. 57, No. 2 (February 1982), p. 235 (Compares the pelvises of *africanus* and "Lucy" and says they are "strikingly similar" — differences are within the range of variation found between human individuals / Says "Lucy" may be *africanus*).

209

☐ William L. Jungers, "Lucy's Limbs: Skeletal Allometry and Locomotion in *Australopithecus Afarensis*," *Nature*, Vol. 24 (June 1982), pp. 676-678 (analysis of "Lucy's" anatomical structure shows she may not normally have walked upright).

☐ Two researchers from New York University have reportedly shown that "Lucy's" thumbs, limb proportions, and toes indicate that much of the time *she probably nested in the trees and lived like other monkeys.*

[Jack T. Stern, Jr. and Randall L. Susman, "The Locomotor Anatomy of *Australopithecus Afarensis*," American Journal of Physical Anthropology, Vol. 60 (March 1983), pp. 279-317.]

[(anonymous author), "The Debate Continues: Lucy in the Trees," *Bible-Science Newsletter*, Vol. 20, No. 10 (P.O. Box 32457, Minneapolis, Minnesota 55432, Phone 612-635-0614: Bible-Science Association, October 1982), p. 4.]

☐ A questioning of "Lucy's" discoverer, Donald Johanson, revealed that the "important" knee joint displayed for "Lucy" was found *"60 to 70 meters* [over 200 feet] *lower in the strata and 2 to 3 kilometers* [1.24 to 1.86 miles] *away."*

[Tom Willis, "'Lucy' Goes to College," *Bible-Science Newsletter*, Vol. 25, No. 10 (P.O. Box 32457, Minneapolis, Minnesota 55432, Phone 612-635-0614: Bible-Science Assn., October 1987), p. 2.]

SOURCES FOR OTHER EVIDENCE AGAINST *AUSTRALOPITHECINES* AS ANCESTORS OF MAN

☐ Paul DuBois, "Creationist Evaluation of *Australopithecus Afarensis*," *Creation Research Society Quarterly*, Vol. 25, No. 2 (P.O. Box 14016, Terre Haute, Indiana 47803: September 1988), pp. 65-69.

☐ Tom Willis, "'Lucy' Goes to College," *Bible-Science Newsletter*, Vol. 25, No. 10 (P.O. Box 32457, Minneapolis, Minnesota 55432: Bible-Science Assn., October 1987), pp. 1-5.

☐ Albert W. Mehlert, Book Review, *Creation Research Society Quarterly*, Vol. 24 (P.O. Box 14016, Terre Haute, Indiana 47803: 1987), pp. 92-102.

☐ Henry M. Morris and Gary E. Parker, *What is Creation Science?* (El Cajon, California: Master Books, 1987).

☐ G.H. Duffett, "Human Origins and the Olduvai Finds," in E.H. Andrews, W. Gitt and W.J. Ouweneel, editors, *Concepts in Creationism* (Phillipsburg, New Jersey: Presbyterian and Reformed Publishing, 1986).

☐ Dennis W. Cheek, "The Creationist and Neo-Darwinian Views Concerning the Origin of the Order Primates Compared and Contrasted: A Preliminary Analysis," *Creation Research Society Quarterly*, Vol. 18, No. 2 (P.O. Box 14016, Terre Haute, Indiana 47803: September 1981), pp. 99-102.

☐ Albert W. Mehlert, "The Australopithecines and (Alleged) Early Man," *Creation Research Society Quarterly*, Vol. 17, No. 1 (P.O. Box 14016, Terre Haute, Indiana 47803: June 1980), pp. 23-27.

210

☐ Paleontologist Adrienne Zihlman, University of California at Santa Cruz:

"Lucy's fossil remains match up remarkably well with the bones of a pygmy chimp" (although there are some differences).

[Adrienne Zihlman, "Pygmy Chimps, People, and the Pundits," *New Scientist*, Vol. 104, No. 1430 (November 15, 1984), pp. 39-40 (quote from: p. 39).]

☐ Herbert Wray, "Lucy's Uncommon Forebear," *Science News*, Vol. 123 (February 5, 1983), p. 89.

☐ *"The evidence given above makes it overwhelmingly likely that Lucy was no more than a variety of pygmy chimpanzee, and walked the same way (awkwardly upright on occasions, but mostly quadrupedal). The 'evidence' for the alleged transformation from ape to man is extremely unconvincing."* (Former Evolutionist and paleoanthropology researcher Albert William Mehlert, Australia)

[Albert W. Mehlert, "Lucy — Evolution's Solitary Claim for an Ape/Man: Her Position is Slipping Away," *Creation Research Society Quarterly*, Vol. 22, No. 3 (P.O. Box 14016, Terre Haute, Indiana 47803: December 1985), p. 145 (emphasis added).]

☐ Albert W. Mehlert, "A Study of Comments by Evolutionist Authorities on the Alleged Hominids Found in the Hadar/Afar Region of Africa," *Contrast: The Creation Evolution Controversy*, Vol. 6, No. 1 (P.O. Box 32457, Minneapolis, Minnesota 55432,

Phone 612-635-0614: January/February 1987), pp. 1-2, 4 (provides evidence that "Lucy" was made up of fossils from two separate sites and was an ape, *"probably a chimp-like ape"*).

HOMO HABILIS

211

☐ Albert W. Mehlert, "Homo Habilis Dethroned," *Contrast: The Creation Evolution Controversy*, Vol. 6, No. 6 (P.O. Box 32457, Minneapolis, Minnesota 55432, Phone 612-635-0614: November/December 1987), pp. 1-2.

☐ Albert W. Mehlert, "Lucy — Evolution's Solitary Claim for an Ape/Man: Her Position is Slipping Away," *Creation Research Society Quarterly*, Vol. 22, No. 3 (P.O. Box 14016, Terre Haute, Indiana 47803: December 1985), pp. 144-145 (p. 145 — concludes that it is *"overwhelmingly likely that Lucy was no more than a variety of pygmy chimpanzee... The 'evidence' for the alleged transformation from ape to man is extremely unconvincing."*).

☐ Duane T. Gish, *Evolution: The Challenge of the Fossil Record* (El Cajon, California: Master Books, 1985).

☐ Paul Lysen, "Was *Australopithecus* Bipedal?: The Evidence from Morphometric Analysis", *Contrast: The Creation Evolution Controversy*, Vol. 3, No. 1 (P.O. Box 32457, Minneapolis, Minnesota 55432, Phone 612-635-0614: January/February 1984), pp. 1-2, 4.

SINANTHROPUS

212

☐ Some researchers have suggested that the mysterious disappearance of the bones of these apes and the concealment of the human remains at the site may have been part of a cover-up by overzealous Evolutionists trying to keep belief in Peking Man alive. Others believe it was just a twist of fate.

> *T*he uniform, continuous transformation of Hyracotherium into Equus, so dear to the hearts of generations of textbook writers, never happened in nature...
>
> *George Simpson, paleontologist and Evolutionist*

213

☐ Patrick O'Connell, *The Science of Today and the Problems of Genesis* (Hawthorne, California: Christ. Book Club, 1969), pp. 108-138.

214

☐ Concerning "Peking Man" skull number 11, it should be noted that the human-like reconstructions were based on the following quality of evidence:

• The skull was badly broken and far from complete.
• The facial bones which were combined with the rest of the skull came from a few feet away, and therefore may not actually belong to "Nellie".
• The toothless lower jaw came from a part of the excavation 80 feet higher than the skull cap fragments!

215

☐ Malcolm Bowden, *Ape-Men: Fact or Fallacy*, 2nd edition (Bromley, Kent, England: Sovereign Publications, 1981).

☐ Ian T. Taylor, *In the Minds of Men: Darwin and the New World Order* (Toronto, Canada: TFE Publishing, 1984), pp. 234-241.

☐ Marcellin Boule and Henri Vallois, *Fossil Men* (New York: Dryden Press, 1957), p. 145 (2 Evolutionists who acknowledged the possibility that *Sinanthropus* was an ape killed by humans).

216

☐ Malcolm Bowden in Willem J.J. Glashouwer and Paul S. Taylor, writers, *The Origin of Mankind* (Mesa, Arizona: Eden Films and Standard Media, 1983) (Creationist motion picture).

PITHECANTHROPUS

217

☐ Dubois also found 2 totally human skulls nearby at approximately the same level in strata which some say are dated similarly (the Wadjak skulls). At the time that Dubois was widely promoting Java Man as a missing link, he never mentioned these skulls — for obvious reasons. If he had shown these very human skulls at the same time that he exhibited his Java Man, nobody would have accepted Java Man as the "missing link". He kept them secret for 30 years. It was not until 1920 that he released this information to the scientific world. See:

Eugene Dubois, "The Proto-Australian Fossil Man of Wadjak, Java," *Koninklijke Akademie van Wetenschappen*, proceedings, Vol. 13 (Amsterdam: Koninklijke Akademie, 1920), p. 1013.

Malcolm Bowden, *Ape-Men: Fact or Fallacy* (Bromley, Kent, England: Sovereign Publications, 1977), p. 131.

Wilbert H. Rusch, Sr., "Human Fossils," in Paul A. Zimmerman, editor, *Rock Strata and the Bible Record* (St. Louis: Concordia Publishing House, 1970), p. 134.

218

☐ Eugene Dubois, "On the Gibbon-like Appearance of *Pithecanthropus erectus*," *Koninklijke Akademie van Wetenschappen*, proceedings, Vol. 38 (Amsterdam: Koninklijke Akademie, 1935), p. 578.

☐ Eugene Dubois, "On the Fossil Human Skulls Recently Discovered in Java and *Pithecanthropus Erectus*," *Man*, Vol. 37 (January 1937), p. 4 (as cited by Dr. Walter T. Brown, Jr.) (Dubois: "*Pithecanthropus* [Java man] was not a man, but a gigantic genus allied to the Gibbons...").

☐ Herbert Wendt, *In Search of Adam* (Westport, Connecticut: Greenwood Press, 1955), p. 299.

☐ C. Loring Brace and Ashley Montagu, *Human Evolution: An Introduction to Biological Anthropology* (New York: MacMillan Publishing Co., 1977), p. 204.

☐ Concerning the "Java Man" skulls, Joseph Birdsell points out that the basal portion was removed in a way that suggests these apes were killed by a human for the purpose of eating the brain.

[Joseph B. Birdsell, *Human Evolution: An Introduction to the New Physical Anthropology* (Chicago: Rand-McNally College Publishing Co., 1975), p. 294.]

SUGGESTED SOURCES FOR FURTHER INFORMATION ON *PITHECANTHROPUS*

☐ Malcolm Bowden, *Ape-Men: Fact or Fallacy*, 2nd edition (Bromley, Kent, England: Sovereign Publications, 1981).

☐ Ian T. Taylor, *In the Minds of Men: Darwin and the New World Order* (Toronto, Canada: TFE Publishing, 1984), pp. 221-225.

NEBRASKA MAN

219

☐ Named after its discoverer, geologist Mr. Harold J. Cook.

220

☐ G. Elliot Smith, "The Ape-Man of the Western World," *The Illustrated London News* (June 24, 1922), p. 944.

☐ G. Elliot Smith, *The Evolution of Man* (London: Oxford University Press, 1924), pp. 7, 9.

☐ Harris H. Wilder, *The Pedigree of the Human Race* (New York: Henry Holt and Company, 1926), pp. 156-157.

221

☐ Henry Fairfield Osborn, "*Hesperopithecus*, The First Anthropoid Primate Found in America," *Science*, Vol. 60, No. 1427 (May 5, 1922), p. 463.

☐ Henry Fairfield Osborn, "*Hesperopithecus*, The First Anthropoid Primate Found in America,", *American Museum Noviates*, No. 37 (1922), p. 2.

☐ Henry Fairfield Osborn, "*Hesperopithecus*, The First Anthropoid Primate Found in America," *Nature*, Vol. 110 (1922), p. 281.

☐ Dr. William K. Gregory and Mr. Milo Hellman, "Further Notes on the Molars of *Hesperopithecus*," *Bulletin of the American Museum of Natural History*, Vol. XLVII (1923), p. 509.

☐ **Henry Fairfield Osborn** (1857-1935): Evolutionist / Paleontologist, specializing in vertebrates / Eugenicist (student of how to improve the human race through selective breeding) / Former president of the American Museum of Natural History (25 years, beginning in 1908) / Former faculty member of Princeton University (1891) / Founded the Department of Biology at Columbia University / Fought against the anti-Evolutionism statute of Tennessee made famous by the Scopes "Monkey" Trial).

222

☐ It is said that Evolutionist Clarence Darrow exhibited a picture of "Nebraska Man" during the trial and said, "See, Bryan, even your own state of Nebraska has a fossil that shows there are missing links and that Evolution is viable."

223

☐ G. Elliot Smith, "Hesperopithecus: The Ape-Man of the Western World," *Illustrated London News*, Vol. 160 (June 24, 1922), pp. 942-944 (two illustrations).

224

☐ The pig was then identified as *Prosthennops serus* (equivalent to *Catagonus wagneri*), but in 1972 it was discovered that the same species is alive today in Paraguay — *Catagonus ameghino*.

[William K. Gregory, "*Hesperopithecus* Apparently Not an Ape nor a Man," *Science*, Vol. 66, No. 1720 (December 16, 1927); Ralph M. Wetzel, et al, "*Catagonus*, An 'Extinct' Peccary, Alive in Paraguay," *Science*, Vol. 189, No. 4200 (August 1, 1975), p. 379.]

☐ Commenting on a similar situation, Dr. Tim White (Evolutionary anthropologist, University of California at Berkeley) is quoted as saying:

"A five million year old piece of bone that was thought to be a collarbone of a humanlike creature is actually part of a dolphin rib... The problem with a lot of anthropologists is that they want so much to find a hominid (a so-called 'ape-man') that any scrap of bone becomes a hominid bone."

[Ian Anderson, "Hominoid Collarbone Exposed as Dolphin's Rib," *New Scientist, Vol. 98, No. 1355 (April 28, 1983), p. 199.]

PILTDOWN MAN

225

☐ **Piltdown Man:** Ape jaw with teeth filed and jaw damaged to hide its true identity / human skull / bones stained to appear old.

☐ Joseph S. Weiner, *The Piltdown Forgery* (London: Oxford University Press, 1955) *(suggests Charles Dawson as the hoaxer)*.

☐ Kenneth P. Oakley and Joseph S. Weiner, "Piltdown Man," *American Scientist*, Vol. 43, No. 4 (October 1955).

☐ Anonymous, "Piltdown Man," *Nature*, Vol. 172, No. 4387 (November 28, 1953), p. 981.

☐ Kenneth P. Oakley and Joseph S. Weiner, "Chemical Examination of the Piltdown Implements," *Nature*, Vol. 172, No. 4389 (December 12, 1953), p. 1110.

☐ Report from meeting of Geological Society, "The Piltdown Bones and Implements," *Nature*, Vol. 174, No. 4419 (July 10, 1954), p. 61.

☐ Joseph S. Weiner, "Obituaries of the Piltdown Remains," *Nature*, Vol. 175, No. 4457 (April 2, 1955), p. 569.

☐ Malcolm Bowden, *Ape-Men: Fact or Fallacy* (Bromley, Kent, England: Sovereign Publications, 1977), pp. 3-43 (provides great detail on the fraud and suggests the hoaxer was the well-known Evolutionist Pierre Teilhard de Chardin S.J.).

☐ Ronald Millar, *The Piltdown Men* (suggests Grafton Smith as the hoaxer).

NEANDERTHAL MAN

226

☐ Neanderthals are officially classified as *Homo sapiens neanderthalensis*.

☐ C. Loring Brace, physical anthropologist and Evolutionist of University of Michigan confirms that Neanderthal traits still persist in some people today:

"*If modern cranial form is appraised worldwide in regard to these same attributes, then it is clear that northwest Europeans can be distinguished from the rest of the people in the world by precisely the same set of characteristics.*"

[Carle Hodge, "Neanderthal Traits Extant, Group Told," *The Arizona Republic*, Vol. 99, No. 186 (Phoenix: November 20, 1988), p. B-5 (emphasis added) (Hodge: "*Neanderthals had short, narrow skulls, large cheekbones and noses and, most distinctive, bunlike bony bumps on the backs of their heads. Many modern Danes and Norwegians have identical features,* Brace reported at the annual meeting of the American Anthropological Association in Phoenix... *Indeed, the present-day European skulls resemble Neanderthal skulls more closely than they resemble the skulls of American Indians or Australian aborigines,* he said. *And their skulls are about the same height and length as those of Neanderthals.* Brace...*measured more than 500 relatively modern northwestern European craniums last year in museums in Denmark, Norway, Finland and England.*" (emphasis added).]

My attempts to demonstrate Evolution by an experiment carried on for more than 40 years have completely failed.

N.H. Nilsson, famous botanist and Evolutionist

SUGGESTED SOURCES FOR FURTHER INFORMATION ON NEANDERTHALS BEING COMPLETELY HUMAN

☐ Boyce Rensberger and Jay Matternes, "Facing the Past," *Science 81*, Vol. 2, No. 8 (October 1981), pp. 41-50 (mentions that the usual portrayals of Neanderthals as bull-necked, slouching brutes was based on a skeleton deformed by age and arthritis, La Chapelle-aux-Saints skeleton / mentions newer evidence that Neanderthals took care of the lame and old, buried loved ones with ceremony, etc. / author concludes: "the story of human evolution has been fictionalized to suit needs other than scientific rigor.").

☐ Erich A. von Fange, "Neanderthal, Oh How I Need You!," *Creation Research Society Quarterly*, Vol. 18, No. 3 (P.O. Box 14016, Terre Haute, Indiana 47803: December 1980), pp. 140-154.

☐ Arthur C. Custance, "The Fallacy of Anthropological Reconstructions," Doorway Paper No. 33 ((P.O. Box 291, Brockville, Ontario, Canada K6V 5V5: Doorway Publications, 1966), pp. 5-12.

☐ Jacob W. Gruber, "The Neanderthal Controversy: Nineteenth-Century Version," *Scientific Monthly*, Vol. 67, (December 1948), pp. 436-439; and *Creation Research Society Quarterly*, Vol. 3, No. 4 (P.O. Box 14016, Terre Haute, Indiana 47803: March 1967), p. 24 (say that in 1947 two skulls of *Homo sapiens-sapiens* were found lower than the tools of Neanderthals).

☐ William Howells, editor, *Ideas on Human Evolution* (NYC: Atheneum, 1962), p. 524 (Homo sapiens predated Neanderthals).

☐ Duane T. Gish, *Evolution: The Fossils Say No!* (San Diego: CLP Publishers, 1979), pp. 106-162.

227

☐ 1600 cubic centimeters was the average brain capacity of Neanderthals.

[Robert Charroux, *Masters of the World* (New York: Berkley Medallion Book, 1974), p. 248.]

☐ The average for humans today is estimated at 1450 to 1500 cubic centimeters.

[M.H. van der Veer and P. Moerman, *Hidden Worlds* (New York: Bantam Books, 1972), p. 31.]

228

☐ George Constable, *The Neanderthals* (New York: Time-Life Books, 1973), pp. 14-17.

☐ Frank E. Poirier, *Fossil Man* (St. Louis: Mosby, 1973), pp. 176-177.

☐ D.J.M. Wright, "Syphilis and Neanderthal Man," *Nature*, Vol. 229, No. 5284 (February 5, 1971), p. 409.

☐ Francis Ivanhoe, "Was Virchow Right About Neanderthal?," *Nature*, Vol. 227, No. 5258 (August 8, 1970), pp. 577-579.

☐ William L. Straus, Jr. and A.J.E. Cave, "Pathology and the Posture of Neanderthal Man," *The Quarterly Review of Biology* (1957), pp. 348-363.

229

☐ See: *University of Nebraska, Lincoln, News, Museum Notes No. 54*, Vol. 55, No. 11 (1975), p. 2 (*Evidence that Neanderthal characteristics are common among historic Indians*).

230

☐ Evolutionist Zuckerman, D.Sc. in Anatomy, M.D.:

"*No scientist could logically dispute the proposition that man, without having been involved in any act of divine creation, evolved from some ape-like creature in a very short space of time — speaking in geological terms — without leaving any fossil traces of the steps of the transformation. As I have already implied, students of fossil primates have not been distinguished for caution... The record is so astonishing that it is legitimate to ask whether much science is yet to be found in this field at all.*"

[Sir Solly Zuckerman, *Beyond the Ivory Tower* (London: Weidenfeld & Nicholson, 1970), p. 64 (emphasis added).]

☐ "*Modern apes, for instance, seem to have sprung out of nowhere. They have no yesterday, no fossil record. And the true origin of modern humans — of upright, naked, toolmaking, big-brained beings — is, if we are to be honest with ourselves, an equally mysterious matter.*" (Evolutionist Dr. L. Watson)

[Lyall Watson, "The Water People," *Science* Digest, Vol. 90, No. 5 (May 1982), p. 44 (emphasis added).]

MOLECULES OF APES AND MEN

231

☐ Evolutionist and paleoanthropologist Joseph Weiner:

"*It is quite obvious that modern man could not have arisen from any ape, let alone monkey, at all similar to those of today... it is ridiculous to describe man as a "naked" or any other kind of ape.*"

[Joseph S. Weiner, *The Natural History of Man* (New York: Universe Books, 1971), p. 33 (emphasis added).]

232

☐ L. James Gibson, "A Creationist View of Chromosome Banding and Evolution," *Origins*, Vol. 13, No. 1 (Loma Linda, California: Geoscience Research Institute, Loma Linda University, 1986) (contains more than 100 citations giving a thorough overview of chromosome banding).

☐ A.J. Jones, "A Creationist Critique of Homology," *Creation Research Society Quarterly*, Vol. 19, No. 3 (P.O. Box 14016, Terre Haute, Indiana 47803: December 1982), pp. 156-175.

MOLECULAR STUDIES ARE NOT PROVIDING THE EVIDENCE EVOLUTIONISTS HAD HOPED.

233

☐ Evolutionist Michael Denton, Ph.D.:

"*The (E)volutionary interpretation of homology is clouded even further by the uncomfortable fact that there are many cases of 'homologous like' resemblance which cannot by any stretch of the imagination be explained by descent from a common ancestor.*"

[Michael Denton, *Evolution: A Theory in Crisis* (Bethesda, Maryland: Adler and Adler Publishers, 1985), p. 151 (emphasis added).]

☐ Wolfgang Smith, Ph.D.:

"*It has often been claimed, moreover, that these new and momentous findings have at last unearthed the true mechanism of (E)volution, and that we are presently on the brink of discovering precisely how macroevolution has come about. However, the truth of the matter is very much the opposite: now that the actual physical structure of what might be termed the biochemical mainstays of life has come into view, scientists are finding — frequently to their dismay — that the evolutionist thesis has become more stringently unthinkable than ever before... on the molecular level, these separations, and this hierarchic order stand out with a mathematical precision which once and for all silences dissent. On the funamental level it becomes a rigorously demonstrable*

fact that there are no transitional types, and that the so-called missing links are indeed non-existent."

[Wolfgang Smith, *Teilhardism and the New Religion: A Thorough Analysis of the Teachings of Pierre Teilhard de Chardin* (P.O. Box 424, Rockford, Illinois 61105: Tan Books and Publishers, Inc., 1988), p. 8 (emphasis added).]

☐ "*Hence, for the gorilla-chimp-human portion of the phylogeny, there is a strong rejection of the molecular clock hypothesis... Moreover, the molecular clock hypothesis was rejected at the 1% level.*" (meaning they are 99% sure that this hypothesis concerning apes and humans is wrong) (Evolutionist Alan Templeton in the journal of the Society for the Study of Evolution)

[Alan Templeton, *Evolution*, Vol. 37, No. 2 (March 1983), pp. 221-244 (quote is from pp. 238 and 242 — emphasis added).]

☐ Biochemist and molecular Evolutionist Christian Schwabe of the Department of Biochemisty at the Medical University of South Carolina strongly *disagrees* with Evolutionists who say molecular biology confirms common descent in every respect:

"*...it seems disconcerting that many exceptions exist to the orderly progression of species as determined by molecular homologies; so many in fact that I think the exception, the quirks, may carry the more important message.*"

[Christian Schwabe, "On the Validity of Molecular Evolution," *Trends in Biochemical Sciences*, Vol. 11, No. 7 (July 1986), pp. 280-283 (quote is from p. 280).]

☐ Evolutionists Lisa Vawter and Wesley Brown suggest throwing out the molecular clock idea altogether, saying there is evidence for:

"*...robust rejection of a generalized molecular clock hypothesis of DNA (E)volution.*"

[Lisa Vawter and Wesley M. Brown, "Nuclear and Mitochondrial DNA Comparisons Reveal Extreme Rate Variation in the Molecular Clock," *Science*, Vol. 234, No. 4773 (October 10, 1986), pp. 194-196 (quote is from their abstract).]

234

☐ Anatomy expert Arthur Keith lists 312 characteristics that are only found in man. [Bernhard Grzimek, editor, *Grzimek's Animal Life Encyclopedia*, Vol. 10, Mammals I, (1975), p. 488.]

SUGGESTED SOURCES FOR MORE INFORMATION ON DIFFERENCES BETWEEN HUMANS AND APES

☐ Kevin C. McLeod, "Studying the Human Brain," *Creation Research Society Quarterly*, Vol. 20, No. 2 (P.O. Box 14016, Terre Haute, Indiana 47803: September 1983), pp. 75-79 (Provides evidence that man and his brain are unique creations).

☐ Jerry Bergman, "Is Language an Exclusive Ability of Man?," *Creation Research Society Quarterly*, Vol. 17, No. 4 (P.O. Box 14016, Terre Haute, Indiana 47803: March 1981), pp. 214-216, 226.

☐ John W. Klotz, "Is the Ability to Use Language Uniquely Human?," *Creation Research Society Quarterly*, Vol. 17, No. 4 (P.O. Box 14016, Terre Haute, Indiana 47803: March 1981), pp. 217-218, 226.

☐ Dennis W. Cheek, "The Creationist and Neo-Darwinian Views Concerning the Origin of the Order Primates Compared and Contrasted: A Preliminary Analysis," *Creation Research Society Quarterly*, Vol. 18, No. 2 (P.O. Box 14016, Terre Haute, Indiana 47803: September 1981), pp. 102-104.

☐ Brian D. Forquer, "The Origin of the Human Speech and Hearing Mechanisms," *Origins Research*, Part I (Vol. 1, No. 2), Part II

(Vol. 1, No. 3), Part III (Vol. 3, No. 2) (Colorado Springs, Colorado 80937-8069: Students for Origins Research, 1980).

235

☐ DIPLOID CHROMOSOME NUMBER IN BODY CELLS

- 2 ......Worm (*Ascaris*)
- 6 ......Mosquito
- 8 ......Vinegar fly
- 12 .....Housefly
- 16 .....Onion (*Allium cepa*)
- 18 .....Cabbage / Radish
- 20 .....Indian corn
- 22 .....Bean
- 24 .....Yellow pine / Tomato
- 32 .....Honeybee (female) / Hydra
- 38 .....Cat
- 40 .....Mouse (*Mus musculus*) / Pig
- 42 .....Rat / Bread wheat (*Trilicum vulgare*)
- 46 .....Human
- 48 .....Tobacco / Rhesus monkey / Platyfish / Potato
- 52 .....Upland cotton
- 54 .....Sheep
- 60 .....Cattle
- 66 .....Horse
- 78 .....Dog / Chicken
- 94 .....Goldfish
- 100 ....Crayfish
- 254 ....Shrimp (*Eupagurus ochotensis*)

[Edmund W. Sinnott, L.C. Dunn, and Theodosius Dobzhansky, *Principles of Genetics*, 5th edition (New York: McGraw-Hill, 1958), p. 11.]

[Frank L. Marsh, *Variation and Fixity in Nature* (Mountain View, California: Pacific Press Publishing Association, 1976), p. 43.]

SUGGESTED SOURCES FOR LAYMAN-LEVEL DISCUSSIONS OF CHROMOSOME NUMBERS AND EVOLUTION

☐ Paul A. Bartz, "Questions and Answers on Creationism: Does the Chromosome Number Have Anything to do with the Supposed Evolutionary Placement of Creatures?", *Bible-Science Newsletter*, Vol. 25, No. 7 (P.O. Box 32457, Minneapolis, Minnesota 55432, Phone 612-635-0614: Bible-Science Association, July 1987), p. 12.

236

☐ Molecular genetics researcher Michael Denton, molecular biologist and medical doctor:

"The really significant finding that comes to light from comparing the proteins' amino acid sequences is that it is impossible to arrange them in any sort of an evolutionary series."

[Michael Denton, *Evolution: A Theory in Crisis* (London: Burnett Books, 1985), p. 289.]

☐ Biochemistry researcher Mark Dwinell concerning the "molecular clock" idea which seeks to show Evolutionary relationships between creatures:

"The seemingly plausible theory, however, is _fraught_ with difficulties for the evolutionists. ..._Any_ attempt to promote this theory as reasonable and valid in light of so _many_ _discrepancies_ seems deceptive or duplicitous."

[Mark Dwinell, "Molecular Evolution or Bust," *Origins Research*, Vol. 8, No. 2 (Colorado Springs, Colorado 80937-8069: Students for Origins Research, 1985), pp. 1-11 (quote from pp. 1 and 11 — emphasis added).]

SUGGESTED SOURCES FOR FURTHER INFORMATION ON THIS AND OTHER QUESTIONS OF HOMOLOGIES

☐ Wendell R. Bird, "The Postulated Evidence for Macroevolution and Darwinism: Darwinian Arguments and the Disintegrating Neo-Darwinian Synthesis — Part II," *Creation Research Society Quarterly*, Vol. 25, No. 2 (P.O. Box 14016, Terre Haute, Indiana 47803: September 1988), pp. 74-81.

☐ Luther D. Sunderland, "Homology," in Luther D. Sunderland, *Darwin's Enigma: Fossils and Other Problems*, 4th edition (Santee, California: Master Books, 1988), pp. 122-130.

☐ Gary E. Parker, "Evidence of Creation in Living Things," in Henry M. Morris and Gary E. Parker, *What Is Creation Science?*, Revised and Expanded edition (San Diego: Master Books, 1987), pp. 52-61.

☐ Michael Denton, *Evolution: A Theory in Crisis* (London: Burnett Books, 1985).

☐ Mark Dwinell, "Molecular Evolution or Bust," *Origins Research*, Vol. 8, No. 2 (Colorado Springs, Colorado 80937-8069: Students for Origins Research, 1985), pp. 1-11.

☐ Dennis W. Cheek, "The Creationist and Neo-Darwinian Views Concerning the Origin of the Order Primates Compared and Contrasted: A Preliminary Analysis," *Creation Research Society Quarterly*, Vol. 18, No. 2 (P.O. Box 14016, Terre Haute, Indiana 47803: September 1981), p. 95.

237

☐ Michael Denton, *Evolution: A Theory in Crisis* (London: Burnett Books, 1985), 368 pp.

HAS MAN ALWAYS BEEN MAN? AND HAVE APES ALWAYS BEEN APES?

238

☐ Evolutionist Stephen Jay Gould of Harvard has admitted:

"We're not just evolving slowly. For all practical purposes _we're not_ _evolving_. There's no reason to think we're going to get bigger brains or smaller toes or whatever — we are what we are."

[Stephen Gould in an October 1983 speech reported in "John Lofton's Journal," *The Washington Times* (February 8, 1984) (emphasis added).]

☐ "Humans are _not_ evolving." (Ronald Strahan, former Senior Research Secretary and Director of Taronga Park Zoo, Sydney, Australia and Honorary Secretary of ANZAAS)

[*The Northern Territory News* (September 14, 1983) (emphasis added).]

239

☐ Frank W. Cousins, *Fossil Man, revised edition* (Emsworth: Evolution Protest Movement, 1971).

> *None of the five museum officials could offer a single example of a transitional series of fossilized organisms that would document the transformation of one basically different type to another.*
>
> *Luther Sunderland, science researcher*

240

☐ REMAINS WHICH SOME RESEARCHERS HAVE SUGGESTED (BUT NOT PROVEN!) AS EVIDENCE THAT THE VARIOUS "MISSING LINKS" WERE CONTEMPORANEOUS, OR THAT MAN AND THESE CREATURES WERE CONTEMPORANEOUS

- **PETRALONA MAN** [Aris N. Poulianos, *Current Anthropology*, Vol. 22, No. 3 (June 1981), p. 287 (Petralona Man found in a stalagmite in Greece, "dated 700 thousand years old"). Also, see: *Chicago Tribune*, Reuters dispatch (June 6, 1976) (Petralona Man — *"The skeleton was found preserved in a stalagmite during an exploration of the Petralona Cave in the Chalkidike Peninsula in southern Greece, said Dr. Aria Poulianos, President of the Greek Anthropological Society, Friday... 'We discovered the cooked meat of rhinoceros, bear and deer, which proves men who lived in the cave made logical use of fire,' Poulianos said."*); mentioned in Henry M. Morris, *Creation and the Modern Christian* (El Cajon, California: Master Books, 1985), pp. 187-189.]
- **CHINESE "HUMAN" JAWBONE** ["Chinese Report Jawbone Goes Back 2 Million Years," *Mesa Tribune* (Mesa, Arizona: November 20, 1988) (*"A human jawbone... with several teeth was discovered in 1986 near the upper reaches of the Yangtze River in Sichuan province..."* / "dated" 2 million years old — "Peking Man" and "Java Man" are generally "dated" at less than 500 thousand years old).]
- **MOUNT CARMEL (PALESTINE)** *HOMO SAPIENS-SAPIENS* **REMAINS** said to be contemporary with Neanderthal remains, discrediting Neanderthal as the ancestor [Malcolm Bowden, *Ape-Men: Fact or Fallacy?* (P.O. Box 88, Bromley, Kent, England BR2 9PF: Sovereign Publications, 1977), p. 155.]
- **CASTENEDOLO MAN SKULL** found in a clay stratum in Castenedolo, Italy (Pliocene). It is said that there was no evidence of intrusive burial through the strata above or below. [Sir Arthur Keith, *The Antiquity of Man*, Vol. 1, 2nd edition (London: Williams and Norgate, 1925), 376 pp., see pp. 334-341; Malcolm Bowden, *Ape-Men: Fact or Fallacy?* (Bromley, Kent, England: Sovereign Publications, 1977), pp. 66-67, 77.]
- **"HUMAN" SKELETON (OLDOWAY MAN)** found by Hans Reck in Bed-II, Olduvai Gorge in the stratum immediately above *Australopithecus robustus* (Zinjanthropus) [Hans Reck, "The Oldoway Skeleton from Tanganyika Territory, *Man*, Vol. 31 (1931), pp. 10-11; Ian T. Taylor, *In the Minds of Men* (Toronto: TFE Publishing, 1984), pp. 244-245; Malcolm Bowden, *Ape-Men: Fact or Fallacy?* (Bromley, Kent, England: Sovereign Publications, 1977), pp. 173-179.] Some have suggested this skeleton is an intrusive burial. [P.G.H. Boswell, "The Oldoway Human Skeleton," *Nature*, Vol. 130 (August 13, 1932), pp. 237-238.]
- **SWANSCOMBE MAN** [Malcolm Bowden, *Ape-Men: Fact or Fallacy?* (Bromley, Kent, England: Sovereign Publications, 1977), pp. 16, 57, 63, 68-70, 71-72, 76, 151-154, 180] W. Fix: *"In conjunction with Swanscombe, Steinheim, and Fontechevade, it certainly shows that there is significant evidence that modern-type humans were in existence long before Neanderthal. Accordingly, it is difficult to see how Neanderthal could have been our ancestor."* [William R. Fix, *The Bone Peddlers* (New York: Macmillan Publishing Company, 1984), p. 105.]
- **VERTESSZOLLOS MAN** [Malcolm Bowden, *Ape-Men: Fact or Fallacy?* (Bromley, Kent, England: Sovereign Publications, 1977), pp. 57, 63, 76, 151, 154.]
- **FONTECHEVADE MAN** [Malcolm Bowden, *Ape-Men: Fact or Fallacy?* (Bromley, Kent, England: Sovereign Publications, 1977), pp. 57, 63, 76, 151, 153, 158.]
- **FOXHALL MAN JAW** from Foxhall, England (Pliocene) [Malcolm Bowden, *Ape-Men: Fact or Fallacy?* (Bromley, Ken, England: Sovereign Publications, 1977), p. 80.]
- **NATCHEZ MAN**, fossilized pelvis (Lower Pleistocene) [Charles Lyell, *Geological Evidence of the Antiquity of Man* (Philadelphia: J.W. Childs, 1863); Arthur Keith, *The Antiquity of Man*, Vol. 2, 2nd edition (London: Williams and Norgate, 1925), 376 pp., see pp. 465-467; Malcolm Bowden, *Ape-Men: Fact or Fallacy?* (Bromley, Kent, England: Sovereign Publications, 1977), pp. 75-76.]
- **GALLEY HILL MAN** skeleton (mid-Pleistocene) [Malcolm Bowden, *Ape-Men: Fact or Fallacy?* (Bromley, Kent, England: Sovereign Publications, 1977), pp. 55, 68-74, 76, 152, 182.]
- **CLICHY MAN** skeleton (mid-Pleistocene) [Arthur Keith, *The Antiquity of Man, Vol. 1, 2nd edition* (London: Williams and Norgate, 1925)., pp. 275-280; Malcolm Bowden, *Ape-Men: Fact or Fallacy?* (Bromley, Kent, England: Sovereign Public., 1977), pp. 74, 76.]
- **ABBEVILLE JAW**, found in 1863 in Abbeville, France (early Pleistocene) [Arthur Keith, *The Antiquity of Man*, Vol. 1, 2nd edition (London: Williams and Norgate, 1925), pp. 267-275; Malcolm Bowden, *Ape-Men: Fact or Fallacy?* (Bromley, Kent, England: Sovereign Publications, 1977), pp. 74, 77.]
- **KANAM JAW** [M. Bowden, *Ape-Men: Fact or Fallacy?* (Bromley, Kent, England: Sovereign Publications, 1977), pp. 180-182.]
- **KANJERA JAW** [Malcolm Bowden, *Ape-Men: Fact or Fallacy?* (Bromley, Kent, England: Sovereign Publications, 1977), pp. 70, 169, 177, 180.]
- **"SOPHISTICATED" STONE TOOLS FOUND IN MEXICO** in beds "dated" at 250 thousand years old [Virginia Steen-McIntyre, et al, "Geologic Evidence for Age of Deposits at Hueyatlaco Archeological Site, Valsequillo, Mexico," *Quaternary Research*, Vol. 16 (1981), pp. 1-17.]
- **EVIDENCE OF MAN AT AUSTRALOPITHECINE SITE** [Malcolm Bowden, *Ape-Men: Fact or Fallacy?* (Bromley, Kent, England: Sovereign Publications, 1977), pp. 167-168.]
- **EVIDENCE OF MAN AT PEKING MAN SITE** [Malcolm Bowden, *Ape-Men: Fact or Fallacy?* (Bromley, Kent, England: Sovereign Publications, 1977), pp. 78-123.]
- **SMALL CLAY FIGURINE OF A HUMAN DISCOVERED NEAR NAMPA, IDAHO**, 1889, under basalt (Tertiary). [G. Frederick Wright, "The Idaho Find," *American Antiquarian*, Vol. 11 (1889), pp. 379-381, and in "An Archaeological Discovery in Idaho," *Scribners* (February 1890); *Proceedings of the Boston Society of Natural History*, Vol. 24 (1890), p. 424; "The Genuineness of the 'Nampa Image'," *Popular Science Monthly*, Vol. 37 (1890).] D. Brinton suggested that this figurine was actually an intrusive burial of a clay toy made by the nearby Pocatello Indians. [D.G. Brinton, "Review of *Man and the Glacial Period*," *Science*, Vol. 20 (October 28, 1892), p. 249.]
- **LAETOLIL FOOTPRINTS WITH A HUMAN APPEARANCE FOUND BY MARY LEAKEY** "dated" at 3.75-million years old, and thus "older" than various supposed "missing links." Laetolil, Africa (Pliocene) [Mary D. Leakey and R.L. Hay, "Pliocene Footprints in the Laetolil Beds at Laetoli, Northern Tanzania," *Nature*, Vol. 278, No. 5702 (March 22, 1979), pp. 317-323; Malcolm Bowden, *Ape-Men: Fact or Fallacy?* (Bromley, Kent, England: Sovereign Publications, 1977), pp. 234-236.]
- **GOLD CHAIN** said to have been found in coal, Morrisonville, Illinois, 1800s (Pennsylvanian). ["A Necklace of a Prehistoric God," *Morrisonville Times* (Morrisonville, Illinois: June 11, 1891); *Mysteries of the Unexplained*, (New York: Reader's Digest, 1982), p. 46; J.R. Jochmans, *Strange Relics From the Depths of the Earth* (Lincoln, Nebraska: Forgotten Ages Research Socty., 1979), p. 17.]
- **"CERAMIC LADLE"** discovered by Myrana Burdick "in bituminous coal", 1937 [Ron Calais, "Fossil Artifacts Found in Coal," *Creation: Ex Nihilo*, Vol. 10, No. 4 (September-November 1988), p. 41 (includes photo, and mentions several other out-of-place artifacts as well); Harry Wiant, "A Curiosity from Coal," *Creation Research Society Quarterly*, Vol. 13, No. 1 (P.O. Box 14016, Terre Haute, Indiana 47803: 1976), p. 74.]
- **IRON 'POT'** (later lost) supposedly found in coal mined near Wilburton, Oklahoma, 1912 (Pennsylvanian).
- **METAL BELL-SHAPED VESSEL** said to have been found in "solid rock" [*Scientific American*, Vol. 7 (June 1851), pp. 298-299.]
- **"CARVED STONES"** said to have been found deep underground [Frank Edwards, *Strange World* (New York: Ace, 1964), p. 109.]
- **"BRONZE COIN OR MEDALLION"** said to have been found at a depth of 114 feet near Chillicothe, Illinois, 1871 [Frank Edwards, *Strangest of All* (New York: Ace, 1962), p. 101; J.R. Jochmans, *Strange Relics From the Depths of the Earth* (Lincoln, Nebraska: Forgotten Ages Research Society, 1979), pp. 13-15.]
- **METAL CUBE** Austria, 1885 (presently at Heimathaus Museum, Vocklabruck) (Paleocene) [*Nature* (November 11, 1886), p. 36; *L'Astronomie* (Paris: 1886), p. 463; J.R. Jochmans, *Strange Relics From the Depths of the Earth* (Lincoln, Nebraska: Forgotten Ages Research Society, 1979), pp. 16-17.]
- **"IRON THIMBLE"**, 1883 [J.Q. Adams, "Eve's Thimble," *American Antiquarian*, Vol. 5 (1883).]
- **SKULLS OF "HOMO ERECTUS" FOUND IN AUSTRALIA** and supposedly "dated" 10 thousand years old and said, therefore, to be contemporaneous with man.
- *HOMO SKULL* **ER-1470** [Henry M. Morris, *Creation and the Modern Christian* (El Cajon, California: Master Books, 1985), pp.

183-185; Malcolm Bowden, *Ape-Men: Fact or Fallacy?* (Bromley, Kent, England: Sovereign Publications, 1977), pp. 183-185.]

- *HOMO SKELETON IN KENYA* [Boyce Rensberger, "Human Fossil Is Unearthed," *Washington Post* (October 19, 1984), p. A-1 ("1.6 million year old" *Homo* skeleton found in Kenya by Richard Leakey and Alan Walker).]
- *HOMO ERECTUS, AUSTRALOPITHECUS, AND HOMO HABILIS SAID TO HAVE BEEN FOUND CONTEMPORARY IN OLDUVAI GORGE BED 2 by Louis Leakey and Bed 1 underneath said to have had the remains of a circular stone "habitation hut"* [Ian T. Taylor, *In the Minds of Men* (Toronto: TFE Publishing, 1984), pp. 243-246; John Reader, *Missing Links* (London: Collins, 1981), p. 173; Louis S.B. Leakey, "New Finds at Olduvai Gorge," *Nature*, Vol. 189 (February 25, 1961), p. 649.]
- KRAPINA REMAINS IN YUGOSLAVIA [Malcolm Bowden, *Ape-Men: Fact or Fallacy?* (Bromley, Kent, England: Sovereign Publications, 1977), p. 155.]
- "HUMAN" SKULL AND ARTIFACTS FOUND IN "135-MILLION YEAR OLD" STRATA NEAR GILMAN, COLORADO, 1867 (Cretaceous) [*Saturday Herald (Iowa City: April 10, 1867)*; J.R. Jochmans, *Strange Relics from the Depths of the Earth* (Lincoln, Nebraska: Forgotten Ages Research Society, 1979 — also reprinted by Bible-Science Association, P.O. Box 32457, Minneapolis, Minnesota 55432, Phone 612-635-0614), p. 4.]
- HUMAN REMAINS SUPPOSEDLY FOUND IN LOWER SILURIAN STRATA IN FRANKLIN COUNTY, MISSOURI, 1880 [J.R. Jochmans, *Strange Relics from the Depths of the Earth* (Lincoln, Nebraska: Forgotten Ages Research Society, 1979 — also reprinted by Bible-Science Association, P.O. Box 32457, Minneapolis, Minnesota 55432, Phone 612-635-0614].
- CALAVERAS MAN SKULL (Pliocene) [B.W.H., "Alleged Discovery of an Ancient Human Skull in California," *American Journal of Science*, Vol. 2, No. 42 (1866), p. 424; Arthur Keith, *The Antiquity of Man*, Vol 2, 2nd edition (London: Williams and Norgate, 1925), pp. 471-473; Malcolm Bowden, *Ape-Men: Fact or Fallacy?* (Bromley, Kent, England: Sovereign Publications, 1977), pp. 76-78.]
- KANAPOI, AFRICA — UPPER ARM BONE (lower Pleistocene) [Charles E. Oxnard, "Human Fossils: New View of Old Bones," *American Biology Teacher* (May 1979); Marvin Lubenow, "Fossil Man," *1983 National Creation Conference*.]

241

☐ **Wilbert Henry Rusch, Sr.:** Creationist / Biologist and paleontologist / L.L.D. (honorary) from Concordia Seminary (1975) / M.S. in biology from University of Michigan (1952) / Specialist in Science degree from Eastern Michigan University (1969) / Has also studied at Purdue University, University of Nebraska (geology), Illinois Institute of Technology / Professor emeritus of Biology and Geology and former head of the Science and Mathematics Division of Concordia College in Ann Arbor (Michigan) (1980) / Board member of the Nebraska Academy of Science (1960-63) / Membership Secretary of Creation Research Society.

242

☐ Wilbert H. Rusch, Sr. in Willem Glashouwer and Paul S. Taylor, writers, *The Fossil Record* (Mesa, Arizona: Eden Films and Standard Media, 1983) (Creationist motion picture). Also see:

Wilbert H. Rusch, Sr., "Human Fossils," in Paul A. Zimmerman, editor, *Rock Strata and the Bible Record* (St. Louis: Concordia Publishing House, 1970), pp. 133-177.

Wilbert H. Rusch, Sr., "The Evolution of Man," in *Possess the Land*, essays and technical papers (P.O. Box 32457, Minneapolis, Minnesota 55432, Phone 612-635-0614: Bible-Science Association, 1979), pp. 182-185 (article mentions Vertesszollos,

Swanscombe Man, Steinheim, Mt. Carmel skulls, Neanderthal, Fontchevade skulls, Krapina remains, KNM-ER-1470).

USE OF ARTISTIC FREEDOM IN RECONSTRUCTIONS

243

☐ Evolutionist Dr. R. Martin, Senior Research Fellow at the Zoological Society of London:

*"In recent years several authors have written popular books on human origins which are based more on fantasy and subjectivity than on fact and objectivity... by and large, written by authors with a formal academic background, but they shared the same tendency (as Robert Ardrey's **African Genesis**) to abandon scientific method for dogmatism. Prominent among them were **On Aggression** by Konrad Lorenz, **The Naked Ape** and **The Human Zoo** by Desmond Morris, **Love and Hate** by Irenaus Eibl-Eibesfeldt, and **The Imperial Animal** by Lionel Tiger and Robin Fox. Ardrey himself followed up with a series of derivative books at roughly five-year intervals: **The Territorial Imperative**, **The Social Contract** and **The Hunting Hypothesis.**"*

[Robert Martin, "Man Is Not an Onion," *New Scientist*, Vol. 75, No. 1063 (August 4, 1977), pp. 283-285 (quote from p. 283, emphasis added).]

244

☐ Evolutionist W. Fix:

"The fossil record pertaining to man is still so sparsely known that those who insist on positive declarations can do nothing more than jump from one hazardous surmise to another and hope that the next dramatic discovery does not make them utter fools... Clearly, some people refuse to learn from this. As we have seen, there are numerous scientists and popularizers today who have the temerity to tell us that there is 'no doubt' how man originated. If only they had the evidence..."

[William R. Fix, *The Bone Peddlers* (New York: Macmillan Publishing Company, 1984), p. 150 (emphasis added).]

☐ *"The fossils that decorate our family tree are so scarce that there are still more scientists than specimens. The remarkable fact is that all the physical evidence we have for human evolution can still be placed, with room to spare, inside a single coffin."*

[Lyall Watson, "The Water People," *Science* Digest, Vol. 90, No. 5 (May 1982), p. 44.]

☐ *"The entire hominid (a so-called 'ape-man' fossil) collection know today would barely cover a billiard table... Ever since Darwin... preconceptions have led evidence by the nose in the study of fossil man."*

[John Reader, "Whatever Happened to Zinjanthropus?," *New Scientist*, Vol. 89, No. 1246 (March 26, 1981), pp. 802-805.]

245

☐ A cover illustration of Neanderthal in *Science* 81, Vol. 2, No. 8 (October 1981) is one of the few exceptions — it shows a completely bald Neanderthal male.

246

☐ Earnest A. Hooton, *Up from the Ape* (New York: Macmillan, 1946), p. 329 (Hooton was a well-known anthropologist at Yale University who said that there is very little, if any, scientific value

*A*s is now well known, most fossil species appear instantaneously in the fossil record.
Tom Kemp of Oxford University

in the alleged reconstructions of ancient man — and they are likely to mislead the public).

247

☐ Evolutionist Dr. Greg Kirby, Senior Lecturer in Population Biology at Flinders University:

"...not being a paleontologist, I don't want to pour too much scorn on paleontologists, but if you were to spend your life picking up bones and finding little fragments of head and little fragments of jaw, there's a very strong desire there to exaggerate the importance of those fragments..."

[Greg Kirby in an address presented at a meeting of the Biology Teachers Association of South Australia (1976) (emphasis added).]

☐ *"It is worth remembering that the generic name Homunculus was actually accorded to an Argentinean fossil primate by Amheghino, its discoverer, in the mistaken belief that it was ancestral to man. Subsequent fossil finds and improvements in techniques of comparative study have demonstrated that this fossil was no more than an early (Miocene) relative of New World monkeys. Yet the tendency for individual paleontologists to trace human history directly back to their own fossil finds has persisted to the present day."* (Evolutionist Dr. R. Martin, Senior Research Fellow at the Zoological Society of London)

[Robert Martin, "Man Is Not an Onion," *New Scientist*, Vol. 75, No. 1063 (August 4, 1977), pp. 283-285 (quote from p. 285).]

☐ Arthur C. Custance, *The Fallacy of Anthropological Reconstructions*, Doorway Paper *No. 33* (P.O. Box 291, Brockville, Ontario, Canada K6V 5V5: Doorway Publications, 1966).

☐ Museums and textbooks controlled by believers in Evolutionism have frequently taught that there is abundant evidence that man and ape evolved from common ancestors. The public is shown imaginative pictures which claim to depict how man's ancestors looked and behaved. But what are the facts? Did the human beings evolve? The safest analysis of the evidence seems to indicate all the fossils involved are either of extinct apes — or humans — or hoaxes.

SUGGESTED SOURCES FOR FURTHER EVIDENCE SUPPORTING THE CLAIM THAT THERE ARE NO VALID TRANSITIONAL FORMS BETWEEN APES AND HUMANS

248

☐ Gary E. Parker, "The Fossil Evidence — Human Beings," in Henry M. Morris and Gary E. Parker, *What Is Creation Science?*, revised and expanded edition (San Diego: Master Books, 1987), pp. 151-163.

☐ John N. Moore, "Teaching About Origin Questions: Origin of Human Beings," *Creation Research Society Quarterly*, Vol. 22, No. 4 (P.O. Box 14016, Terre Haute, Indiana 47803: March 1986), pp. 183-188.

☐ William R. Fix, *The Bone Peddlers* (New York: Macmillan Publishing Company, 1984) (Written by an Evolutionist — shows "there are formidable objections to all the subhuman and near-human species that have been proposed as ancestors").

☐ Dennis W. Cheek, "The Creationist and Neo-Darwinian Views Concerning the Origin of the Order Primates Compared and Contrasted: A Preliminary Analysis," *Creation Research Society Quarterly*, Vol. 18, No. 2 (P.O. Box 14016, Terre Haute, Indiana 47803: September 1981), pp. 93-110, 134.

☐ Albert W. Mehlert, "Alleged Evolution of the Order Primates, Including Monkeys and Apes," *Creation Research Society Quarterly*, Vol. 18, No. 1 (P.O. Box 14016, Terre Haute, Indiana 47803: June 1981), pp. 20-21.

☐ Malcolm Bowden, *Ape-Men: Fact or Fallacy*, 2nd edition (Bromley, Kent, England: Sovereign Publications, 1981).

☐ Chris C. Hummer, "Unthinking *Homo Habilis*," *Creation Research Society Quarterly*, Vol. 15, No. 4 (P.O. Box 14016, Terre Haute, Indiana 47803: March 1979), pp. 204, 212-214 (*"The evidence is poor, fragmentary, uncertain and fraught with controversy. Evolutionists assign the material to Homo because they think it evolved into Homo, not because of what the creature looked like... In reality, the small-brained, primitive creature looks like an australopithecine."*)

☐ Arthur C. Custance, *Evolution or Creation* (Grand Rapids: Zondervan, 1976).

THE FOSSIL RECORD

INTERPRETING THE STRATA'S ORGANIZATION AND DISORGANIZATION

249

☐ Also called "geologic periods."

250

☐ It is interesting to note that the Geologic Column was originally constructed, not mostly by Evolutionists, but Christians (Creationists who believed in catastrophism) – many of whom thought the Earth was only thousands of years old. Those who believed Earth's strata were formed mostly by catastrophe included Adam Sedgwick, Roderick Murchison, and William Coneybeare.

[Luther D. Sunderland, "The Geologic Column: Its Basis and Who Constructed It," *Bible-Science Newsletter*, Vol. 24, No. 12 (P.O. Box 32457, Minneapolis, Minnesota 55432, Phone 612-635-0614: Bible-Science Association, December 1986), pp. 1-2, 5-6, 14.]

[R. Ritland, "Historical Development of the Current Understanding of the Geologic Column: Part II," *Origins*, Vol. 9 (Loma Linda, California: Geoscience Research Institute, Loma Linda University, 1982), pp. 28-47.]

251

☐ Glenn R. Morton, "Fossil Succession," *Creation Research Society Quarterly*, Vol. 19 (P.O. Box 14016, Terre Haute, Indiana 47803: 1982), pp. 90, 103-111.

☐ Gary E. Parker, "The Fossil Evidence," in Henry M. Morris and Gary E. Parker, *What Is Creation Science?*, revised and expanded edition (San Diego: Master Books, 1987), pp. 163-176.

☐ *"It is worth mentioning that continuous 'Evolutionary' series derived from the fossil record can in most cases be simulated by chronoclines — successions of a geographical cline population imposed by the changes of some environmental gradients."* (Evolutionist V. Krassilov)

[Valentin Krassilov, "Causal Biostratigraphy," *Lethaia*, Vol. 7, No. 3 (1974), p. 174.]

☐ Evolutionist David Raup (Ph.D. from Harvard University, Curator of Geology at the Field Museum in Chicago, and former Professor of Geology at the University of Rochester) pointed out that there is actually little or no real orderly progression in the fossils which Creationists need accommodate in constructing Flood geology theories.

[David M. Raup, "Evolution and the Fossil Record," letter, *Science*, Vol. 213 (July 17, 1981), p. 289. Also see: David M. Raup,

"Geology and Creationism," *Field Museum Bulletin*, Vol. 54 (March 1983), pp. 16-25.]

Also see Woodmorappe quotations in endnotes (see index).

IS THE EVOLUTIONARY TIME SCALE BASED ON STRONG GLOBAL EVIDENCE?

252

☐ Eminent Evolutionist Edmund Spieker admits:

"No... I wonder how many of us realize that the time scale was frozen in essentially its present form by 1840...? How much world geology was known in 1840? A bit of western Europe, none too well, and a lesser fringe of North America. All of Asia, Africa, South America, and most of North America were virtually unknown. How dared the pioneers (of this theory) assume that their scale would fit the rocks in these vast areas, by far most of the world? Only in dogmatic assumption — a mere extension of the kind of reasoning developed by Werner from the facts in his little district of Saxony. And in many parts of the world, notably India and South America, it does not fit. But even there it is applied! The followers of the founding fathers went forth across the earth and in Procrustean fashion made it fit the sections they found, even in places where the actual evidence literally proclaimed denial. So flexible and accommodating are the 'facts' of geology."

[Edmund M. Spieker, "Mountain-Building and Nature of Geologic Time-Scale," *Bulletin of the American Association of Petroleum Geologists*, Vol. 40 (August 1956), p. 1803 (emphasis added).]

253

☐ Geologist John Woodmorappe states that:

Two-thirds of Earth's land surface has only *"5 or fewer of the 10 geologic periods in place".* (p. 46)

"Eighty to eighty-five percent of Earth's land surface does not have even 3 geologic periods appearing in 'correct' consecutive order." (p. 46)

"A significant percentage of every geologic period's rocks does not overlie rocks of the next older geologic period... Some percentage of every geologic period rests directly upon Precambrian 'basement'..." (p. 67)

"Since only a small percentage of the earth's surface obeys even a significant portion of the geologic column, it becomes an overall exercise of gargantuan special pleading and imagination for the evolutionary-uniformitarian paradigm to maintain that there ever were geologic periods. The claim of their having taken place to form a continuum of rock/life/time of ten biochronologic 'onion skins' over the earth is therefore a fantastic and imaginative contrivance." (p. 69)

[John Woodmorappe, "The Essential Non-Existence of the Evolutionary Uniformitarian Geologic Column: A Quantitative Assessment," *Creation Research Society Quarterly*, Vol. 18, No. 1 (P.O. Box 14016, Terre Haute, Indiana 47803: June 1981), pp. 46-71.]

☐ Geologist Steven Austin, Ph.D. says there are ten common major "MISCONCEPTIONS" about the geologic column. He states that the evidence is clear and overwhelming that NONE of the following beliefs is true:

"1. The geologic column was constructed by geologists who, because of the weight of evidence that they had found, were convinced of the truth of uniformitarian theory and organic evolution.

2. Geologists composed the geologic column by assembling the 'periods' and 'eras' which they had recognized.

3. The strata systems of the geologic column are worldwide in their occurrence with each strata system being present below any point on the earth's surface.

4. Strata systems always occur in the order required by the geologic column.

5. Because each strata system has distinctive lithologic composition, a newly discovered stratum can be assigned easily to its correct position in the geologic column.

6. Fossils, especially the species distinctive of specific systems, provide the most reliable method of assigning strata to their level in the geologic column.

7. Sedimentary evidence proves that periods of millions of years' duration were required to deposit individual strata systems.

8. Radiometric dating can supply 'absolute ages' in millions of years with certainty to systems of the geologic column.

9. The environmental 'pictures' assigned to certain portions of the geologic column allow us to accurately visualize what its 'geologic ages' were like.

10. The geologic column and the positions of fossils within the geologic column provide proof of amoeba-to-man [E]volution."

[Steven A. Austin, "Ten Misconceptions About the Geologic Column," Impact series No. 137, *Acts & Facts* (P.O. Box 2667, El Cajon, California 92021: Institute for Creation Research, November 1984), 4 pp.]

---

*T**he curious thing is that there is a consistency about the fossil gaps; the fossils are missing in all the important places.***

Francis Hitching, archaeologist

254

☐ William Waisgerber, George F. Howe, and Emmett L. Williams, "Mississippian and Cambrian Strata Interbedding: 200 Million Years Hiatus in Question," *Creation Research Society Quarterly*, Vol. 23, No. 4 (P.O. Box 14016, Terre Haute, Indiana 47803: March 1987), pp. 160-167.

☐ Creationists do not generally believe that most of the layers are actually missing; they believe these layers simply never existed. Some say the evidence indicates the sedimentary layers of the Grand Canyon were actually laid more or less continuously during truly massive flood conditions.

255

☐ *Science News* reported:

"In many places, the oceanic sediments of which mountains are composed are inverted, with the older sediments lying on top of the younger."

[(anonymous author), "Mountain Building in the Mediterranean," (News of the Week section under "Marine Biology"), *Science News*, Vol. 98, No. 16 (October 17, 1970), p. 316 (emphasis added).]

SUGGESTED SOURCES FOR LISTS OF SCIENTIFIC REFERENCES TO SUCH "WRONG ORDER" FORMATIONS AND "OUT-OF-ORDER" FOSSILS

☐ Duane T. Gish, "More Creationist Research (14 Years) - Part I: Geological Research," *Creation Research Society Quarterly*, Vol. 25, No. 4 (P.O. Box 14016, Terre Haute, Indiana 47803: March 1989), pp. 161-170 (includes discussion of overthrusts, Thornton Quarry deposits, evidence from the Grand Canyon / includes 50 references to other articles).

☐ Walter E. Lammerts, "Recorded Instances of Wrong-Order Formations or Presumed Overthrusts in the United States: A Bibliography," in multiple parts, *Creation Research Society Quarterly*, Vol. 23, No. 3 (P.O. Box 14016, Terre Haute, Indiana 47803: December 1986), p. 38, Vol. 22 (1986), pp. 188-189, Vol. 22 (1985), p. 127, Vol. 21 (1985), p. 200, Vol. 21 (1984), pp. 88, 150.

☐ George F. Howe, "Creation Research Society Studies on Precambrian Pollen," *Creation Research Society Quarterly*, Vol. 23, No. 3 (P.O. Box 14016, Terre Haute, Indiana 47803: December 1986), pp. 99-104.

☐ William R. Corliss, *Remarkable Unconformities, Unknown Earth: A Handbook of Geologic Enigmas* (Glen Arm, Maryland: The Sourcebook Project, 1980).

☐ John Woodmorappe, "An Anthology of Matters Significant to Creationism and Diluviology: Report 2," *Creation Research Society Quarterly*, Vol. 18, No. 4 (P.O. Box 14016, Terre Haute, Indiana 47803: March 1982), pp. 208-216 (Includes a listing of over 200 published instances of anomalously-occurring fossils).

☐ John G. Read, *Fossils, Strata and Evolution* (Culver City, California: Scientific-Technical Presentations, 1979).

☐ Henry M. Morris, *Creation and the Modern Christian* (El Cajon, California: Master Books, 1985), pp. 252-260.

☐ William R. Corliss, "Inverted Strata," in William R. Corliss, *Strange Planet: A Sourcebook of Unusual Geological Facts*, Vol. E-1 (Glen Arm, Maryland: Sourcebook Project, 1975), pp. 177-184.

INFORMATION CONCERNING THE EXISTENCE OF DINOSAURS WITHIN HUMAN HISTORY

256

☐ Paul S. Taylor, *The Great Dinosaur Mystery and the Bible* (Denver, Colorado: Accent Books, 1987), 63 pp.

☐ And other works by Paul S. Taylor on dinosaurs.

DATING FOSSILS

257

☐ There is presently no radioactive dating method which can be used to directly date a dinosaur bone (or any other part of the body), and prove it to be tens of millions of years old.

☐ Radiometric dating:

"*is an exceedingly crude instrument with which to measure our strata and I can think of no occasion where it has been put to an immediate practical use. Apart from very 'modern' examples, which are really archaeology, I can think of no cases of radioactive decay being used to date fossils. ... Ever since William Smith at the beginning of the 19th century, fossils have been and still are the best and most accurate method of dating and correlating the rocks in which they occur.*" (Geologist and Evolutionist Dr. Derek Ager, former President of the British Geological Association)

[Derek Ager, "Fossil Frustrations," *New Scientist*, Vol. 100, No. 1383 (November 10, 1983), p. 425 (emphasis added).]

☐ "*As yet there is no radiometric method (that is, one based on radioactivity) for the direct absolute dating of dinosaurs.*" (Paleontologist and Evolutionist Alan Charig, head of the British Museum's paleontological laboratory)

[Alan Charig, *A New Look at the Dinosaurs* (New York: Mayflower Books, 1979), p. 36 (emphasis added.]

☐ Also, see first half of chapter in this book, titled "The Earth, A Young Planet?".

258

☐ Geology researcher and Creation/Evolution specialist Dr. H. Morris:

"*Since there is no way to tell the geologic age of rocks except on the assumption of (E)volution, there is no way to be sure that any one 'age' is different from any other. Thus, they could all well be the same age, exactly as the Biblical Flood model requires. The rocks and fossil beds were all formed catastrophically, and by the same catastrophe at that.*"

[Henry M. Morris, *King of Creation* (San Diego: CLP Publishers, 1980), p. 160 (emphasis added).]

☐ **Henry M. Morris**: Creationist (former Evolutionist) / Hydraulicist / Lecturer / Ph.D. from University of Minnesota (1950) (hydrology, geology, mathematics) / Fellow of the American Association for the Advancement of Science and the American Society of Civil Engineers / Former Professor of Hydraulic Engineering and Chairman of the Department of Civil Engineering at Virginia Polytechnic Institute (1957-1970) / Current President of the Institute for Creation Research in San Diego / Further information can be found in Who's Who: — in the World, — in America, — in Science, and — in Engineering.

259

☐ J.E. Ransom, *Fossils in America* (New York: Harper & Row, 1964), p. 43.

☐ "*Certain fossils appear to be restricted to rocks of a relatively limited geological age span. These are called index fossils. Whenever a rock is found bearing such a fossil, its approximate age is automatically established. This method is not foolproof. Occasionally an organism, previously thought to be extinct, is found to be extant. Such 'living fossils' obviously cannot function as index fossils except within the broader time span of their known existence.*" (Dr. W. Stansfield, Biology Department of California Polytech State University)

[William D. Stansfield, *Science of Evolution* (New York: Macmillan, 1977), p. 80.]

260

☐ See Ager quotation in endnotes (see index).

☐ Evolutionist O. Schindewolf:

"*The only chronometric scale applicable in geologic history for the stratigraphic classification of rocks and for dating geologic events is furnished by the fossils. Owing to the irreversibility of evolution, they offer an unambiguous time-scale for relative age determinations and for worldwide correlations of rocks.*"

[O.H. Schindewolf, *American Journal of Science*, Vol. 255, No. 6 (June 1957), p. 394 (emphasis added).]

☐ "*Historic geology relies chiefly on paleontology, the study of fossil organisms... The geologist utilizes knowledge of organic evolution, as preserved in the fossil record, to identify and correlate the lithic records of ancient time.*" (Evolutionary geologists Engeln and Caster)

[O.D. von Engeln and K.E. Caster, *Geology* (New York: McGraw-Hill, 1952), p. 423.]

☐ This method of dating rocks is still the chief method used to this day.

☐ A.E. Wilder-Smith, Ph.D., Dr.es.Sc., D.Sc., F.R.I.C.:

"So firmly does the modern geologist believe in evolution up from simple organisms to complex ones over huge time spans, that he is perfectly willing to <u>use the theory of evolution to prove the theory of evolution</u> (p. 128) ...one is applying the <u>theory of evolution</u> to prove the correctness of evolution. For we are <u>assuming</u> that the oldest formations contain only the most primitive and least complex organisms, which is the basic <u>assumption</u> of Darwinism...(p. 127) If we now <u>assume</u> that only simple organisms will occur in <u>old</u> formations, we are assuming the basic premise of Darwinism to be correct. To use, therefore, for dating purposes, the <u>assumption</u> that only simple organisms will be present in old formations is to thoroughly beg the whole question. It is arguing in a circle." (p. 128)

[Arthur E. Wilder-Smith, *Man's Origin, Man's Destiny* (Wheaton, Illinois: Harold Shaw Publishers, 1968), pp. 127-128 (emphasis added).]

SUGGESTED SOURCES CONCERNING CIRCULAR REASONING, THE GEOLOGIC COLUMN, AND DATING

☐ Luther D. Sunderland, "The Geologic Column: Its Basis and Who Constructed It," *Bible-Science Newsletter*, Vol. 24, No. 12 (P.O. Box 32457, Minneapolis, Minnesota 55432, Phone 612-635-0614: Bible-Science Association, December 1986), pp. 1-2, 5-6, 14 (p. 6 cites a 1979 interview with Dr. Donald Fisher, state paleontologist of New York in which he admits the circular reasoning and says, "Of course; how else are you going to do it?").

☐ Larry Azar, "Biologists, Help!", *Bioscience*, Vol. 28, No. 11 (November 1978) (p. 714 — *"Are the authorities maintaining, on the one hand, that Evolution is documented by geology and, on the other hand, that geology is documented by Evolution? Isn't this a circular argument?"*).

☐ J.E. O'Rourke, "Pragmatism versus Materialism in Stratigraphy," *American Journal of Science*, Vol. 276, No. 1 (January 1976), pp. 47-55.

EVOLUTIONISTS COMMENT ON CIRCULAR REASONING

☐ Evolutionist and paleontologist Niles Eldredge:

"And this poses something of a problem: If we date the rocks by their fossils, how can we then turn around and talk about patterns of evolutionary change through time in the fossil record?"

[Niles Eldredge, *Time Frames* (New York: Simon and Schuster, 1985), p. 52.]

☐ Evolutionist Tom Kemp, Curator of the University Museum of Oxford University:

"A circular argument arises: Interpret the fossil record in terms of a particular theory of evolution, inspect the interpretation, and note that it confirms the theory. Well, it would, wouldn't it?"

[Tom Kemp, "A Fresh Look at the Fossil Record," *New Scientist*, Vol. 108, No. 1485 (December 5, 1985), p. 66.]

☐ Evolutionist researcher J. O'Rourke:

"The intelligent layman has long suspected circular reasoning in the use of rocks to date fossils and fossils to date rocks. The geologist has never bothered to think of a good reply, feeling the explanations are not worth the trouble as long as the work brings results. This is supposed to be hard-headed pragmatism."

[J.E. O'Rourke, "Pragmatism Versus Materialism in Stratigraphy," *American Journal of Science*, Vol. 276, No. 1 (January 1976), p. 48.]

☐ Evolutionist R.H. Rastall, Lecturer in Economic Geology, Cambridge University:

"It cannot be denied that from a strictly philosophical standpoint, geologists are here arguing in a circle. The succession of organisms has been determined by the study of their remains imbedded in the rocks, and the relative ages of the rocks are determined by the remains of the organisms they contain."

[R.H. Rastall, *Encyclopedia Britannica*, Vol. 10 (Chicago: William Benton, Publisher, 1956), p. 168.]

261

☐ Michael Oard:

"Few people realize that the index fossil dating system, despite its <u>poor assumptions</u> and <u>many</u> problems, is actually the <u>primary</u> dating tool for geologic time. Even though 'absolute' dating methods have been widely touted to be accurate, this is <u>not</u> the case at all. They have many <u>serious</u> problems... In other words, radiometric dating methods are actually fit into the geological column, which was set up by fossil dating over 100 years ago."

[Michael J. Oard, "Ice Ages: The Mystery Solved?, Part II: The Manipulation of Deep-Sea Cores," *Creation Research Society Quarterly*, Vol. 21, No. 3 (P.O. Box 14016, Terre Haute, Indiana 47803: December 1984), p. 132 (emphasis added).]

262

☐ Concerning the popular potassium/argon system, radiometric dating researcher A. Hayatsu confirms:

"In conventional interpretation of K-Ar age data, it is common to <u>discard ages</u> which are substantially too high or too low compared with the rest of the group or with other available data such as the geological time scale. The discrepancies between the rejected and the accepted are <u>arbitrarily</u> attributed to excess or loss of argon."

[A. Hayatsu, "K-Ar Isochron Age of the North Mountain Basalt, Nova Scotia," *Canadian Journal of Earth Sciences*, Vol. 16, No. 4, (1979), p. 974 (emphasis added).]

☐ *"In general, dates in the 'correct ball park' are <u>assumed to be correct</u> and are published, but <u>those in disagreement with other data are seldom published</u> nor are discrepancies fully explained."* (Geologist Richard Mauger, Ph.D., Associate Professor of Geology at East Carolina University)

[Richard L. Mauger, "K-Ar Ages of Biotites from Tuffs in Eocene Rocks of the Green River, Washakie and Uinta Basins...," *Contributions to Geology, University of Wyoming*, Vol. 15, No. 1 (1977), p. 37 (emphasis added).]

☐ It has been reported that a London lab once gave Evolutionist Richard Leakey a date of 220 million years on a volcanic tuff associated with bones he discovered. It is said that because this date did not at all fit his theories, he requested a new dating which yielded a much more acceptable 2.6 million years.

[E.T. Hall, article in *Sunday Telegraph* (November 3, 1974), p. 15.]

*E*volution requires intermediate forms between species and paleontology does not provide them.

David Kitts, paleontologist and Evolutionist

MACROEVOLUTION AND THE FOSSIL RECORD

263

☐ Evolutionist Dr. George Gaylord Simpson admitted that complex life forms are found in the Cambrian rocks, and he calls this:

"the major mystery of the history of life."

[George G. Simpson, *The Meaning of Evolution* (New Haven, Connecticut: Yale University Press, 1953), p. 18.]

☐ *"Of those earliest stages of evolution we have no direct evidence... we cannot make any definite statements about it."* (Evolutionist author and Professor G.S. Carter, Fellow of Corpus Christi College, Cambridge, England)

[G.S. Carter, *Structure and Habit in Vertebrate Evolution* (Seattle: University of Washington Press, 1967), 520 pp. (quote from p. 8 — emphasis added).]

SUGGESTED SOURCE FOR EVIDENCE THAT "DEEPEST" FOSSILS REVEAL GREAT COMPLEXITY

☐ Luther D. Sunderland, *Darwin's Enigma: Fossils and Other Problems* (El Cajon, California: Master Book Publishers, 1984), pp. 43-53.

ARTICLES BY EVOLUTIONISTS WHICH REVEAL THE PUZZLE THEY ARE CONFRONTED WITH ON THIS POINT:

☐ Mark McMenamin, "The Emergence of Animals," *Scientific American*, Vol. 256, No. 4 (April 1987), pp. 94-102 (includes useful illustrations and photos — and summarizes new speculation on the problem by Evolutionists).

☐ Simon Morris, "The Search for the Precambrian-Cambrian Boundary," *American Scientist*, Vol. 75, No. 2 (March/April 1987), pp. 157-167 (p. 157 — admits that "the problems set by the fossil record across the Precambrian-Cambrian boundary remain for the most part unsolved.").

THE ORIGIN OF FLIGHT

264

☐ Concerning the abrupt appearance of bats

"The fossil record of bats extends back to the early Eocene... and has been documented... on five continents... (A)ll fossil bats, even the oldest, are clearly fully developed bats and so they shed little light on the transition from their terrestrial ancestor." (Evolutionists Hill and Smith)

[John E. Hill and James D. Smith, *Bats: A Natural History* (London: British Museum of Natural History, 1984), p. 33 (emphasis added).]

☐ Glenn L. Jepsen, "Early Eocene Bat from Wyoming," *Science*, Vol. 154, No. 3754 (1966), pp. 1333-1339.

☐ Marvin L. Lubenow, "Significant Fossil Discoveries Since 1958: Creationism Confirmed," *Creation Research Society Quarterly*, Vol. 17, No. 3 (P.O. 14016, Terre Haute, Indiana: 1980), p. 159.

265

☐ Robert R. Sanders and George F. Howe, "Insects Indicate Creation," *Creation Research Society Quarterly*, Vol. 22, No. 4 (P.O. Box 14016, Terre Haute, Indiana 47803: March 1986), pp. 166-170.

☐ Stephen Butt, "Insect Flight: Testimony to Creation," *Creation Research Society Quarterly*, Vol. 16, No. 4 (P.O. Box 14016, Terre Haute, Indiana 47803: March 1980), p. 195.

266

☐ Paleontologist and Evolutionist expert Dr. John Ostrom:

"There can be no doubt that Archaeopteryx was a true bird..."

[John Ostrom in *The Beginning of Birds* (Eichstatt, West Germany: Jura Museum, 1985), p. 174 — as cited by Ronald C. Calais, "Response to Padian," *Creation Research Society Quarterly*, Vol. 25, No. 4 (P.O. Box 14016, Terre Haute, Indiana 47803: March 1989), p. 203.]

SUGGESTED SOURCES FOR ADDITIONAL EVIDENCE AGAINST *ARCHAEOPTERYX* AS A MACROEVOLUTIONARY TRANSITIONAL FORM

267

☐ Michael Denton, *Evolution: A Theory in Crisis* (London: Burnett Books, 1985), 368 pp.

☐ Luther D. Sunderland, *Darwin's Enigma: Fossils and Other Problems* (El Cajon, California: Master Book Publishers, 1984), pp. 69-76.

☐ Francis Hitching, *The Neck of the Giraffe: Where Darwin Went Wrong* (New Haven, Connecticut: Ticknor and Fields, 1982), pp. 34-36 (Shows that *"every one of its supposed reptilian features can be found in various species of undoubted birds"*).

☐ Colin Brown, "Another Look at the *Archaeopteryx*," *Creation Research Society Quarterly*, Vol. 17, No. 2 (P.O. Box 14016, Terre Haute, Indiana: 1980), pp. 87, 109.

☐ Frank W. Cousins, "The Alleged Evolution of Birds," in Donald W. Patten, editor, *A Symposium on Creation III* (Grand Rapids, Michigan: Baker Book House, 1971), pp. 89-99.

IS *ARCHAEOPTERYX* A FAKE?

Some Evolutionists (and a few creationists) have claimed that the *Archaeopteryx* fossils were partial forgeries. This appears to have been disproven by the recent splitting-open of a new rock sample which was supposedly found to contain an *Archaeopteryx* fossil (the 6th), complete with feather shaft impressions, which was said to have been found by the mayor of Solnhofen, West Germany.

ANTI-HOAX REFERENCES

☐ Henry Gee, "Ruffled Feathers Calmed by Fossil Bird," *Nature*, Vol. 334, No. 6178 (July 14, 1988), p. 104.

☐ Stephen J. Gould, "The Fossil Fraud That Never Was," *New Scientist*, Vol. 113, No. 1551 (March 12, 1987), pp. 32-36.

PRO-HOAX REFERENCES

☐ Fred Hoyle and N. Chandra Wickramasinghe, *Archaeopteryx* (Swansea, England: Christopher Davies, Ltd., 1986).

☐ Ian Taylor, "The Berlin Archaeopteryx," *Creation Science Association of Ontario FEATURE*, No. 9 (P.O. Box 821, Station A, Scarborough, Ontario M1K 5C8: Fall 1988), 4 pp.

☐ Ian Taylor, "Archaeopteryx — A Case of Fossil Forgery," *Creation Science Association of Ontario FEATURE*, No. 8 (P.O. Box 821, Station A, Scarborough, Ontario M1K 5C8: Summer 1988), 4 pp.

268

- L.D. Martin, et al "The Origin of Birds: Structure of the Tarus and Teeth," *The Auk*, Vol. 97 (1980), pp. 86-93 (*Shows that "Archaeopteryx had unserrated teeth with constricted bases and expanded roots like those of other Mesozoic birds"*).

- All sub-classes of vertebrates have some species with and without teeth.

- Also, it is said that *Archaeopteryx*'s teeth are not like those of any known dinosaur, despite the claim of some Evolutionists that *Archaeopteryx* evolved from dinosaurs. See: L. Martin, "The Relationship of *Archaeopteryx* to Other Birds," in *The Beginning of Birds* (Eichstatt, West Germany: Jura Museum, 1985), p. 179.

269

- Juvenile touraco (*Touraco corythaix*), native to North Africa.

270

- Juvenile hoatzin (*Opisthocomus hoatzin*), native to South America.

SUGGESTED SOURCES ON THE HOATZIN AS IT RELATES TO *ARCHAEOPTERYX*

- Colin Brown, "The Hoatzin," *Creation Research Society Quarterly*, Vol. 18, No. 2 (P.O. Box 14016, Terre Haute, Indiana 47803: September 1981), pp. 92, 111.

- Frank L. Marsh, "The Strange Hoatzin," *Creation Research Society Quarterly*, Vol. 11, No. 3 (P.O. Box 14016, Terre Haute, Indiana 47803: 1974), p. 139.

271

- A number of species from 9 Families of birds with wing-claws were displayed in 1983 at the British Museum of Natural History.

272

- These feathers were not reptilian scale partially changed into a primitive feather. This animal had full-blown flying feathers. The shaft went down the leading edge, which is considered a unique characteristic of birds that are strong flyers.

[Alan Feduccia and Harrison Tordoff, "Feathers of *Archaeopteryx*: Asymmetric Vanes Indicate Aerodynamic Function," *Science*, Vol. 203, No. 4384 (March 9, 1979), pp. 1021-1022 (Shows that flight feathers of *Archaeopteryx* were asymmetrical — identical to those of modern flying birds).]

SUGGESTED SOURCES FOR INFORMATION ON THE DIFFICULTIES OF EVOLVING FEATHERS

- Michael Denton, *Evolution: A Theory in Crisis* (London: Burnett Books, 1985) (shows the implausibility of a reptilian scale transforming into a feather), 368 pp.

- Willis E. Keithley, "Feathers: Flight or Fancy?," *Creation Research Society Quarterly*, Vol. 9, No. 4 (P.O. Box 14016, Terre Haute, Indiana 47803: March 1973), p. 203.

---

*F*ossils are a great embarrassment to Evolutionary theory and offer strong support for the concept of Creation.

Gary Parker, Ph.D., biologist/paleontologist and former Evolutionist

---

273

- Evolutionist Feduccia:

"*Feathers are features unique to birds, and there are no known intermediate structures between reptilian scales and feathers.* Notwithstanding speculations on the nature of the elongated scales found on such forms as *Longisquama* ... as being featherlike structures, there is simply *no demonstrable evidence* that they in fact are. They are very interesting, highly modified and elongated *reptilian scales*, and are *not* incipient feathers."

[Alan Feduccia, "On Why Dinosaurs Lacked Feathers," in *The Beginning of Birds* (Eichstatt, West Germany: Jura Museum, 1985), p. 76.]

274

- G. Russell Akridge, "*Archaeopteryx* Aerodynamics," *Creation Research Society Quarterly*, Vol. 16, No. 3 (P.O. Box 14016, Terre Haute, Indiana 47803: 1979), p. 185.

275

- The hoatzin has a similarly shallow breastbone.

276

- Storrs L. Olson and Alan Feduccia, "Flight Capability and the Pectoral Girdle of *Archaeopteryx*," *Nature*, Vol. 278, No. 5701 (March 15, 1979), pp. 247-248.

277

- Ronald C. Calais:

"It is nothing short of absurdity to believe Ostrom has demonstrated the evolution of birds from small carnivorous dinosaurs. His research demonstrates nothing of the sort. Ostrom has merely formulated an hypothesis... Ostrom's thesis is by no means universally accepted among paleobiologists..."

[Ronald C. Calais, "Response to Padian," *Creation Research Society Quarterly*, Vol. 25, No. 4 (P.O. Box 14016, Terre Haute, Indiana 47803: March 1986), p. 205.]

- Ron C. Calais, "Response to Padian," *Creation Research Society Quarterly*, Vol. 25, No. 4 (P.O. Box 14016, Terre Haute, Indiana 47803: March 1989), pp. 202-207.

278

- *Archaeopteryx* was found in sediments classified as Jurassic (upper) by Evolutionists. The most recent "bird" find has been called "Proavis" by Evolutionists. It was discovered in the Dockum sediments classified by Evolutionists as Triassic (lower-upper to middle-upper) — which they date as about 75 million years earlier than the Late Jurassic. Its discover has identified it as avian (a bird).

- Describing this find, *Scientific American* said:

"Two sets of bones found in western Texas have turned out to be those of crow-sized *birds*..."

[Anonymous, "Fossil Revisionism," *Scientific American*, Vol. 255, No. 4 (1986), pp. 84-89 (quote is from p. 84 — emphasis added).]

- Tim Beardsley, "Fossil Bird Shakes Evolutionary Hypotheses," *Nature*, Vol. 322, No. 6081 (August 21-27, 1986), p. 677.

- Marvin L. Lubenow, "Significant Fossil Discoveries Since 1958: Creationism Confirmed," *Creation Research Society Quarterly*, Vol. 17, No. 3 (P.O. Box 14016, Terre Haute, Indiana 47803: December 1980), p. 158.

□ *"It is obvious that we must now look for the ancestors of flying birds in a period much older than that in which Archaeopteryx lived."* (Prof. James A. Jepsen of Brigham Young University)

[John Ostrom, "Bone Bonanza: Early Bird and Mastodon," *Science* News, Vol. 112, No. 13 (September 24, 1977), p. 198 (Bird in strata supposedly 60 million years older than *Archaeopteryx*.]

DO FOSSIL HORSES PROVE THAT MACROEVOLUTION REALLY HAPPENS?

279

□ One such claim was made by Evolutionist William Matthew, former curator of vertebrate paleontology of the American Museum of Natural History.

[William D. Matthew, "Three-Toed Horses: A Fossil Record That Provides Direct Evidence of Evolution," *Natural History* (September/October 1920), reprinted in *Natural History, Vol. 89, No. 4 (April 1980), pp. 125-126.*]

280

□ **Gary E. Parker**: Creationist / Former Evolutionist author and professor / Biologist and paleontologist / Ed.D. from Ball State University in biology with a cognate in geology and paleontology / American Society of Zoologists / Former Chairman of the Biology Department of the Institute for Creation Research / Former Chairman of the Natural Science Department at Christian Heritage College / Current head of the Science Department at Clearwater Christian College, Clearwater, Florida.

CONCERNING LACK OF EVIDENCE FOR THE MACROEVOLUTION OF HORSES

281

□ *"The supposed pedigree of the Equidae [horses, asses, zebras] is a deceitful delusion, which ...in no way enlightens us on the palaeontological origin of the Horse."* (French paleontologist and Evolutionist C. Deperet)

[Charles J.J. Deperet in *Transformations of the Animal World* (New York: Arno Press, 1980), p. 105 (emphasis is Deperet's).]

□ *"Classic cases ...such as the (E)volution of the horse in North America have had to be modified or discarded as the result of more detailed information."* (Paleontologist and Evolutionist Dr. David Raup, Curator of the Field Museum of Natural History, Chicago)

[David Raup, "Conflicts Between Darwin and Paleontology," *Field Museum of Natural History Bulletin*, Vol. 50, No. 1 (1979), pp. 22-29 (emphasis added).]

Unknown to most laypeople, even back in the 1950s the erroneous Horse Evolution story was being admitted by various prominent Evolutionists:

□ Evolutionist Professor G. Kerkut, Department of Physiology and Biochemistry, University of Southampton:

"The (E)volution of the horse provides one of the keystones in the teaching of (E)volutionary doctrine, though the actual story depends to a large extent upon who is telling it and when the story is being told. In fact one could easily discuss the evolution of the story of the (E)volution of the horse."

[G.A. Kerkut, *Implications of Evolution* (London: Pergamon Press, 1960) (emphasis added).]

□ Evolutionist Professor Heribert Nilsson:

"The family tree of the horse is beautiful and continuous only in the textbooks. In the reality provided by the results of research it is put together from 3 parts, of which only the last can be described as including the horses. The forms of the first part are just as much little horses as the present-day damans are horses. The construction of the whole Cenozoic family tree of the horse is therefore a very artificial one, since it is put together from non-equivalent parts, and cannot therefore be a continuous transformation series."

[N. Heribert Nilsson, *Synthetische Artbildung* (Lund, Sweden: Verlag CWE Gleerup, 1954) (emphasis added).]

□ Ardent Evolutionist George Gaylord Simpson, although somehow persisting in acceptance of the various horse fossils as evidence of Evolution, admitted:

"The uniform, continuous transformation of Hyracotherium into Equus, so dear to the hearts of generations of textbook writers, never happened in nature..." (p. 125)

"The (E)volution of the horse family, Equidae, is now no better known than that of numerous other groups of organisms..." (p. 127)

[George G. Simpson, *Life of the Past* (New Haven, Connecticut: Yale University Press, 1953), pp. 125, 127 (emphasis added).]

□ Evolutionist Richard Goldschmidt, Ph.D., M.D., D.Sc., former Professor of Genetics and Cytology, University of California:

"Moreover, within the slowly evolving series, like the famous horse series, the decisive steps are abrupt and without transition."

[Richard B. Goldschmidt, "Evolution, As Viewed By One Geneticist," *American Scientist*, Vol. 40, No. 1 (1952), pp. 84-94 (emphasis added).]

282

□ Gary E. Parker in Willem J.J. Glashouwer and Paul S. Taylor, writers, *The Fossil Record* (Mesa, Arizona: Eden Films and Standard Media, 1983) (Creationist motion picture).

SUGGESTED SOURCES FOR FURTHER EVIDENCE AGAINST THE MACROEVOLUTION OF HORSES

□ Erich A. von Fange, "The Litopterna — A Lesson in Taxonomy: The Strange Story of the South American 'False' Horses," *Creation Research Society Quarterly*, Vol. 25, No. 4 (P.O. Box 14016, Terre Haute, Indiana 47803: March 1989), pp. 184-190 (von Fange, p. 184 — *"The supposed [E]volution of the horse was confronted by contradictory fossil evidence from South America. The solution in 1910 was to banish the contradictions into an obscure separate order of mammals. This paper illustrates the strange and wonderful contortions of taxonomists to remain mindlessly loyal when the theory of [E]volution fails them."*).

□ Luther D. Sunderland, *Darwin's Enigma: Fossils and Other Problems*, 4th edition (Santee, California: Master Books, 1988).

□ Francis Hitching, *The Neck of the Giraffe: Where Darwin Went Wrong (New Haven, Connecticut: Ticknor and Fields, 1982), p. 30 (Shows that fossils of modern horses, Equus nevadensis and Equus occidentalis have been found in strata with Eohippus — formerly called Hyracotherium).*

□ Duane T. Gish, *Evolution: The Fossils Say No!* (San Diego: CLP Publishers, 1979).

□ Frank W. Cousins, "The Alleged Evolution of the Horse," in Donald W. Patten, editor, *A Symposium on Creation III* (Grand Rapids, Michigan: Baker Book House, 1971), pp. 69-85.

□ Frank W. Cousins, "A Note On the Unsatisfactory Nature of the Horse Series of Fossils As Evidence for Evolution," *Creation Research Society Quarterly*, Vol. 8, No. 2 (P.O. Box 14016, Terre Haute, Indiana 47803: 1971), pp. 99-108.

283

□ Niles Eldredge in Luther D. Sunderland, *Darwin's Enigma: Fossils and Other Problems*, 4th edition (Santee, California: Master Books, 1988), p. 78 (emphasis added).

IS THERE, OR IS THERE NOT, SUBSTANTIAL FOSSIL EVIDENCE OF MACROEVOLUTION?

PLANTS

284

☐ Evolutionist Dr. Edred J.H. Corner, Professor of Botany at Cambridge University, England:

"...I still think that to the unprejudiced, _the fossil record of plants is in favor of special creation._"

[Edred J.H. Corner in A.M. MacLeod and L.S. Copely, editors, _Evolution in Contemporary Botanical Thought_ (Chicago: Quadrangle Books, 1961), p. 97 (emphasis added).]

☐ "_My attempts to demonstrate (E)volution by an experiment carried on for more than 40 years have completely failed._ At least, I should hardly be accused of having started from a preconceived anti-Evolutionary standpoint... It may be firmly maintained that it is not even possible to make a caricature of an Evolution out of paleo-biological facts. The fossil material is now so complete that it has been possible to construct new classes, and the lack of transitional series cannot be explained as being due to the scarcity of material. The deficiencies are real, they will never be filled. (Famous botanist and Evolutionist Dr. Heribert Nilsson)

[N. Heribert Nilsson, as quoted in Arthur C. Custance, _The Earth Before Man_, Part II, Doorway Paper No. 20 (P.O. Box 291, Brockville, Ontario, Canada K6V 5V5: Doorway Publications), p. 51 (emphasis added).]

☐ "As yet we have _not_ been able to track the phylogenetic history of a _single group_ of modern plants from its beginning to the present." (Evolutionist Chester Arnold, University of Michigan)

[Chester A. Arnold, _Introduction to Paleobotany_ (New York: McGraw-Hill, 1947), p. 7 (emphasis added).]

FISH

285

☐ Zoologist J. Norman:

"The geological record has so far provided _no_ evidence as to the origin of the fishes..." (Evolutionist J.R. Norman, Assistant Keeper of the Department of Zoology, British Museum of Natural History, London)

[J.R. Norman in P.H. Greenwood, _A History of Fishes_, 2nd edition (New York: Hill and Wang, 1963), p. 296 (emphasis added).]

AMPHIBIANS

286

☐ Evolutionist Gordon Taylor:

"There are _no_ intermediate forms between finned and limbed creatures in the fossil collections of the world." (Award-winning science writer Gordon Rattray Taylor, former editor of the British Broadcasting Corporation's "Horizon" series)

[Gordon R. Taylor, _The Great Evolution Mystery_ (New York: Harper & Row, 1983), p. 60 (emphasis added).]

☐ "Each must have required a long and complex series of genetic changes, which needed to be correlated with each other at all times so that the animal remained viable throughout. Evolution of this kind must always need long periods of time, but in spite of this _the fossils give us little evidence of its course in the (E)volution of the Amphibia._ Even the most primitive amphibians we know, the Ichthyostegalia, were as adults _fully adapted to terrestrial life_ in many of their characters, for instance in their pentadactyl limbs." (Evolutionist G. Carter speaking of the various differences between amphibians, reptiles, mammals, and birds)

[G.S. Carter, _Structure and Habit in Vertebrate Evolution_ (Seattle: University of Washington Press, 1967), 520 pp. (quote is from p. 263 — emphasis added).]

REPTILES

287

☐ "Unfortunately _not a single specimen_ of an appropriate reptilian ancestor is known prior to the appearance of _true_ reptiles. The absence of such ancestral forms leaves many problems of the amphibian-reptilian transition unanswered." (Evolutionist Robert Carroll)

[Robert L. Carroll, "Problems of the Origin of Reptiles," _Biological Reviews of the Cambridge Philosophical Society_, Vol. 44, No. 3 (July 1969), p. 393.]

☐ Recently a "340 million year old" 8 inch long lizard was found in southern Scotland by Stan Wood, a commercial fossil hunter. It was found in Lower Carboniferous strata. This is "40 million" years older than any other known reptile. Wood said, "It was below the level at which I previously found what were regarded as the ancestors of the reptiles."

[Graham Heathcote, "Oldest Reptile Found; Owner Aims to Sell It," Associated Press dispatch from London, _The Arizona Republic_, Vol. 99, No. 186 (Phoenix: November 20, 1988), p. AA-4.]

MAMMALS

288

☐ "_Each_ species of mammal-like reptile that has been found _appears suddenly_ in the fossil record and is _not preceded_ by the species that is directly ancestral to it. It disappears some time later, equally abruptly, without leaving a directly descended species..." (Evolutionist Dr. Tom Kemp, Curator of Zoological Collections at the Oxford University Museum, England)

[Tom Kemp, "The Reptiles that Became Mammals," _New Scientist_, Vol. 92 (March 4, 1982), p. 583 (emphasis added).]

☐ "The (Evolutionary) transition to the first _mammal_, which probably happened in just one or, at most, two lineages, is _still an enigma._" (Evolutionist Roger Lewin, science writer)

[Roger Lewin, "Bones of Mammals' Ancestors Fleshed Out," _Science_, Vol. 212, No. 4502 (June 26, 1981), p. 1492 (emphasis added).]

Anyone with the slightest understanding of the hydraulics of moving water and the hydrodynamic forces associated with it would know that a worldwide 'tranquil' flood is about as reasonable a concept as a worldwide tranquil explosion!
Henry Morris, hydraulicist and flood specialist

CONCERNING FOSSIL EVIDENCE FOR THE MACROEVOLUTION OF ALL ANIMALS

289

☐ On behalf of the New York State Board of Regents, origins researcher Luther Sunderland interviewed the <u>top</u> paleontology experts at five of the world's <u>greatest</u> fossil museums. The result:

"*<u>No</u> museum official offered <u>any</u> real fossil evidence that <u>any</u> <u>one</u> of the various <u>invertebrates evolved into vertebrate fish</u>.*" (Sunderland, p. 63)

"*<u>None</u> of the museum officials could produce <u>any</u> fossil evidence of an intermediate ancestor connecting the <u>amphibians with fishes</u>.*" (Sunderland, p. 64)

"*<u>None</u> of the five museum officials could offer a <u>single</u> example of a transitional series of fossilized organisms that would document the transformation of <u>one</u> basically different type to another.*" (Sunderland, p. 88)

[Luther D. Sunderland, *Darwin's Enigma: Fossils and Other Problems*, 4th edition (Santee, California: Master Books, 1988) (emphasis added).]

☐ "*As is now <u>well known</u>, most fossil species appear <u>instantaneously</u> in the fossil record.*" (Evolutionist Tom Kemp, Curator of the University Museum at Oxford University)

[Tom Kemp, "A Fresh Look at the Fossil Record," *New Scientist*, Vol. 108, No. 1485 (December 5, 1985), p. 66 (emphasis added).]

☐ "*The curious thing is that there is a <u>consistency</u> about the fossil gaps; the fossils are missing <u>in all the important places</u>.*" (Francis Hitching, Royal Institute of Archaeology)

[Francis Hitching, *The Neck of the Giraffe or Where Darwin Went Wrong* (Bergenfield, New Jersey: Penguin Books, 1982), p. 19.]

☐ "*In any case, <u>no real evolutionist</u>, whether gradualist or punctuationist, <u>uses the fossil record as evidence in favour of the theory of evolution as opposed to special creation</u>...*" (Mark Ridley, Professor of Zoology at Oxford University)

[Mark Ridley, "Who Doubts Evolution?," *New Scientist*, Vol 90, No. 1259 (June 25, 1981), pp. 830-832 (quote from p. 831 — emphasis added.)]

☐ "*The more scientists have searched for the transitional forms that lie between species, the more they have been <u>frustrated</u>.*"

[John Adler with John Carey, "Is Man a Subtle Accident?", *Newsweek*, Vol. 96, No. 18 (November 3, 1980), p. 95 (emphasis added).]

☐ "*All paleontologists know that the fossil record contains precious little in the way of intermediate forms; transitions between major groups are characteristically abrupt.*"

[Stephen J. Gould, "The Return of Hopeful Monsters," *Natural History*, Vol. 86 (1977), p. 22.]

☐ "*The <u>absence</u> of fossil evidence for intermediary stages between major transitions in organic design, indeed our inability, even in our imagination, to construct functional intermediates in many cases, has been a <u>persistent and nagging problem</u> for gradualistic accounts of evolution.*" (Stephen J. Gould, ardent Evolutionist and Professor of Geology and Paleontology at Harvard University)

[Stephen Gould, "Is a New and General Theory of Evolution Emerging?," *Paleobiology*, Vol. 6 (January 1980), p. 127 (emphasis added).]

☐ "*The known fossil record <u>fails</u> to document a <u>single</u> example of phyletic (E)volution accomplishing a major morphologic transition...*" (Evolutionist Steven M. Stanley)

[Steven Stanley, *Macroevolution: Pattern and Process* (San Francisco: W.M. Freeman and Company, 1979), p. 39 (emphasis added).]

☐ "*...most people assume that fossils provide a very important part of the general argument made in favor of Darwinian interpretations of the history of life. Unfortunately, this is <u>not</u> strictly true.*" (Dr. David Raup, Curator of the Field Museum of Natural History in Chicago)

[David Raup, "Conflicts Between Darwin and Paleontology," *Field Museum of Natural History Bulletin*, Vol. 50, No. 1 (1979), pp. 22-29 (emphasis added).]

☐ "*The family trees which adorn our textbooks are based on inference, however reasonable, not the evidence of fossils.*" (Evolutionist Gould)

[Stephen J. Gould, "Evolution's Erratic Pace," *Natural History*, Vol. 86, No. 5 (May 1977), p. 13.]

☐ "*Despite the bright promise that paleontology provides us a means of 'seeing' Evolution. It has presented some <u>nasty difficulties for evolutionists</u>, the most notorious of which is the presence of <u>'gaps'</u> in the fossil record. Evolution requires intermediate forms between species and <u>paleontology does not provide them</u>.*" (David Kitts, Ph.D. in Zoology, well-known Evolutionary paleontologist, Head Curator of the Department of Geology of the Stoval Museum)

[David B. Kitts, "Paleontology and Evolutionary Theory," *Evolution, Vol. 128 (September 1974), p. 467 (emphasis added).]*

☐ "*It must also be remembered that we never have available for our discussions the actual forms from which a later group evolved, for, as we have seen, <u>we never find among the fossils a record of the exact point of divergence of one group from another</u>.*" (Carter, p. 11)

"*...many of the forms that would be of the greatest interest to us are missing. In particular, we have no direct fossil evidence of the steps in these early stages of vertebrate evolution by which any of the major groups arose from earlier forms.*" (Carter, p. 187) (Evolutionist author and Professor G.S. Carter, Fellow of Corpus Christi College, Cambridge, England)

[G.S. Carter, *Structure and Habit in Vertebrate Evolution* (Seattle: University of Washington Press, 1967), 520 pp.]

☐ "*It remains true, <u>as every paleontologist knows</u>, that most new species, genera, and families, and that nearly all categories above the level of families, appear in the (fossil) record <u>suddenly</u>, and are <u>not</u> led up to by gradual, completely continuous transitional sequences.*" (Dr. George Simpson, ardent Evolutionist and fossil expert)

[George G. Simpson, *The Major Features of Evolution* (New York: Columbia University Press, 1953), p. 360 (emphasis added).]

290

☐ Dr. Colin Patterson, Senior Principal Scientific Officer of the Paleontology Department of the British Museum of Natural History, London:

"*<u>I fully agree</u> with your comments on the lack of direct illustration of evolutionary transitions in my book. <u>If I knew of any, fossil or living, I would certainly have included them</u>... Yet Gould and the American Museum people are hard to contradict when they say <u>there are no transitional forms</u>... I will lay it on the line — <u>there is not one such fossil for which one could make a watertight argument</u>.*"

[Colin Patterson in a personal letter to Luther D. Sunderland (April 10, 1979) — See: Luther D. Sunderland, *Darwin's Enigma: Fossils and Other Problems*, 4th edition (Santee, California: Master Books, 1988), p. 89 (emphasis added).]

291

☐ Charles Darwin on the lack of fossil evidence:

"*But, as by this theory <u>innumerable</u> transitional forms <u>must</u> have existed, <u>why</u> do we <u>not</u> find them embedded in <u>countless</u> numbers in the crust of the earth?* (p. 206, Chapter 6 on 'Difficulties on Theory')

"*But just in proportion as this process of extermination has acted on an enormous scale, so <u>must</u> the numbers of intermediate varieties, which have formerly existed on the earth, be truly <u>enormous</u>. Why then is <u>not</u> every geological formation and every stratum <u>full</u> of such intermediate links? Geology assuredly does <u>not</u> reveal <u>any</u> such finely graduated organic chain; and this, perhaps, is the most obvious and <u>gravest</u> objection which can be urged against my theory (of Evolution).*" (p. 292, first paragraph of Chapter 9 "On the Imperfection of the Geologic Record")

[Charles Robert Darwin, *The Origin of Species by Means of Natural Selection*, first edition reprint (New York: Avenel Books, 1979) (emphasis added).]

292

☐ Evolutionist Neville George:

"*There is no need to apologize any longer for the poverty of the fossil record. In some ways it has become almost unmanageably rich...*"

[T. Neville George, "Fossils in Evolutionary Perspective," *Science Progress*, Vol. 48, No. 1 (January 1960).]

CONCERNING A CONTINUING LACK OF EVIDENCE FOR MACROEVOLUTION IN A FOSSIL RECORD WHICH IS RICH

293

☐ Evolutionist and paleontologist David Raup:

"*Darwin... was embarrassed by the fossil record... we are now about 120 years after Darwin and the knowledge of the fossil record has been greatly expanded. We now have a quarter of a million fossil species, but the situation hasn't changed much... <u>We have even fewer examples of Evolutionary transition than we had in Darwin's time</u>.*"

[David M. Raup, "Conflicts Between Darwin and Paleontology," *Field Museum of Natural History*, Vol. 50, No. 1 (January 1979), p. 22 (emphasis added).]

☐ "*Now, <u>after over 120 years of the most extensive and painstaking geological exploration of every continent and ocean bottom, the picture is</u> infinitely more vivid and complete than it was in 1859. Formations have been discovered containing hundreds of billions of fossils and our museums now are filled with over 100 million fossils of 250,000 different species. The availability of this profusion of hard scientific data should permit objective investigators to determine if Darwin was on the right track. What is the picture which the fossils have given us? ...<u>The gaps between major groups of organisms have been growing even wider and more undeniable. They can no longer be ignored or rationalized away with appeals to the imperfection of the fossil record</u>.*" (Creation/Evolution researcher Luther Sunderland)

A growing number of respectable scientists are defecting from the evolutionist camp, ...moreover, for the most part these 'experts' have abandoned Darwinism, not on the basis of religious faith or biblical persuasions, but on strictly scientific grounds, and in some instances, regretfully."
Wolfgang Smith, Ph.D., physicist and mathematician

[Luther D. Sunderland, *Darwin's Enigma: Fossils and Other Problems*, 4th edition (Santee, California: Master Books, 1988), p. 9 (emphasis added).]

☐ "*All one can learn about the history of life is learned from systematics, from groupings one finds in nature. The rest of it is <u>story-telling</u> of one sort or another. We have access to the tips of a tree; the <u>tree itself is theory</u> — and people who pretend to know about the tree and to describe what went on with it... I think, are telling stories.*" (Evolutionist Dr. Colin Patterson, Senior Paleontologist of the British Museum of Natural History, London)

[Colin Patterson in a British Broadcasting Corporation television program (March 4, 1982) (emphasis added).]

☐ "*At the present stage of geological research, we <u>have to admit that there is nothing in the geological records that runs contrary to the view of conservative creationists</u>, that God created each species (Creationists would say 'baramin', not 'species') separately, presumably from the dust of the earth.*" (Dr. Edmund J. Ambrose, Emeritus Professor of Cell Biology at the University of London)

[Edmund Ambrose, *The Nature and Origin of the Biological World* (New York: John Wiley & Sons, 1982), p. 164 (emphasis added).]

SUGGESTED SOURCES FOR FURTHER INFORMATION ON THIS TOPIC

☐ Luther D. Sunderland, *Darwin's Enigma: Fossils and Other Problems*, 4th edition (Santee, California: Master Books, 1988).

☐ Gary Parker, "The Fossil Evidence," in Henry M. Morris and Gary E. Parker, *What Is Creation Science?*, revised and expanded edition (San Diego: Master Books, 1987), pp. 125-184.

☐ Duane T. Gish, *Evolution: The Challenge of the Fossil Record* (El Cajon: CLP Publishers, 1986).

☐ Duane T. Gish, *Evolution: The Fossils Say No!* (El Cajon, California: Master Book Publishers, 1981).

☐ Richard B. Bliss, Gary E. Parker, and Duane T. Gish, *Fossils: Key to the Present* (El Cajon: CLP Publishers, 1980).

☐ Randy L. Wysong, *The Creation-Evolution Controversy* (Midland, Michigan: Inquiry Press, 1976).

As a result of all these findings, an increasing number of scientists have lost faith in Evolutionism

☐ "*<u>Hundreds</u> of scientists who once taught their university students that the bottom line on origins had finally been figured out and settled are today <u>confessing</u> that they were <u>completely wrong</u>. They've discovered that their previous conclusions, once held so <u>fervently</u>, were based on very <u>fragile</u> evidences and <u>suppositions</u> which have since been <u>refuted</u> by new discoveries.*" (Creation/Evolution researcher Luther D. Sunderland)

[Luther D. Sunderland, *Darwin's Enigma: Fossils and Other Problems*, 4th edition (Santee, California: Master Books, 1988), pp. 7-8 (emphasis added).]

☐ A number of formerly ardent Evolutionists have accepted part or all of the concepts of Creationism. Biologist and paleontologist Dr. Gary Parker is one of these. He comments:

"In most people's minds, fossils and Evolution go hand in hand. In reality, fossils are a great embarrassment to Evolutionary theory and offer strong support for the concept of Creation. If Evolution were true, we should find literally millions of fossils that show how one kind of life slowly and gradually changed into another kind of life. But, missing links are the trade secret, in a sense, of paleontology. The point is, the links are STILL MISSING. What we really find are gaps that sharpen up the boundaries between kinds. It's those gaps which provide us with the evidence of Creation of separate kinds. As a matter of fact, there are gaps between each of the major kinds of plants and animals. Transition forms are missing by the millions. What we do find are separate and complex kinds, pointing to Creation."

[Gary E. Parker in Willem J.J. Glashouwer and Paul S. Taylor, writers, *The Origin of Species* (Mesa, Arizona: Eden Films and Standard Media, 1983) (Creationist motion picture) (emphasis is Dr. Parker's).]

☐ *"The extreme rarity of transitional forms in the fossil record persists as the trade secret of paleontology."* (Evolutionist Stephen Jay Gould)

[Stephen J. Gould, "Evolution's Erratic Pace," *Natural History*, Vol. 86, No. 5 (May 1977), p. 14.]

294

☐ Figures supplied by Evolutionist Matthews indicate that less than 10% of all the species are known only as fossils; 90% are living. There are approximately 1,105,000 *living* species of animals and only about 130,000 *extinct* species discovered thus far.

[William H. Matthews, III, *Fossils* (New York: Barnes and Noble, Inc., 1982), p. 8.]

295

☐ **Duane T. Gish**: Creationist / Biochemist / Lecturer / Ph.D. in Biochemistry from University of California at Berkeley / Research Associate, Research Division, The Upjohn Company, Kalamazoo, Michigan (1960-1971) / Assistant Research Associate in Biochemistry, University of California (Berkeley), Virus Laboratory (1956-1960) / Assistant Professor of Biochemistry, Cornell University Medical College (NYC) (1955-1956) / Lilly Postdoctoral Fellow, Cornell University Medical College (1953-1955) / Phi Beta Kappa, University of California, Los Angeles / Vice President of the Institute for Creation Research / Foremost debater on Creation-Evolution.

296

☐ Duane T. Gish in Willem J.J. Glashouwer and Paul S. Taylor, writers, *The Fossil Record* (Mesa, Arizona: Eden Films and Standard Media, 1983) (Creationist motion picture).

297

☐ All basic kinds of animals appear abruptly in the fossil record. Excellent documentation of this can be found in the following paleontological report: W.B. Harland, et al, *The Fossil Record* (London: Geological Society of London, 1967).

298

☐ Fossilization experiments in the sediment-rich Mississippi River delta region showed that it takes far greater than normal sedimentation to prevent the total disintegration of fish by bacteria and scavengers.

[Ranier Zangerl and Eugene S. Richardson, Jr., "The Paleoecological History of Two Pennsylvanian Black Shales," *Fieldiana: Geology Memoirs*, Vol. 4 (Chicago: Field Natural History Museum, 1963), pp. 20-21, 167-169.]

☐ Luther D. Sunderland, *Darwin's Enigma: Fossils and Other Problems*, Revised Edition (Santee, California: Master Book Publishers, 1988), pp. 111-114.

WORLDWIDE EVIDENCE OF RAPID, CATASTROPHIC BURIAL AND EROSION

299

☐ Creationist Albert W. Mehlert:

"The fossil record does not support any long-age concept... No! — time is the <u>enemy</u> of historical geologists. <u>The record only makes sense if the world's strata were laid down fairly recently</u>."

[Albert W. Mehlert, "Diluviology and Uniformitarian Geology — A Review," *Creation Research Society Quarterly*, Vol. 23, No. 3 (P.O. Box 14016, Terre Haute, Indiana 47803: December 1986), pp. 104, 106 (emphasis added).]

☐ Luther Sunderland, Creation/Evolution researcher:

*"The scientific establishment's acceptance of worldwide catastrophism and mass extinction does not signify their abandonment of materialistic Evolution. Neither has their grudging acquiescence to <u>the fact that great catastrophes caused the deposition of many of the fossils</u> forced them to consider that <u>virtually no fossils are in the process of forming on the bottom of any lake or sea today</u>. This is a **verboten** subject. When I asked the editors of several of the most prestigious scientific journals the reason for this silence, I was met with more silence."*

[Luther D. Sunderland, "Mass Extinction and Catastrophism Replace Darwinism and Uniformitarianism," *Contrast: The Creation Evolution Controversy*, Vol. 4, No. 2 (P.O. Box 32457, Minneapolis, Minnesota 55432, Phone 612-635-0614: March/April 1986), pp. 1-2 (emphasis added).]

☐ Geologist and Evolutionist Derek Ager:

"The hurricane, the flood, or the tsunami may do more in an hour or a day than the ordinary processes of nature achieved in a thousand years."

[Derek V. Ager, *The Nature of Stratigraphical Record* (New York: John Wiley & Sons Publishers, 1973), p. 49.]

☐ For evidence of catastrophe in the fossil record, see index.

300

☐ The fossils of millions of fish worldwide speak of death by catastrophe. A *Science* magazine article reported a 4-square-mile area where "more than a billion fish" were killed and densely packed in the sediment.

[H.S. Ladd, "Ecology, Paleontology, and Stratigraphy," *Science* (January 9, 1959), p. 72.]

Also see: David S. Jordon, "A Miocene Catastrophe," *Natural History*, Vol. 20 (1920), pp. 18-22.

☐ *"It can <u>definitely</u> be said that, through all the geologic formations in which fish remains occur, a large proportion of the remains consists of entire fishes or of sections in which every scale is in position... All of this <u>conclusively proves that when myriads of fish were simultaneously killed, their bodies were deposited... and preserved intact either immediately or within a day or two at most after death</u>."* (J.M. MacFarlane of the University of Pennsylvania states)

[J.M. MacFarlane, *Fishes, The Source of Petroleum* (New York: Macmillan, 1923), p. 400 (emphasis added).]

301

☐ Experiments by Dr. George R. Hill and Dr. Don C. Adams at the University of Utah have shown that plant matter can be turned into coal in a matter of hours.

[George R. Hill, "Some Aspects of Coal Research," *Chemical Technology* (May 1972), p. 296.]

[George R. Hill and Don C. Adams, *Exothermal Metamorphosis of Coal Precursors* (Salt Lake City: University of Utah, College of Mines and Mineral Industries, 1970).]

[Don C. Adams, *Exothermal Metamorphosis of Coal Precursors*, doctoral dissertation (Salt Lake City: University of Utah, Dept. of Mineral Engineering, August 1970).]

☐ The scientific journal *Research and Development* reported the rapid formation of coal when plant material (lignin) was heated together with illite clay or montmorillite:

"A group at Argonne National Laboratory near Chicago, Illinois, recently uncovered some clues as to the origin of coal. The studies indicate that currently accepted theories of the development of coal probably are wrong..."

[(author not listed), "Basic Coal Studies Refute Current Theories of Formation," *Research and Development*, (February 1984), p. 92.]

☐ Similarly, experiments by the U.S. Bureau of Mines showed that petroleum (oil) can be produced from organic matter in only 20 minutes.

[Hayden R. Appell, Y.C. Fu, Sam Friedman, et al, "Converting Organic Wastes to Oil," RL-7560 (Washington, D.C.: United States Department of the Interior, Bureau of Mines, 1971).]

Also, see: *Science* News, Vol. 125 (March 24, 1984), p. 187.

302

☐ **Steven A. Austin**: Creationist / Geologist / Ph.D. from Pennsylvania State University, doctoral dissertation on coal formation / Professor of Geology, Institute for Creation Research Graduate School / Consulting geologist for government and industry.

303

☐ Steven A. Austin, *Depositional Environment of the Kentucky No. 12 Coal Bed (Middle Pennsylvanian) of Western Kentucky, With Special Reference to the Origin of Coal Lithotypes*, doctoral dissertation (Pennsylvania State University, 1979), 390 pp. (University Microfilms International, Ann Arbor, MI, Order No. 8005972.)

☐ Steven A. Austin, *Catastrophes in Earth History* (P.O. Box 2667, El Cajon, California 92021: Institute for Creation Research, 1984), 318 pp. (includes large bibliography of recent secular geology books and papers supporting catastrophism).

☐ Stuart E. Nevin (Steven A. Austin), "The Origin of Coal," Impact Series No. 41, *Acts & Facts* (P.O. Box 2667, El Cajon, California 92021: Institute for Creation Research, November 1976).

304

☐ Dr. Austin made this discovery by producing ultra-thin cross-slices of numerous coal samples for microscopic analysis.

SUGGESTED SOURCES FOR FURTHER DETAILS ON POLYSTRATE TREE FOSSILS

305

☐ Mats Molen, *Vart Ursprung?: Om Universums, Jordens Och Livets Uppkomst Samt Historia* (Box 3110, 13603, Haninge, Sweden:

1988), 302 pp. (includes a good selection of photos and references concerning polystrate fossils / text is in Swedish).

☐ Harold G. Coffin, "Erect Floating Stumps in Spirit Lake, Washington," *Geology*, Vol. 11 (May 1983), pp. 298-299.

☐ Harold G. Coffin, "Vertical Flotation of Horsetails (*Equisetum*): Geological Implications," *The Geological Society of America Bulletin*, Vol. 82 (July 1971), pp. 2019-2022.

☐ N.A. Rupke, "Prolegomena to a Study of Cataclysmal Sedimentation," in Walter E. Lammerts, editor, *Why Not Creation?* (Grand Rapids, Michigan: Baker Book House, 1970), pp. 152-157.

☐ Harold G. Coffin, "Research on the Classic Joggins Petrified Trees," *Creation Research Society Quarterly*, Vol. 6, No. 1 (P.O. Box 14016, Terre Haute, Indiana 47803: June 1969), pp. 34-44, 70.

☐ Byron C. Nelson, *The Deluge Story in Stone* (Minneapolis: Bethany Fellowship, 1968), pp. 111-112 (re: Craiglieth Quarry).

☐ F.M. Broadhurst, "Some Aspects of the Paleoecology of Non-Marine Faunas and Rates of Sedimentation in the Lancashire Coal Measures," *American Journal of Science*, Vol. 262 (Summer 1964), pp. 858-869.

☐ George McCready Price, *The New Geology* (Mountain View: Pacific Press, 1923), p. 462.

☐ E.A. Newell Arber, *The Natural History of Coal* (England: Cambridge University Press, 1912), pp. 101, 114.

☐ C.O. Dunbar, *Geology*, 2nd edition (New York: Wiley and Sons, 1960), p. 227.

☐ A. Geikie, *Textbook of Geology*, 4th edition (London: Macmillan Publishing Company, 1903), pp. 654-655.

☐ Robert R. Schrock, *Sequence in Layered Rocks* (New York: McGraw-Hill Book Co., 1948), p. 293.

☐ H. Witham, "A Description of a Fossil Tree Discovered in the Quarry of Craiglieth," *Transactions of the Royal Society of Edinburgh*, Vol. 12 (1832), pp. 147-152.

☐ Another interesting evidence for the rapid burial of trees comes from the research of Dr. Robert Gentry. In numerous samples of coalified wood he found microscopic radiohalos produced by Polonium-210. The halos were elliptical, rather than perfectly round.

☐ "This indicated that the halos were formed while the wood was still in a *soft* condition, *before* it was compressed by the weight of overlying sediment. After careful analysis it was found that the elliptical polonium halos in wood specimens taken from *three different* geological strata — the Triassic, Jurassic and Eocene — were virtually *identical*. Evidence suggested that all the wood had been infiltrated with the *same* uranium-bearing solution during a *single* event. These findings had *disturbing* implications for conventional geochronology. The Triassic, Jurassic and Eocene formations are thought by most scientists to have been deposited tens of *millions* of years apart... The simplest scenario to account for their infiltration would be a major flood which uprooted trees, soaking them in water which had absorbed large amounts of uranium from nearby ground deposits, and finally compressing them between layers of sediment. A flood like the one described in the biblical book of Genesis would have done just that." (Reporter Dennis Crews)

[Dennis Crews, "Mystery in the Rocks," *The Inside Report* (March/April 1988), pp. 3-4 (emphasis added).]

*I*t is not the duty of science to defend the theory of Evolution, and stick by it to the bitter end — no matter what illogical and unsupported conclusions it offers...
I. Cohen, mathematician and archaeologist

306

☐ **Arthur V. Chadwick**: Creationist / Geologist / Ph.D. in Geology from University of Miami (1969) / Professor of Geology and Biology at Southwestern Adventist College, Keene, Texas.

CONCERNING THE ENORMOUS POWER OF LARGE AMOUNTS OF FAST-MOVING WATER

307

☐ The speed of moving water *greatly* increases erosive force and sediment transporting capacity (increases at a rate of a 3rd or 4th power of its velocity).

[A. Holmes, *Principles of Physical Geology* (New York: The Ronald Press Company, 1965), p. 512 (as cited by John C. Whitcomb in *The World That Perished*, 2nd edition (1988), p. 133.]

☐ Increasing the flow speed 10 times results in an increased sediment carrying capacity of 1 thousand times greater or even 10 thousand times greater.

[John C. Whitcomb in *The World That Perished*, 2nd edition (1988), p. 133.]

☐ A process called "cavitation" is also an astoundingly powerful erosive force involved in flooding. During rapid discharge at the Glen Canyon Dam, U.S.A., cavitation once eroded over 62 thousand cubic feet of solid rock (equivalent to a 12 foot thick slab of rock the size of a basketball court) in about one minute. Engineer and educator Paul MacKinney:

"Vacuum bubbles formed within turbulent fluids (including water) possess unimaginable capability for rapidly reducing materials. Evidence from constantly monitored civil engineering projects, aerodynamics, marine acoustics, engine design, etc.; combine to witness that cavitation: unavoidable in floods, must be avoided in fluid dynamics design. Rampant cavitation explains flood sediment origins within minimum time. ...Laboratory tests at Stanford University demonstrate impacts as high as 350,000 pounds per square inch resulting from shock waves initiated by the collapse of vacuum bubbles (cavitation). Other investigators suggest forces as high as 30,000 atmospheres, or about 450,000 psi... The certainty of its widespread activity in floods is beyond question both theoretically and from observation. ...Ongoing cavitation during the historical Flood and the breaking up of the fountains of the deep would have resulted in sequential subsidence of large sections of the crust of the earth down into the exhausted fountain cavities. These reservoirs supported the crust prior to all being broken up in one day. ...Impact, electrical and thermal shock from cavitation event may make cement instantaneously, providing rapid sedimentary lithification."

[Paul M. Mackinney, "Abstract: 'Nothing' Can Reduce 'Everything,'" (3468 Don Juan Drive, Carlsbad, California 92008: P. MacKinney, 1989) (emphasis added).]

308

☐ Geologist A. Chadwick, Ph.D.:

"One thing that supports this view is the fact that these layers are continuous for mile after mile through the Canyon. You can pick any one of these layers and follow it through for 100 or 200 miles in the Canyon, with very little change. This kind of continuity and uniformity suggests that deep water was involved in the process."

[Arthur V. Chadwick in the Creationist motion picture, *The Fossil Record* (Mesa, Arizona: Eden Films and Standard Media, 1983).]

☐ Also, see: Arthur V. Chadwick, "Megabreccias: Evidence for Catastrophism," *Origins*, Vol. 5 (Loma Linda, California: Geoscience Research Institute, Loma Linda University, 1978), pp. 39-46.

309

☐ Albert Mehlert, Creationist researcher:

"A week's study of the Grand Canyon should be a good cure for Evolutionary geologists as it is a perfect example of Flood geology with its paraconformities and striking parallelisms of the under strata. The whole area was obviously laid down quickly, then uplifted and then the whole sedimentary area split open like a rotten watermelon."

[Albert W. Mehlert, "Diluviology and Uniformitarian Geology — A Review," *Creation Research Society Quarterly*, Vol. 23, No. 3 (P.O. Box 14016, Terre Haute, Indiana 47803: December 1986), p. 106 (emphasis added).]

310

☐ See examples of very rapid, mature-appearing canyon erosion after the eruption of Mount St. Helens, U.S.A.

[Steven A. Austin, "Rapid Erosion at Mount St. Helens," *Origins*, Vol. 11, No. 2 (Loma Linda, California: Geoscience Research Institute, Loma Linda University, 1984), pp. 90-98.]

311

☐ Hydraulicist and flood geology specialist Dr. Henry Morris says there is no doubt that a worldwide flood would be accompanied by geological upheaval, earthquakes and massive volcanic activity:

"Anyone with the slightest understanding of the hydraulics of moving water and the hydrodynamic forces associated with it would know that a worldwide 'tranquil' flood is about as reasonable a concept as a worldwide tranquil explosion!"

[Henry M. Morris, *King of Creation* (San Diego: CLP Publishers, 1980), p. 151.]

312

☐ John Woodmorappe, "The Antediluvian Biosphere and Its Capability of Supplying the Entire Fossil Record," in Robert E. Walsh, et al., editors, *Proceedings of the First International Conference on Creationism*, Vol. 2 (August 4-9, 1986), pp. 205-218.

SOME LINES OF EVIDENCE SUGGESTED IN SUPPORT OF AN ANCIENT, WORLDWIDE FLOOD CATASTROPHE — involving massive amounts of water, earthquakes, volcanic eruptions, "tsunamis", turbidity currents, massive erosion, etc.

313

☐ **EXISTENCE OF EXTREMELY LARGE NUMBERS OF FOSSILS** — Fossilization requires rapid burial. Yet such burial is exceedingly rare today, and fossilization is almost nonexistent in modern times. The existence of massive numbers of fossils worldwide is clear evidence of quick, deep, mass burial. A global flood catastrophe would offer conditions most ideal to the formation of great numbers of fossils. Many (if not most) fossils give evidence that the animals were killed suddenly — most likely connected with their entombment. There is no strong evidence to the contrary. And, in fact, there are often good indicators of this.

☐ **RAPID FOSSILIZATION, AS EVIDENCED BY PRESERVATION OF DELICATE PARTS**

• Thousands and millions of fish fossils which retain all the body parts indicating very rapid burial. Under normal conditions, fish do not fossilize. Dead fish are torn apart by scavengers and disintegrated by bacteria.

- The existence of fossils of such soft invertebrates as jellyfish and sponges.
- Preservation of animal tracks, fish odors, dung, rain prints, mud cracks, amino acids, proteins, epidermal hairs in plants, cell details, chlorophyll, etc.

□ **WHALE FOSSILS** — Such huge animals as ancient whales can be found completely and quickly buried in sediment.

[Example. K.M. Reese, "Workers Find Whale in Diatomaceous Earth Quarry," *Chemical and Engineering News*, Vol. 54, No. 42 (October 11, 1976), p. 40.]

□ **POLYSTRATE FOSSILS** — The existence of fossils (trees, shells, etc.) extending into two, three or more layers of strata.

□ **RANDOM ORDER OF FOSSILS** — The sediments do not exhibit strong evidence of a record of Evolution with simple animals at the bottom, progressing type by type up to more and more complex animals. The order is often random or completely upside down or out of order for Evolution. But, this would be expected in a global flood catastrophe.

□ **MASSIVE SEDIMENTATION** — The global existence of massive amounts of sediment. Most of Earth's crust is covered with layer upon layer of sediment and evidence of strong sorting action produced by moving water. Frequently the sediment bears strong evidence of having been laid under flood conditions. Where can one find dolomite, siliceous iron, etc. forming in large quantity today?

□ **DOLOSTONE BEDS** — The global existence of massive amounts of dolostone. Beds are sometimes thousands of feet thick. Dolostone is not forming today.

[Stuart E. Nevins, "Stratigraphic Evidence of the Flood," in Donald W. Patten, editor, *Symposium on Creation III* (Grand Rapids, Michigan: Baker Book House, 1971), pp. 46-48.]

□ **CHERT BEDS** — The global existence of large amounts of chert. Beds are up to 50 feet thick (or more). No chert is forming today.

[Stuart E. Nevins, "Stratigraphic Evidence of the Flood," in Donald W. Patten, editor, *Symposium on Creation III* (Grand Rapids, Michigan: Baker Book House, 1971), pp. 48-49.]

□ **CONGLOMERATE** — The global existence of massive amounts of conglomerate rock indicating deposition under flood conditions over extremely wide areas with very strong currents. (Conglomerate consists of cemented gravel, sand and boulders.)

[Stuart E. Nevins, "Stratigraphic Evidence of the Flood," in Donald W. Patten, editor, *Symposium on Creation III* (Grand Rapids, Michigan: Baker Book House, 1971), pp. 50-51 (p. 51 — *"such a present-day widespread conglomerate in the process of formation has not been found."*]

□ **GRAYWACKE** — The global existence of massive amounts of graywacke (greywacke) sandstone. Very rapid deposition is implied. No graywacke sediments have been found forming today.

[Stuart E. Nevins, "Stratigraphic Evidence of the Flood," in Donald W. Patten, editor, *Symposium on Creation III* (Grand Rapids, Michigan: Baker Book House, 1971), pp. 51-53.]

□ **MASSIVE PRECIPITATIONS OF GYPSUM, COMMON SALT, AND ANHYDRITE** — Enormous, relatively pure beds of these minerals are found globally, sometimes thousands of feet thick — without clear evidence of other sediments (waterborne or air-borne). Some claim these beds are much easier to explain in terms of a rapid precipitation in "deep" water, than it is over thousands of years.

[Duane T. Gish, "Precipitation Brought About by Mixing Brines," in "More Creationist Research (14 Years) — Part I: Geological Research," *Creation Research Society Quarterly*, Vol. 25, No. 4 (P.O. Box 14016, Terre Haute, Indiana 47803: March 1989), pp. 168-169.]

[Stuart E. Nevins, "Stratigraphic Evidence of the Flood," in Donald W. Patten, editor, *Symposium on Creation III* (Grand Rapids, Michigan: Baker Book House, 1971), pp. 53-54.]

□ **FLUID DYNAMICS EXPERIMENTS** — have yielded evidence for how cyclic turbulence during a global flood might naturally produce a layering effect in the sediments. Layers of clay, sand, lime, organic material, and the like, could naturally tend to be piled on top of each other in repeated patterns in very short periods.

[Marlyn E. Clark and H.D. Voss, "Computer Simulation of Large-Scale Wave Motions Associated with the Genesis Flood," *Creation Research Society Quarterly*, Vol. 17, No. 1 (P.O. Box 14016, Terre Haute, Indiana 47803: June 1980), pp. 28-40.

[H.D. Voss, M.E. Clark, et al., "Investigation of a Global Flood Using a Large Circular Flume" (2020 Zuppke Drive, Urbana, IL 61801: The Genesis Research Laboratory, 1980+).]

□ **COAL** — The existence of coal in enormous amounts. No uniformitarian theory adequately explains the evidence of coal as well as does catastrophic flooding.

□ **MASSIVE VOLCANISM** — The existence of thousands of cubic miles of volcanic and granitic rock types, as would be expected during a global catastrophic geologic upheaval.

□ **WARM GLOBAL CLIMATE** — evidence of a worldwide climate that was more uniformly warm before the Flood. No evidence of frozen Poles.

□ **EVIDENCE OF SIGNIFICANT PAST GLOBAL TEMPERATURE CHANGES.** This would be an expected result of a worldwide catastrophe involving massive volcanic releases into the atmosphere, worldwide flooding and, later, great evaporation from wet continents.

□ **CORRELATION OF DEATH DATES BY RADIOCARBON** — When the Carbon-14 dating method is "correctly" calibrated, and 25 thousand radiocarbon dates are graphed, the result shows evidence of a great peak of death about 4 thousand years ago.

[Robert L. Whitelaw, "Time, Life and History in the Light of 15,000 Radiocarbon Dates," *Creation Research Society Quarterly*, Vol. 7, No. 1 (P.O. Box 14016, Terre Haute, Indiana 47803: June 1970), pp. 56-71, 83.]

□ **EVIDENCE OF RAPID DEPOSITION IN THE INTERNAL CHARACTERISTICS OF STRATA SEQUENCES** — "The widespread physical similarity in the order of strata in each

The fact that a theory so vague, so insufficiently verifiable, and so far from the criteria otherwise applied in 'hard' science has become a dogma can only be explained on sociological grounds.
Ludwig von Bertalanffy, biologist

sequence indicates that virtually identical conditions were prevalent laterally over broad areas. Sandstones and conglomerates, which form the basal and best preserved parts of many sequences, indicate that widespread flood conditions once prevailed. ... Sequences are often thousands of feet in thickness. ...with the coarsest material at the base progressively decreasing in coarseness toward the top."

[Stuart E. Nevins, "Stratigraphic Evidence of the Flood," in Donald W. Patten, editor, *Symposium on Creation III* (Grand Rapids, Michigan: Baker Book House, 1971), pp. 60-62 (quote is from pp. 60-61).]

☐ **MOUNTAINS UPLIFTED AFTER MOST SEDIMENTATION** — "Many mountain ranges can be shown to have been uplifted *after* nearly all of the stratigraphic record was deposited."

[Stuart E. Nevins, "Stratigraphic Evidence of the Flood," in Donald W. Patten, editor, *Symposium on Creation III* (Grand Rapids, Michigan: Baker Book House, 1971), p. 64 (quote is from p. 64).]

☐ **"UNDERFIT" STREAMS AND RIVERS** — Evidence that most natural drainage systems globally at one time drained off far larger amounts of water.

☐ **MASSIVE, RAPID EROSION** — evidenced at many locations worldwide, including the Grand Canyon. Also, see evidence of rapid erosion based on widespread "sequence-bounding discontinuities."

[Stuart E. Nevins, "Stratigraphic Evidence of the Flood," in Donald W. Patten, editor, *Symposium on Creation III* (Grand Rapids, Michigan: Baker Book House, 1971), pp. 60-62.]

☐ **EXISTENCE OF GREAT "PLUNGEPOOLS"** (created as torrents of floodwater mud plunged off the continents).

[Reginald Daly, *Earth's Most Challenging Mysteries* (Vancouver, Washington: The Craig Press, 1972), pp. 296-311.]

☐ **EXISTENCE OF SUBMARINE CANYONS.**

☐ **ENCLOSED LAKE BASINS** — Evidence of formerly huge inland lakes and seas on all continents that dried up as the Floodwaters receded over the centuries.

☐ **WATERLINES** — found on the coasts of every continent.

☐ **EVIDENCE FROM STUDIES OF SMALLER-SCALE CATASTROPHES** — Studies of modern floods, volcanic eruptions (e.g., Krakatoa, Mount St. Helens), tsunamis, turbidity currents, and ocean waves — showing these formidable forces of nature are capable of producing rapid and significant geologic changes.

☐ **FLOOD LEGENDS** throughout the world. See index.

☐ **GENESIS RECORD** of the Flood, and other Biblical references.

SUGGESTED SOURCES FOR FURTHER EVIDENCE OF A WORLDWIDE CATASTROPHIC FLOOD

☐ John C. Whitcomb, Jr., *The World That Perished*, 2nd edition (Grand Rapids, Michigan: Baker Book House, 1988) (sequel to The Genesis Flood by Whitcomb and Morris).

☐ Albert W. Mehlert, "Diluviology and Uniformitarian Geology — A Review," *Creation Research Society Quarterly*, Vol. 23, No. 3 (P.O. Box 14016, Terre Haute, Indiana 47803: December 1986), pp. 104-109.

☐ Steven A. Austin, "Did Noah's Flood Cover the Entire World? Yes.", in Ronald Youngblood, editor, *The Genesis Debate* (Nashville: Thomas Nelson Publishers, 1986), pp. 210-228.

☐ Glenn R. Morton, "Global, Continental and Regional Sedimentation Systems and Their Implications," *Creation Research Society Quarterly*, Vol. 21, No. 1 (P.O. Box 14016, Terre Haute, Indiana 47803: June 1984), pp. 23-33 (*"The geologic record displays a trend in which certain lithologies are more prominently deposited during certain geologic periods. The trend is a worldwide phenomenon which seems to better fit within Creationist views of earth history."*)

☐ Steven A. Austin, *Catastrophes in Earth History* (P.O. Box 2667, El Cajon, California 92021: Institute for Creation Research, 1984), 318 pp. (includes large bibliography of recent secular geology books and papers supporting catastrophism).

☐ Henry M. Morris, *The Biblical Basis for Modern Science* (Grand Rapids, Michigan: Baker Book House, 1984), pp. 270-364.

☐ Harold S. Coffin, "Mount St. Helens and Spirit Lake," *Origins*, Vol. 10, No. 1 (Loma Linda, California: Geoscience Research Institute, Loma Linda University, 1983), pp. 9-17 (Mount Saint Helens eruption and aftermath provides interesting parallels to phenomena associated with the Flood).

☐ Henry M. Morris, "Catastrophism in Geology," in Henry M. Morris and Gary E. Parker, *What Is Creation Science?* (San Diego: CLP Publishers, 1982), pp. 189-218.

☐ James H. Shea, "Twelve Fallacies of Uniformitarianism," *Geology*, Vol. 10, No. 9 (September 1982), pp. 455-460.

☐ Stanley E. Taylor, writer, *The World That Perished* (Mesa, Arizona: Films for Christ Association, 1977) (Creationist motion picture and video).

☐ Stuart E. Nevins (Steven Austin), "Stratigraphic Evidence of the Flood," in Donald W. Patten, editor, *A Symposium on Creation III* (Grand Rapids, Michigan: Baker Book House, 1971), pp. 33-65.

☐ Henry M. Morris, "Sedimentation and the Fossil Record: A Study in Hydraulic Engineering," in Walter E. Lammerts, editor, *Why Not Creation?* (Grand Rapids, Michigan: Baker Book House, 1970), pp. 114-137.

☐ N.A. Rupke, "Prolegomena to a Study of Cataclysmal Sedimentation," in Walter E. Lammerts, editor, *Why Not Creation?* (Grand Rapids, Michigan: Baker Book House, 1970), pp. 141-179.

☐ Byron C. Nelson, *The Deluge Story in Stone* (Minneapolis: Bethany Fellowship Publishers, 1968).

☐ Melvin A. Cook, *Prehistory and Earth Models* (London: Max Parrish, 1966).

☐ John C. Whitcomb, Jr. and Henry M. Morris, *The Genesis Flood* (Philadelphia: The Presbyterian and Reformed Publishing Company, 1967, copyright 1961) (the single most comprehensive book on this subject and the basis for further research by many subsequent authors).

FLOOD LEGENDS

314

☐ If a worldwide flood catastrophe took place, and if all subsequent humans have been descendants of the few survivors (the Bible indicates 8), one would expect to find some record of this deluge in ancient records. This is exactly the case. Legends and mythologies of nations and tribes around the world tell of a time when the entire Earth was devastated by water. Anthropologists have collected at least 59 Flood legends from the aborigines of North America, 46 from Central and South America, 31 from Europe, 17 from the Middle East, 23 from Asia, and 37 from the South Sea Islands and Australia. They all agree on at least 3 things:

- A worldwide flood destroyed both man and animals.
- There was a vessel of safety provided.
- An extremely small remnant of people thus survived.

[James A. Strickling, "A Statistical Analysis of Flood Legends," *Creation Research Society Quarterly*, Vol. 9, No. 3 (P.O. Box 14016, Terre Haute, Indiana 47803: December 1972), pp. 152-155.]

[Alfred M. Rehwinkel, *The Flood* (St. Louis: Concordia Publishing House, 1951), p. 128.]

SOURCES FOR FURTHER INFORMATION ON FLOOD LEGENDS AND/OR EVIDENCE THAT THE GENESIS ACCOUNT IS BASED ON AN ORIGINAL SOURCE

☐ William H. Shea, "A Comparison of Narrative Elements in Ancient Mesopotamia Creation-Flood Stories with Genesis 1-9," *Origins*, Vol. 11, No. 1 (Loma Linda, California: Geoscience Research Institute, 1984), pp. 2-3, 9-29.

☐ William H. Shea, "The Structure of the Genesis Flood Narrative and Its Implications," *Origins*, Vol. 6, No. 1 (Loma Linda, California: Geoscience Research Institute, 1979), pp. 3-4, 8-29.

☐ Stanley E. Taylor, writer, *The World That Perished* (Mesa, Arizona: Films For Christ Association, 1977) (a Creationist motion picture — includes excerpts from numerous legends).

☐ Tim F. LaHaye and John D. Morris, *The Ark on Ararat* (San Diego: CLP Publishers, 1976), chapter 30.

☐ Arthur C. Custance, "Flood Traditions of the World," in Donald W. Patten, editor, *Symposium on Creation — IV* (Grand Rapids, Michigan: Baker Book House, 1972), pp. 9-44.

☐ Theodor H. Gaster, *Myth, Legend, and Custom in the Old Testament* (New York: Harper and Row, 1969).

☐ Byron C. Nelson, *The Deluge Story in Stone* (Augsburg, Minnesota: Augsburg Publishing House, 1931), Appendix I, also (Grand Rapids, Michigan: Baker Book House, 1968).

☐ Johannes Riem, *Die Sintflut in Sage und Wissenschaft* (Hamburg, Germany: Agentur des Rauhen Hauses, 1925).

☐ Sir James George Frazer, *Folk-Lore in the Old Testament*, Vol. I (London: Macmillan and Co., 1918), pp. 104-361.

☐ William Restelle, "The Traditions of the Deluge," *Bibliotheca Sacra*, Vol. 64 (1907), pp. 148-167.

☐ Richard Andree, *Die Flutsagen: Ethnographisch Betrachtet* (Braunschweig, Germany: Friedrich Bieweg und Sohn, 1891).

315

☐ **John Wolfgang Smith**: Mathematician and physicist / Ph.D. in Mathematics from Columbia University (1957) / M.S. in Physics from Purdue University (1950) / B.S. from Cornell University (at age 18) in physics, philosophy and mathematics / Currently Professor of Mathematics at Oregon State University / Formerly an Aerodynamicist with Bell Aircraft Corporation / Provided the "theoretical key to the solution of the famed re-entry problem for space flight" / Former math instructor at Massachusetts Institute of Technology / Former Assistant and Associate Professor at the University of California, Los Angeles

/ Active research mathematician / Published in various scientific journals.

316

☐ Wolfgang Smith, *Teilhardism and the New Religion: A Thorough Analysis of The Teachings of Pierre Teilhard de Chardin* (P.O. Box 424, Rockford, Illinois 61105: Tan Books & Publishers, Inc., 1988), 248 pp. (quote from p. 5 — emphasis is Smith's) (p. 2 — "*We are told dogmatically that Evolution is an established fact; but we are never told who has established it, and by what means. We are told, often enough, that the doctrine is founded upon evidence, and that indeed this evidence 'is henceforward above all verification, as well as being immune from any subsequent contradiction by experience'; but we are left entirely in the dark on the crucial question wherein, precisely, this evidence consists."*).

317

☐ Michael Denton, *Evolution: A Theory in Crisis* (Bethesda, Maryland: Adler and Adler Publishers, 1985), p. 358.

COMMENTS ON THE THEORY OF EVOLUTION AND THE CURRENT STATE OF SCIENCE

318

☐ Wolfgang Smith:

"*Today, a hundred and twenty-eight years after it was first promulgated, the Darwinian theory of evolution stands under attack as never before. There was a time, not too long ago, when it seemed to the world at large that the theory had triumphed once and for all, and that the issue was henceforth closed. And yet, within the last two or three decades the debate about (E)volution has not only revived but is showing signs of heating up. Indeed, the question whether the evolutionist claims are justified is currently being discussed and argued, not just in fundamentalist circles, but also on occasion in research institutes, and in the prestigious halls of academe. The fact is that in recent times there has been increasing dissent on the issue within academic and professional ranks, and that a growing number of respectable scientists are defecting from the evolutionist camp. It is interesting, moreover, that for the most part these 'experts' have abandoned Darwinism, not on the basis of religious faith or biblical persuasions, but on strictly scientific grounds, and in some instances regretfully, as one could say.*"

[Wolfgang Smith, *Teilhardism and the New Religion: A Thorough Analysis of the Teachings of Pierre Teilhard de Chardin* (Rockford, Illinois: Tan Books & Publishers, Inc., 1988), p. 1 (emphasis added).]

☐ "*Any suppression which undermines and destroys that very foundation on which scientific methodology and research was erected, evolutionist or otherwise, cannot and must not be allowed to flourish. In a certain sense, the debate transcends the confrontation between evolutionists and creationists. We now have a debate within the scientific community itself: it is a confrontation between scientific objectivity and ingrained prejudice — between logic and emotion — between fact and fiction. (pp. 6-7) ... In the final analysis, objective scientific logic has to prevail — no matter what the final result is — no matter how many time-honored idols have to be discarded in the process. (p. 8) ... After all, it is not the duty of science to defend the theory of evolution, and stick by it to the bitter end — no matter what illogical and unsup-*"

> *The theory of Evolution... will be one of the great jokes in the history books of the future. Posterity will marvel that so flimsy and dubious an hypothesis could be accepted with the incredible credulity that it has.*
>
> Malcolm Muggeridge, well-known philosopher

ported conclusions it offers. ...If in the process of impartial scientific logic, they find that creation by outside superintelligence is the solution to our quandary, then let's cut the umbilical cord that tied us down to Darwin for such a long time. It is choking us and holding us back. (pp. 214-215) ...every single concept advanced by the theory of evolution (and amended thereafter) is imaginary as it is not supported by the scientifically established facts of microbiology, fossils, and mathematical probability concepts. Darwin was wrong. (p. 209) The theory of evolution may be the worst mistake made in science." (p. 210)

[I.L. Cohen, *Darwin Was Wrong — A Study in Probabilities* (P.O. Box 231, Greenvale, New York 11548: New Research Publications, Inc., 1984), 225 pp. (emphasis added).]

☐ "We have had enough of the Darwinian fallacy. It is time that we cry: 'The emperor has no clothes.'" (K. Hsu, geologist at the Geological Institute at Zurich)

K. Hsu, "Darwin's Three Mistakes," *Geology*, Vol. 14 (1986), p. 534 — as cited by Wendell R. Bird, "The Anti-Darwinian Scientists," Impact series no. 173, *Acts & Facts* (P.O. Box 2667, El Cajon, California 92021: Institute for Creation Research, November 1987), p. iv.]

☐ "Far from being an established fact of science that it is so typically portrayed to be, (E)volution is, in reality, an unreasonable and unfounded hypothesis that is riddled with countless scientific fallacies."

[Scott M. Huse, *The Collapse of Evolution* (Grand Rapids, Michigan: Baker Book House, 1983), 172 pp. (quote is from p. 127 — emphasis added).]

☐ **Scott M. Huse:** Former Evolutionist and former atheist / Lecturer on college campuses / Creationist / Computer scientist / Ph.D. in Philosophy and Religion from Bethany Theological / Th.D. from International Bible Institute and Seminary / Former teacher and principal of Pinecrest Bible Training Center, Salisbury Center, New York.

☐ "The fact that a theory so vague, so insufficiently verifiable, and so far from the criteria otherwise applied in 'hard' science has become a dogma can only be explained on sociological grounds." (Biologist Ludwig von Bertalanffy)

[Ludwig von Bertalanffy as quoted by Huston Smith, *Beyond the Post-Modern Mind* (New York: Crossroads, 1982), p. 173 (emphasis added).]

☐ "If living matter is not, then, caused by the interplay of atoms, natural forces and radiation, how has it come into being? There is another theory, now quite out of favor, which is based upon the ideas of Lamarck: that if an organism needs an improvement it will develop it, and transmit it to its progeny. I think we need to go further than this and admit that the only acceptable explanation is creation. I know this is an anathema to physicists, as indeed it is to me, but we must not reject a theory that we do not like if the experimental evidence supports it." (H.S. Lipson, Professor of Physics at the University of Manchester)

[H.S. Lipson, in a paper published by The Institute of Physics (Techno House, Redcliff Way, BSI CNX, England: Institute of Physics, IOP Publishing Ltd., 1980) (emphasis added).]

☐ "Unfortunately, many scientists and non-scientists have made Evolution into a religion, something to be defended against infidels. In my experience, many students of biology — professors and textbook writers included — have been so carried away with the arguments for Evolution that they neglect to question it. They preach it... College students, having gone through such a closed system of education, themselves become teachers, entering high schools to continue the process, using textbooks written by former classmates or professors. High standards of scholarship and teaching break down. Propaganda and the pursuit of power replace the pursuit of knowledge. Education becomes a fraud." (Science writer and biologist G. Kocan)

[George Kocan, "Evolution Isn't Faith But Theory," *Chicago Tribune* (Monday, April 21, 1980) (emphasis added).]

☐ "Evolutionism is a fairy tale for grown-ups. This theory has helped nothing in the progress of science. It is useless." (Dr. Louis Bounoure, Director of Research at the French National Center for Scientific Research, Director of the Zoological Museum, and former president of the Biological Society of Strassbourg)

[As quoted in: Wilbert H. Rusch, "Analysis of So-Called Evidences for Evolution," *Bible-Science Newsletter*, Vol. 5, No. 6 (P.O. Box 32457, Minneapolis, Minnesota 55432, Phone 612-635-0614: Bible-Science Association, 1967), p. 1., and *The Advocate* (March 8, 1984), p. 17 (emphasis added).]

☐ "Scientists who go about teaching that Evolution is a fact of life are great con men, and the story they are telling may be the greatest hoax ever. In explaining Evolution we do not have one iota of fact." (Dr. T.N. Tahmisian, a U.S. Atomic Energy Commission physiologist)

[As quoted in: *The Fresno Bee* (August 10, 1959), and Robert Whitelaw, "Voices of Science on Evolution," *Bible-Science Newsletter*, Vol. 10, No. 8 (P.O. Box 32457, Minneapolis, Minnesota 55432, Phone 612-635-0614: Bible-Science Association, 1972), p.11, and N.J. Mitchell, *Evolution and the Emperor's New Clothes* (3D Enterprises Limited, 1983), title page.]

☐ "I, myself, am convinced that the theory of evolution, especially to the extent to which it's been applied, will be one of the great jokes in the history books of the future. Posterity will marvel that so very flimsy and dubious an hypothesis could be accepted with the incredible credulity that it has." (Malcolm Muggeridge, well-known philosopher and journalist)

[Malcolm Muggeridge, Pascal Lectures (Ontario, Canada: University of Waterloo) (emphasis added).]

☐ "The result we believe must be striven for can therefore only be the following: biology will receive no advantage from following the teachings of Lamarck, Darwin and the modern hyper-Darwinists; indeed, it must as quickly as possible leave the narrow straits and blind alleys of the evolutionistic myth and resume its certain journey along the open and illuminated paths of tradition." (G. Sermonti, Professor of Genetics at the University of Perugia, former director of the Genetics Institute of the University of Palermo, Senior Editor of the Biology Forum, and R. Fondi, paleontologist — both scientifically reject macroevolution)

[G. Sermonti and R. Fondi, *Dopo Darwin: Critica all Evoluzionismo* (1980), translated by Montalenti, *Darwinism Today*, 77 Scientia 21, 29 (1983) (emphasis is from Sermonti and Fondi) — as cited by Wendell R. Bird, "More on the Anti-Darwinian Scientists," Impact series no. 176, *Acts & Facts* (P.O. Box 2667, El Cajon, California 92021: Institute for Creation Research, February 1988), p. iii.]

Index

Index

ILLUSTRATIONS

Front cover. Cover illustration of man and ape. From the motion picture *The Origin of Mankind*, Eden Films and Standard Media International.
   Artist: Todd Tennant.

Back cover. *ORIGINS* poster illustration. Eden Films. Artist: Edward Rice.

Page 3.   Solar system, elliptical view from the motion picture *The Earth, A Young Planet?*, Eden Films and Standard Media International.
   Artist: Charles Needham.

   Evolution from amoeba to man. From the motion picture *The Origin of Species*, Eden Films and Standard Media. Artist: Todd Tennant.

Page 4.   Scientist on pedestal. From the motion picture *The Genesis Solution*, Films for Christ Association. Artists: Dan Peeler Associates.

Page 5.   Scientist excavating dinosaur fossils at Dinosaur National Monument. Photographer: Joop van der Elst.

   Big bang. National Aeronautics and Space Administration, U.S.A.

Page 6.   Train and galaxy. From the motion picture *The Origin of the Universe*, Eden Films and Standard Media. Artists: Image Associates.

   City and volcano spewing rock. From the motion picture *The Origin of the Universe*, Eden Films and Standard Media. Artist: Todd Tennant.

Page 7.   Solar system, circular view. From the motion picture *The Earth, A Young Planet?*, Eden Films and Standard Media. Artist: Charles Needham.

   Two arrows. From the motion picture *The Origin of the Universe*, Eden Films and Standard Media International. Artist: Paul S. Taylor.

Page 8.   Skyline of New York City. From the motion picture *The Origin of Mankind*, Eden Films and Standard Media. Photographer: Jan Bodzinga.

   Earth and graph. From the motion picture *The Origin of the Universe*, Eden Films and Standard Media International. Artist: Paul S. Taylor.

Page 9.   Butterflies. Copyright © 1989, Paul S. Taylor. Photographer: Paul S. Taylor.

   Rose flower. From the motion picture *The Origin of Life*, Eden Films and Standard Media International. Photographer: Jan Bodzinga.

   Dr. A.E. Wilder-Smith. From *ORIGINS* motion picture series, Eden Films and Standard Media International. Photographer: Jan Bodzinga.

Page 11.   Earth as seen from the Moon. National Aeronautics and Space Administration, U.S.A.

   Scientist in Carbon-14 laboratory. From the motion picture *The Earth, A Young Planet?*, Eden Films and Standard Media.
      Photographer: Jan Bodzinga.

Page 12.   Buried fossils. From the motion picture *The Earth, A Young Planet?*, Eden Films and Standard Media International. Artist: Todd Tennant.

Page 13.   Chain and block, "calculated date". Eden Films. Artist: Charles Zilch.

   Earth as seen from space. National Aeronautics and Space Administration, U.S.A.

Page 14.   Earth's magnetic field. From the motion picture *The Earth, A Young Planet?*, Eden Films and Standard Media International.
      Artists: Image Associates.

Page 15.   Comet.

   Moon from Apollo 17. National Aeronautics and Space Administration.

Page 16.   Shrinking Sun with Earth. From the motion picture *The Earth, A Young Planet?*, Eden Films and Standard Media International.
      Artists: Image Associates.

   Sun with flares. National Aeronautics and Space Administration.

Page 17.   Astronaut on Moon. National Aeronautics and Space Administration, U.S.A.

Page 18.   Tree of Evolution. From the motion picture *The Origin of the Universe*, Eden Films and Standard Media International. Artist: Paul S. Taylor.

Page 21.   Various animals. From the motion picture *The Origin of Life*, Eden Films and Standard Media International. Artist: Charles Zilch.

Page 21.   Louis Pasteur. Parke-Davis, Warner-Lambert Company.

Page 22.   Dr. Stanley Miller with apparatus. From the motion picture *The Origin of Life*, Eden Films and Standard Media International.

   Amoeba.

Page 23.   DNA. From the motion picture *The Origin of Life*, Eden Films and Standard Media International. Artist: Charles Zilch.

Page 24.   Hundreds of books. From the motion picture *The Origin of Life*, Eden Films and Standard Media International. Photographer: Paul S. Taylor.

Page 25.   Ducklings swimming. Copyright © 1989, Paul S. Taylor. Photographer: Paul S. Taylor.

Page 26.   Infant and father. Copyright © 1989, Paul S. Taylor. Photographer: Star Taylor.

   Swan. Copyright © 1989, Paul S. Taylor. Photographer: Paul S. Taylor.

Page 27.   Tree and forest of trees. From the motion picture *The Origin of Species*, Eden Films and Standard Media International.
      Artists: Charles Zilch and Paul S. Taylor.

Dedication

This book is dedicated with special appreciation to the two most special ladies in my life:
   Star Taylor – my beloved and faithful wife
   Marian Taylor – my mother, continuing supporter and friend
Both have generously given of their love, help, and advice. Without their endless support and patience, projects such as this might never reach completion.

Acknowledgments

Many individuals were involved in one way or another in the production of this book. A special thanks goes to Dr. Arthur E. Wilder-Smith, the host of the motion picture series *ORIGINS: How the World Came to Be* which inspired this book. For their various special contributions, sincere appreciation goes to:

(in alphabetical order)
Gerald Aardsma, Ph.D. (Astrophysicist/Geophysicist)
Steven Austin, Ph.D. (Geologist)
Thomas Barnes, Ph.D. (Physicist)
Dudley Benton, Ph.D. (Mechanical Engineer)
Malcolm Bowden (Engineer)
Arthur Chadwick, Ph.D. (Geologist)
Melvin Cook, Ph.D. (Physical Chemist)
John Cuozzo (Orthodonist)
Donald DeYoung, Ph.D. (Astrophysicist/Geophysicist)
Duane Gish, Ph.D. (Biochemist)
Henry Morris, Ph.D. (Hydraulicist)
Willem Ouweneel, Ph.D. (Genetic Biologist)
Gary Parker, Ph.D. (Biologist/Paleontologist)
Wilbert Rusch, Sr., M.S., L.L. (Hon.) (Biological Sciences)
Harold Slusher, Ph.D. (Geophysicist/Astrophysicist)
Andrew Snelling, Ph.D. (Geologist)
Arthur Wilder-Smith, Ph.D., Dr.es.Sc., D.Sc., F.R.I.C. (Organic Chemist/Pharmacologist)